Change a Life,
Change Your Own

Change a Life, Change Your Own

Child Sponsorship, the Discourse of Development, and the Production of Ethical Subjects

Peter Ove

FERNWOOD PUBLISHING
HALIFAX & WINNIPEG

Editing: Fazeela Jiwa
Cover design: John van der Woude
Printed and bound in Canada

This book has been published with the help of a grant from the
Federation for the Humanities and Social Sciences, through the
Awards to Scholarly Publications Program, using funds provided by the
Social Sciences and Humanities Research Council of Canada.

Published by Fernwood Publishing
32 Oceanvista Lane, Black Point, Nova Scotia, B0J 1B0
and 748 Broadway Avenue, Winnipeg, Manitoba, R3G 0X3
www.fernwoodpublishing.ca

Fernwood Publishing Company Limited gratefully acknowledges the financial support
of the Government of Canada, the Manitoba Department of Culture, Heritage and
Tourism under the Manitoba Publishers Marketing Assistance Program and the
Province of Manitoba, through the Book Publishing Tax Credit, for our publishing
program. We are pleased to work in partnership with the Province of Nova Scotia
to develop and promote our creative industries for the benefit of all Nova Scotians.
We acknowledge the support of the Canada Council for the Arts, which last year
invested $153 million to bring the arts to Canadians throughout the country.

Library and Archives Canada Cataloguing in Publication

Ove, Peter, 1975-, author
Change a life, change your own : child sponsorship, the discourse of
development and the production of ethical subjects / Peter Ove.

Includes bibliographical references and index.
Issued in print and electronic formats.
ISBN 978-1-77363-014-4 (softcover).—ISBN 978-1-77363-015-1 (EPUB).—
ISBN 978-1-77363-016-8 (Kindle)

1. Child welfare—Developing countries. 2. Humanitarian assistance—
Moral and ethical aspects. 3. Fund raising. I. Title.

HV713.O94 2018   362.7'7569   C2017-907907-7   C2017-907908-5

Contents

Acknowledgements

This project has been a long time in the making. It started over a decade ago as a PhD dissertation funded in part by the Social Sciences and Humanities Research Council. I owe an enormous debt of gratitude to my doctoral supervisor at UBC, Dr. Dawn Currie, as well as all the members of my committee, Drs. Thomas Kemple, Renisa Mawani, and Sunera Thobani. A special thanks goes to my editor Candida Hadley for her guidance and patience, to my copyeditor Fazeela Jiwa for her meticulous eye for detail, and to all the people at Fernwood Publishing for their help turning this manuscript into a book. I would also like to acknowledge the interview participants, including the sponsorship staff and their respective organizations, without whom this research would not have been possible. Finally, I would like to say that I would never have completed this project without the fierce love and relentless support of my wife, Jette Midtgaard.

Studying Child Sponsorship

In May 1995, Lisa Anderson began sponsoring a twelve-year-old Malian girl named Korotoumou Kone through the American branch of Save the Children. Lisa sent the organization US$20 each month in return for a picture of Korotoumou and assurances that the sponsorship would help "change her life and make it better" (Anderson, 1998b: 1). However, when Lisa went to visit her sponsored child two years later, she found out that Korotoumou had died shortly after the sponsorship began. She had been struck by lightning while working in a rice patty. Although the local representatives of Save the Children had been informed of the incident, Lisa never received any information about Korotoumou's death. What she did receive, after her visit, was a letter of apology from Save the Children's vice president of international programs and a cheque refunding the $480 that she had contributed.

As sad as it is, the sensational circumstances of Korotoumou's death turned out to be beneficial for Lisa, who was a journalist with the *Chicago Tribune*. At the time, she was one of a number of reporters and editors from the *Tribune* working on a "special report" on child sponsorship, a fundraising technique that ostensibly works by pairing poor children in the South with donors in the North.[1] The report, indelicately titled "The Miracle Merchants: The Myths of Child Sponsorship," examines the practices of child sponsorship agencies to determine the accuracy of their advertising and the effectiveness of their intervention. While the report was released twenty years ago in 1998, it remains one of the most thorough and effective editorial critiques of child sponsorship. Despite numerous articles, reports, and blog posts on the topic of child sponsorship over the last few decades, no agency has publicly tackled the issue with the same degree of scrutiny and breadth.

Four organizations were included in the *Chicago Tribune* report: Save the Children US, Childreach (now known as Plan International US), Children International, and Christian Children's Fund (now known as ChildFund

International). Over a two-year period, twelve children were sponsored by reporters from the *Tribune*, and then, without the sponsorship agencies' knowledge, these reporters set out to find their sponsored children and assess the impact of their contributions. The results of this "inquiry" covered almost thirty pages and appeared in two separate weekend editions in March of 1998. Throughout the report, child sponsorship organizations were accused of commonly misrepresenting the state of sponsored children and the benefits they receive through sponsorship. They were also criticized for having overly expensive and bureaucratic administrations that allow children to fall through the cracks. At a more fundamental level, sponsorship agencies were charged with duping Northern donors into a relationship that is largely a "marketing myth" (Anderson, 1998a: 1).

On the first day of the report's publication, Korotoumou's disembodied and washed-out face appeared on the front page of the paper beside the boldfaced heading "Relentless campaigns of hollow promises." Her sad eyes accompanied the reader through the introduction of the inquiry. The story of her death — and of Lisa's ensuing search to find out what went wrong with Save the Children's Mali operations — occupied the next four pages. Another full page was dedicated to the results of a follow-up investigation conducted by Save the Children that found an additional twenty-two cases in which donors had been sponsoring children who had died. In one of these cases, an American family discovered that they had still been receiving letters from their sponsored child even though he had been dead nearly three years. Apparently, the letters were written by a member of the organization's local staff. According to the *Tribune*, this case illustrates how "donors can be betrayed by the sponsorship system" (Dellios and Anderson, 1998: 6). Taking up more than a third of the first set of articles, these stories of death and "betrayal" not only provided a compelling lead-in to the *Tribune* report but also offered a glimpse at some of the worst organizational problems associated with child sponsorship.

Both the tone of these stories and the results of the follow-up investigation, which ended in several local staff being "reprimanded," drew attention to a supposedly shocking problem with child sponsorship. As in many classic critiques of child sponsorship (for example, see Hancock, 1989: 16; Maren, 1997: 136), the problem was presented as an appalling lack of efficacy, transparency, and oversight on the part of sponsorship agencies. Whether wilfully negligent or not, these organizations were depicted as failing to live up to their responsibilities to sponsored children and to sponsors. In placing the blame squarely at the figurative feet of the sponsorship agencies, however, these articles not only described the problem of child sponsorship as one of organizational ineptitude, but they also inferred a predominantly administrative solution. The clear message from the sad tale of Korotoumou and her counterparts was that, to "fix" child sponsorship, these organizations need to improve their development practices in the South and their accountability in the North. In this way, the *Tribune* report is representative of many mainstream critiques of child sponsorship and, therefore, ideally suited to serve as a point of departure for the present study.

The fact that Lisa and others had not been informed about the deaths of their sponsored children is a dramatic illustration of the potential problems with child sponsorship, but the *Tribune's* focus on sensational examples of organizational negligence avoids many interesting and challenging questions. While it is important that sponsorship agencies are held accountable for their actions, seeing the central problem and solution of child sponsorship as chiefly administrative neglects the influence of broader social, cultural, political, and economic contexts on the past and present practice of sponsorship. For example, knowing that some organizations have not provided the advertised benefits to each sponsored child does not tell us what it is about child sponsorship that has made it — and continues to make it — so remarkably successful in attracting donors. Furthermore, knowing that some donors have been misled, intentionally or not, does not help us understand how child sponsorship fits into the contemporary development industry or the political, cultural, and economic climate of global relations.

Addressing issues like these involves looking beyond the faults of sponsorship agencies, although these cannot be ignored, to the ways in which child sponsorship is marketed by organizations and perceived by sponsors as a reasonable response to Southern "underdevelopment." That is to say, instead of only exploring the misconduct of child sponsorship organizations, it becomes necessary to examine how the problem of development is constructed such that child sponsorship is seen to be a rational and ethical solution. In shifting the critical lens from the problem of sponsorship organizations to the problem of development, the results (or lack thereof) of specific sponsorship programs become less important than the way that the practice of child sponsorship reveals how individuals and institutions think about development and act in its name. Such an emphasis on the relationship between child sponsorship and what is commonly called the "discourse of development" makes it easier to formulate a critique of sponsorship that not only comments on organizational difficulties but also addresses the enormous historical and contemporary complicity of Northern societies, governments, and businesses in the current state of global poverty and inequality. This move toward a more general critique of child sponsorship and its relationship to contemporary development practices can then help make sense of the appeal of child sponsorship without tired references to the guilt that emotion-laden advertisements supposedly foster.

This book emerges out of these concerns to better understand the relationship between the practice of child sponsorship and the broader material and discursive contexts of international development. Rather than emphasize extraordinary examples of problems with child sponsorship, this study analyzes the everyday activities of sponsorship and how they are ordered, negotiated, and rationalized by those involved. It is grounded in a desire to shed light on how particular ideas about development are produced and reproduced at organizational and individual levels. Consequently, the aim of this study is to explore child sponsorship both as a prominent feature of the contemporary development industry and as a significant facet of the mainstream development discourse (the way that international development and its actors are imagined, discussed, and acted upon). In other words, this study examines child sponsorship not only as a successful fundraising tool but also — and more importantly — as an influential component of identity formation in the North.

A focus on what happens in the North may seem counterintuitive given the apparent objective of raising funds for development in the South, but it fits well with the contemporary nature of child sponsorship. Most of what goes on nowadays in relation to sponsorship is more about opening Northern wallets than feeding Southern bellies. An underappreciated but substantial divide between how sponsorship programs raise money in the North and how they spend it in the South is one of the reasons that the *Tribune* journalists referred to child sponsorship as a "marketing myth" (Anderson, 1998a: 1). Although a direct social and financial relationship between sponsor and child is usually inferred from sponsorship advertising, this is not often the case. With most sponsorship agencies, money is pooled at the national level and sent in bulk to partner agencies or local affiliates to be spent on projects at community and regional levels. There are few guarantees that these projects, funded by sponsorship dollars, will meet the advertised needs of the children being sponsored. On a related note, the content of letters and reports coming from sponsored children, their families, or local field offices is often generic and superficial. Although it is possible for meaningful relationships between sponsors and sponsored children to exist, these seem to be rare and are not essential to the process. These features indicate that, in many although not all cases, child sponsorship is better understood as an elaborate fundraising technique than as a comprehensive development strategy.

As a fundraising technique, child sponsorship is remarkably successful. In fact, it has been one of the most lucrative fundraising tools in terms of private donations for development assistance in the South (Smillie, 1995: 136). It is used by a bewildering array of both faith-based and secular non-governmental organizations (NGOs), the largest of which have annual revenues in the hundreds of millions. For example, the international networks Plan International and the ChildFund Alliance (Christian Children's Fund of Canada) report revenues of around US$900 million and US$500 million respectively (ChildFund Alliance, 2017; Plan International, 2017a). World Vision, the world's largest relief and development network offering child sponsorship, had a worldwide revenue of about US$2 billion in 2016 (World

Vision International, 2017a). While a portion of these funds now comes from things like corporate donations and government contracts, child sponsorship is still a central element of these organizations' fundraising strategies. With millions of sponsors across the globe giving more than CAN$450 per year, how could the situation be otherwise?

We should not forget, however, that child sponsorship is more than a means to garner donations; it is also a powerful apparatus for shaping the way that Northern audiences understand and respond to global poverty and inequality. It is no coincidence that images of destitute children are often the first thing that comes to many Northerners' minds when thinking of the South. Years of sponsorship advertising have made the hollowed-out faces of black[2] children iconic symbols of poverty and have arguably taken the place of colonial imagery in Northern popular culture. The images in these ads are heartrending, the language seductive. The overwhelming use of these kinds of images has even resulted in many commentators arguing that people have become inured to them and now respond with apathy and even resistance, so-called compassion fatigue (for example, see Moeller, 1999). Others have argued that this imagery is one of the foremost factors perpetuating stereotypes about the South and its people (Smillie, 1995: 136). Whatever the case, child sponsorship and its associated imagery are now regular features of the cultural landscape in the North. Sponsorship appeals can commonly be found in newspapers, magazines, and on the Internet, and sponsorship infomercials are a standard element of daytime television in North America. These marketing campaigns are independently publicized by the news media, churches, and other development organizations and are often endorsed by high-profile spokespersons. Child sponsorship has now become so powerful and so commonplace that it has been described as "not only *the* most successful fundraising tool in the North, but the pre-eminent lens through which a very large and growing majority of Northern citizens view the South" (Smillie, 1998: 30).

This understanding of the enormous power of child sponsorship to influence thought and action in the North — irrespective of its actual contributions in the South — is central to the way this book is formulated. It is based on a vision of child sponsorship as primarily a fundraising technique with serious implications for the way Northerners view themselves in relation to the world. Such an emphasis on the subject positions of Northerners in relation to child sponsorship, and international development in general, is not completely novel. There have been several critiques of sponsorship that address such things as the role of organization staff in sponsorship scandals, the emotional state of sponsors upon signing up, the stereotypical portrayal of Southerners within sponsorship advertising, the problematic role of religion in sponsorship, or the antipathetic role that sponsorship has played in international affairs (for example, see Bornstein, 2001; Fieldston,

2014; Hancock, 1989; Jefferess, 2002a; Maren, 1997). Unlike such analyses of child sponsorship, however, the present study focuses more generally on the way sponsorship is constructed as an ethical practice in contemporary North American society. Rather than analyze specific sponsorship ads, for example, this research focuses on the broader discursive mechanisms through which sponsorship staff and sponsors (are able to) position themselves as doing something that is almost unquestionably good.

An emphasis on the ethical nature of sponsorship and its relationship to the subject positions of Northerners involved in sponsorship fits well within a focus on the discourse of development, which refers to the way that relations of power define the "appropriate and legitimate ways of practicing development as well as speaking and thinking about it" (Grillo, 1997: 12). After all, what is understood by the term development has an enormous influence on the staff members who produce the promotional material of sponsorship programs and on the sponsors who interpret this material, but it is also inherently tied up in particular visions of progress and the values associated with those visions. Based on these analytical priorities, this book examines why child sponsorship is commonly seen as a rational and ethical response to global poverty.

Within the scope of this problem, the following chapters explore the relationship among sponsorship programs (Chapters 2 and 3), the promotional material they produce (Chapter 4), and the sponsors they attract (Chapters 5 and 6). These three components of sponsorship represent specific sites within which different aspects of the discourse of development can be usefully seen to operate. Along with an introduction to the history and context of child sponsorship (Chapter 1), these components form distinct but related sections of this project. Drawing on in-depth interviews with sponsorship staff and sponsors, the following chapters present a discourse analysis that highlights how sponsorship programs and sponsors are represented — and represent themselves — as trying to "make a difference" in the world, and how these representations relate to contemporary understandings of poverty and development.

For Foucault (2002 [1969]: 54), discourses are not only "words and things" but also "practices that systematically form the objects of which they speak." This means that a discourse is not just a "group of signs" and what they signify; it is also the "group of rules" that both determines the meaning of words and, crucially, the truth of statements in any given context (54). According to Foucault (1990 [1978]: 100), then, the study of discourse(s) should be less concerned with revealing the "true" significance of communicative acts and more concerned with understanding how truth is produced through the strategic use of discursive elements within particular contexts. This emphasis on strategy is important because it indicates the active nature of the interface between people and discourses, which both shape the subjectivities of individuals and are themselves shaped by these individuals. In the end, however, the goal of discourse analysis is simply to highlight how certain areas of life, and the practices with which they are associated, become normalized through the use of language and the production of knowledge.

In light of this Foucauldian understanding of discourse and discourse analysis, this study looks at the way sponsorship organizations and sponsors understand and position their activities within the broader contexts of international development and charitable donation. The objective is to explore the way mainstream understandings of development are taken up by sponsorship agencies and sponsors to help construct a vision of the purpose and ethical value of child sponsorship. This objective is implicit in the overarching questions that guide this research: What is the relationship between the discourse of development and the practice of child sponsorship? How does this relationship help produce a situation in which sponsoring a child is seen as both a rational and ethical response to global poverty? Exploring these questions across the scope of sponsorship practice in the North, this book draws on a modified version of another Foucauldian concept, governmentality, to examine the supposed transformation of the sponsor.

Developmentality and the transformation of the sponsor

Representations of sponsored children and the South they symbolize are probably the most conspicuous feature of child sponsorship and its promotional material, and these representations make sponsorship a central site for the construction of Northern worldviews. More than this, however, sponsorship represents a significant force in the formation of Northern identities. Representations of Southern "Others" play a formative role in the way Northerners view themselves, but sponsorship advertising also places significant emphasis on the sponsors themselves and how they should think and feel about the act of sponsorship. As with many commercial products, sponsorship marketing is often more about the buyer and their (potential) lifestyle than about the object or service being sold. Although images of children are a necessary ingredient of sponsorship promotion, the narrative of child sponsorship often revolves around how the sponsor transforms both the life of the sponsored child and their own life in the process. This transformation is a major selling point in sponsorship advertising, and it is captured in the long-time World Vision slogan "Change a life. Change your own."

Through the "magic" of child sponsorship, individuals are not only transformed from simple donors into sponsors, but sponsors are also (supposedly) transformed into better people. The key to this transformation is that it occurs in an ethical realm largely removed from the respective lives of the sponsor and the child. Even if the sponsorship funds have no bearing on the well-being of the child (as in the case of

Korotoumou) and even if the sponsor donates for less than altruistic reasons (as in the case of Lisa), the act of sponsorship itself is often seen to be undeniably good. After all, it is almost impossible to dispute the ethical nature of helping to support a child who is poor. Why else should it seem so appropriate that Lisa be offered a refund when her reason for sponsorship was as conceivably fraudulent as the organization's portrayal of Korotoumou's life? This ethical quality of sponsorship helps constitute Northern subjects who are always already good. As part of a movement that sees people doing good by enjoying or improving themselves (as with marathon runs that help cure cancer and massive rock concerts that help save the environment), child sponsorship presents individuals with an almost instantaneous way of becoming better people — possibly better than they have otherwise made themselves. Because of the apparently miraculous capacity of their donations to forever alter some poor child's life, sponsors move closer to attaining the status of "extraordinary person" that is so desirable in modern Western culture. In this way, child sponsorship and its advertising help position what it means to live ethically in an unequal and unjust world.

By examining the way sponsors are transformed through sponsorship into ethical subjects, it is possible to highlight the relationships among the structures and practices of sponsorship programs, the thoughts and actions of sponsors, and the representations of sponsorship that unite them. An appreciation for these relationships, in turn, helps clarify the connections between the practice of child sponsorship and a discourse of development that is historically constructed and indelibly racialized. To facilitate the analysis of these connections, this research draws on a modified version of Michel Foucault's (2007; 2003 [1978]) concept of governmentality (see also Foucault, 2003 [1982a]; 2003 [1982b]; 2003 [1984a]). By exploring the connections between the government of others and the government of the self, Foucault's concept helps trace the particular relationships between freedom and control that characterize contemporary life in modern liberal states (for more explanation, see Barry, Osborne, and Rose, 1996; Bratich, Packer, and McCarthy, 2003; Burchell, Gordon, and Miller, 1991; Dean, 1999; Dean and Hindess, 1998; Larner and Walters, 2004; Lemke, 2001, 2002, 2007; Rose, 1998, 1999; Rose and Miller, 1992).

Governmentality studies have tended to emphasize the management of populations through the self-management of individuals. It is important to remember, however, that "government has as its purpose not the act of government itself, but the *welfare* of the population, the *improvement* of its condition, the *increase* of its wealth, longevity, health, and so on" (Foucault, 2003 [1978]: 241, emphasis added). The fact that the purpose of government, for Foucault, is basically synonymous with that of development makes it possible and desirable within this framework to study not only the way individuals regulate themselves (as a facet of the regulation of others) but also the way they develop themselves (as a facet of the development of others). Foucault talks about governmentality in this way when he refers to his concept of "technologies of the self" (Foucault, 2003 [1982b]). A technology of the self is a practice that "permit[s] individuals to effect by their own means, or with the help of others, a certain number of operations on their own bodies and souls, thoughts, conduct, and way of being, so as to transform themselves in order to attain a certain state of happiness, purity, wisdom, perfection, immortality" (Foucault, 2003 [1982b]: 146). Because Foucault sees governmentality as an "encounter between the technologies of domination of others and those of the self" (Foucault, 2003 [1982b]: 147), this perspective helps explain the relationship between the mechanisms of control and ideas of improvement that so often go together in international development.

Due to this focus on the development (as in improvement) rather than government (as in management) of people, this research makes use of a perspective that can be usefully termed developmentality (see Ove, 2013, for a full explanation). An adapted version of governmentality, developmentality is a portmanteau of "developmental rationality" or "development mentality." While not the first appearance of this term (see for example, see Deb, 2009; Fendler, 2001; Ilcan and Phillips, 2006; Lie, 2005; Mawuko-Yevugah, 2010), it is used here in a different manner that incorporates some of Foucault's later work on the way individuals constitute themselves as ethical subjects within particular moral environments (Foucault, 1990 [1984]). In this light, developmentality is used to describe the way in which the various meanings or uses of the term development (personal, biological, organizational, and international) articulate with each other in important and disturbing ways. It is also used to incorporate a discussion of how a concern for Southern Others fits into, and usefully expands, a more traditional understanding of governmentality.

The first element of developmentality, the articulation of the idea of development across various sites, is primarily related to a metaphorical relationship founded upon the all-too-straightforward association between social life and maturational or evolutionary processes. Through this relationship, particular practices of economic development, social development, personal development, and so on, are rationalized using an organic model of progress that features such things as directionality (growth has a purpose and follows a number of well-defined stages to get there), continuity (there is some degree of "permanence through change" during this process), cumulativeness (every stage is necessarily more advanced than what came before), and irreversibility (in the "natural" order of things, it is not possible to go back to previous stages) (Rist, 2002: 27). The prevalence of these features within the discourse of development has resulted in, among other things, an image of all societies as moving naturally and consistently "up" on a route from poverty, barbarism, despotism, and ignorance to riches, civilization, democracy and rationality, expressed at its highest in Science. This is also an irreversible movement from endless diversity of particularities, wasteful of human energies and economic resources, to a world unified and simplified into the one most rational arrangement. It is therefore movement from badness to goodness and from mindlessness to knowledge. (Shanin, 1997: 65)

The idea that societies develop through well-defined stages that simultaneously mirror the evolution of the human species and the maturation of the individual human body has long been taken for granted (the classic example being Rostow [1960]). Not only has this idea justified the treatment of whole societies like children, but it has also firmly located the "mature" form of society, and therefore the goal of all societal development, in the North. Even with contemporary modifications, this value-laden image of societal progress has been surprisingly durable and forms the basic connotation of most of what falls under the label of international development.

Analysis of these metaphorical underpinnings of societal development is not new to international development studies (for example, see Esteva, 1992; Porter, 1995; Rist, 2002), but what is commonly left out of these discussions is an understanding of the equivalent metaphorical processes that occur in other uses of the term "development" and the connections that link them together. The common features of the organic metaphor foster broad, thematic linkages between such things as the development of the child and the development of society (think of the banality of phrases linking children to the future of society or comparing colonial subjects to children needing guidance) and the development of individuals, companies, or organizations and the development of the national economy (think of the use of protectionist policies in international trade or the value placed on entrepreneurial "personalities"). These linkages are important because they often help provide the justification for policies and programs that seek to improve society. For example, tax breaks are often directly rationalized using the language of indirect collective improvement. As *Canada's Economic Action Plan* (Government of Canada, 2010) states: "Tax reductions are an essential part of the government's effort to stimulate the economy. Permanent tax reductions also help create a solid foundation for future economic growth, more jobs and higher living standards for Canadians" (n.p.). This metaphorical linkage between individual economic development and the collective good is so taken for granted that no evidence is usually required, which runs contrary to the fact that the Scandinavian societies, for example, have robust national economies despite high levels of personal taxation.

As with governmentality, developmentality offers a perspective that attempts to draw connections between the daily actions of individuals and the formation of specific discourses that structure these actions through the construction of truth and, ultimately, the determination of ethical conduct. This emphasis on everyday practices and the rationalities behind them is a critical element in following a Foucauldian theoretical framework (for example, see Foucault 2003 [1980b]: 251). In this light, then, a developmentality approach is more about locating and analyzing particular articulations and their significance than it is about justifying the overarching impact of the development metaphor. This element of developmentality guides the analysis in this book by privileging certain kinds of questions, such as: what are the connections between developing a (sponsorship) organization and helping to improve the lives of (sponsored) children (Chapters 2 and 3)? How does the notion of "proper" child development in modern liberal society influence the location of children and sponsors in sponsorship advertising (Chapter 4)? And how is the relationship between developing or improving oneself and helping others incorporated into child sponsorship (Chapters 5 and 6)?

While this first element of developmentality helps focus the analysis of child sponsorship on the personal and organizational development of sponsors and NGOs in the North, the second element of developmentality ensures that this analysis does not exclude a consideration for (the representation of) people in the South. Expanding on Foucault's understanding of governmentality as the "encounter between the technologies of domination of others and those of the self" (Foucault, 2003 [1982b]: 147), this second element shifts the focus of governmentality from a national frame of reference that examines individuals within their larger "imagined community" to an international one that links in-groups to (representations of) out-groups (Anderson, 1991). To accomplish this, the socio-psychological and postcolonial concept of the Other (see Bhabha, 1994; Lacan, 2006 [1977]; Levinas, 1969; Said, 1994) is used to move attention from the traditional problem of the relationship between individuals and others (within their local political entity) to the problem of the relationship between individuals and Others (people from different political and ethnic groups).

The concept of governmentality does not, at first glance, lend itself to a critical analysis of the racialization processes involved in supposed development interventions like child sponsorship. In fact, this is one reason why a specific focus on colonial governmentality was thought to be necessary (see Dutton, 2009; Pels, 1997; Scott, 1995). The injection of a focus on Others into Foucault's theorizing around governmental techniques plays a central role in the shift from governmentality to developmentality and is intended to help address this difficulty (insofar as Othering processes are almost always racialized and processes of racialization are almost always Othering). An understanding of racialization is brought to the fore in the present adaptation of governmentality not to highlight the way race is deployed in overt discussions of Southern people(s); rather, it is employed to draw attention to the way the very categories of development (North and South or sponsor and child) are themselves products of racialized historical practices such as colonialism.

The relationship between the representation of Southern Others and the production of ethical subjects in the North did not, of course, originate with child sponsorship. This relationship is rooted, at least in part, in the racialized interactions stemming from the colonial era and its civilizing mission. By focusing exclusively on the help provided to the child and the corresponding generosity of the donor, these historical relationships, which undergird the very categories of North and South, are elided. Even though the contemporary structure of the world is based on this legacy of imperialism and colonialism, the racialized aspects of these relationships are absent from many present-day discussions of child sponsorship. Consequently, rather than say that the ethical transformation of the sponsor is wholly removed from the lives of sponsor and child, it is perhaps more appropriate to say that this transformation simultaneously draws on and negates the racialized relationships associated with these lives. Categories of race are too often (and paradoxically) invisible nowadays, but they still maintain an organizing frame of reference for most international activities, including child sponsorship. Therefore, processes of racialization (the creation or maintenance of racialized categories and their consequences) provide a powerful but largely unacknowledged context for the ethical transformation of sponsors. In particular, it should be kept in mind that the construction of good (white) people or peoples is predicated upon an historically oppressive association with helping poor (black) Others. In this way, the work of international development in general, and child sponsorship in particular, can never truly be separated from the perspective of "the white man's burden" (see William Easterly's [2006] book on contemporary foreign aid for a discussion of the modern incarnations of Kipling's well-known phrase).

In addition to bringing issues of ethnicity and race to the fore, the infusion of the concept of the Other into governmentality highlights the role played by Christian evangelism in the motivation behind development efforts. Within some, if not most, of the evangelical community involved in international development, there is a common overlap between the motivations to "help" other people through development efforts and through exposure to Christian teachings. This connection apparently manifests itself in two ways: one, individuals working for Christian NGOs often see their development work as an expression of their faith, and two, the transformation (understood as improvement) of development subjects is seen as a parallel process in the transformation of their faith (Bornstein, 2002). Consequently, this perspective on development and the spread of the Gospel reflects a division of the world into the categories of Christian/non-Christian or evangelized/unevangelized that mirrors the division into those of developed and "underdeveloped." The importance of this link between Christian evangelism and international development is that the ethical justification for the development of others is often linked to their status as Others. That is to say, it is the status of development subjects as Others that allows for them to be objects of developmental and evangelical techniques simultaneously. Moreover, it is the simultaneity of this link that helps constitute Northerners as subjects who are seen to be good because of their religious motivations and not in spite of them.

One final but crucial consideration with respect to the theme of the Other in theorizing development and governmentality deals with the understanding of charity in contemporary liberal thought. The idea of charity occupies a significant position in the moral calculations of liberal philosophy in that it corresponds to a broad area of literature dealing with obligations related to distributive justice (for example, see Rawls, 1971, 1999; Fabre, 2007; Kelly, 2005). This literature revolves around what people's ethical obligations to others should be in terms of redistributing wealth and, consequently, what is owed to others as a matter of course and not as an aspect of charity. This distinction defines what could be considered generous or not depending on the extent to which a person is morally obliged to redistribute their wealth. For example, even though taxes are used in part to help the destitute or unemployed, individuals tend not feel that paying their taxes is an altruistic gesture because it is obligatory. On the other hand, when they give money to a shelter or a food bank, this donation is considered charitable, and therefore generous, because it goes beyond what is considered ethically necessary.

What is important about the level of this trade-off between obligation and generosity is that there is almost always felt to be a lesser degree of obligation to Others than to those within one's own political (as well as cultural or racial) group. In other words, arguments about obligatory redistribution at the international level are almost always more tenuous within liberal theory than those at the national level (for arguments, see Fabre, 2007; for examples, see Fishkin, 1986; Lomasky, 2007). This means that any redistribution of wealth to Others is much more likely to be deemed charitable — to be considered a gift — than to those of one's own imagined community. This quality of Otherness has at least two implications. First, for charitable donations to be charitable, there cannot be any perceived connection between, for example, one person's poverty and another's wealth. For example, if a person's poverty is understood to be a result of exploitation, then assisting them should be seen as a matter of justice and not charity. Consequently, liberal models of charity at the international level implicitly disregard such connections. Second, because most charitable gifts cannot be reciprocated, the receiver could be seen to be forever in debt to the giver and so continuously lower in status (a feature that is undoubtedly evident in most forms of development assistance). This is one way in which charity can be understood as a method of maintaining the social order as much as ameliorating it, and it illustrates the famous etymological link between the words present and poison (see Mauss, 1954).

The moral positioning of the charitable gift within liberal thought illustrates a key aspect of developmentality: namely, the perceived ethical value of (privately given) development assistance precisely because of its association with Others. By emphasizing the particular (racialized) relationship between (Southern) Others and (Northern) selves rather than the relationship between the self and others (within the same politico-cultural body), the term developmentality highlights the fact that individuals in the North, through their development-related charity, are able become better people than they otherwise could be without the existence of Others.

In shifting the concept of governmentality toward an analytics of development, the concept of the Other is important because it helps illuminate some practical and theoretical difficulties in liberal ethics. While it is not without its own problems, the concept of the Other is particularly useful in that it facilitates an understanding of governmentality wherein development does not simply represent the welfare of the population within which one is located (and, therefore, define ethical action in light of one's relationship with this population only). Instead, the idea of development in all its manifestations is part of numerous parallel processes involving individuals from many different ethno-political collectivities, such that the importance of the discourse of development stems from these differences rather than transcends them. For example, the fact that the majority of sponsored children are from the South (and usually seen to be darker-skinned) while the majority of sponsors are from the North (and usually seen to be lighter-skinned) is more than a coincidence. This typical relationship between selves and Others within development aid expresses more than a geography of economic inequality; it reflects an organizing principle of ethical action — one that offers selective and disproportionate access to the ability to "do good" in contemporary society. Developmentality can be summed up, consequently, as a specific extension of governmentality that orients analysis toward the ethical connections among different understandings of development and what these connections tell us about the reproduction of unequal relations of power on a global level. To this end, this approach simply tries to highlight that perceptions of what makes a person good are tied to a specific pattern of relationships with others (or, in this case, Others) and to broader fields of knowledge and power related to the idea of improvement. These broader fields of knowledge and power are often referred to in terms of the "discourse of development."

The discourse of development

Writing about international development in terms of discourses is a relatively new and specialized practice within the field of development studies (for example, see Crush, 1995; Rist, 2002). As noted above, the Foucauldian concept of discourse that is used in this context is broader than a simple focus on what people say. Rather, discourses are inseparably related to the concepts of power, knowledge, truth, and subjectivity. Foucault does not say that knowledge is power (a common and unfortunate misreading) but that the "production, regulation, distribution, circulation, and operation of statements" always occurs in a field of power relations (Foucault, 2003 [1977]: 317). These relations of power are supported and extended, in turn, through the resulting configuration of knowledge. Because of this relationship, truth is not something external to discourse — something against which discursive elements can be measured. Instead, truth relies on discourse for its very production, and the resulting "regime of truth" has a subtle yet powerful influence on the way people understand the world and act within it. Consequently, discourses are both "an instrument and an effect of power" relations and, as such, they are more than a linguistic component of social interaction (Foucault, 2003 [1978]: 101). Not only are discourses specific to particular social formations, locations, and time periods, but they are also inseparably related to the multitude of everyday practices that define these situations.

This understanding of discourse led Arturo Escobar (1995: 10), one of the best-known importers of Foucault's work into the field of development studies, to focus on what he calls the "three axes" of development:

> the forms of knowledge that refer to it [development] and through which
> it comes into being and is elaborated into objects, concepts, theories, and
> the like; the systems of power that regulate its practice; and the forms of
> subjectivity fostered by this discourse, those through which people come
> to recognize themselves as developed or underdeveloped.

In structuring his analysis around these "axes," Escobar indicates what he means by the discourse of development and how he studied it. Although the theme of development can be seen as encompassing a wide range of elements — including a conception of time and space, a way of representing ourselves and Others, and a regime of governance (Rojas, 2001) — Escobar (1995: 40) stresses that to "understand development as discourse, one must look not at the elements themselves but at the system of relations established among them. It is this system that ... determines what can be thought and said." An emphasis on the system of relations that coordinates thought and action around development is a shift away from the common practice of development studies, which centres on studying the economics of projects and policies to figure out how best to "unleash" the latent forces of development. Because of this emphasis, the discourse of development is best "characterized not by a unified object [a reified vision of what development is and how to achieve it] but by the formation of a vast number of objects and strategies" (Escobar, 1995: 44). The discursive connections among these objects and strategies are so pervasive that it is almost "impossible to conceptualize social reality in other terms" (5).

Wolfgang Sachs (2000: 7, 13) underscores this point when he writes that development can be understood as nothing less than "a secular salvation story," which for fifty years "has been much more than just a socio-economic endeavour; it has been a perception which models reality, a myth which comforts societies, and a fantasy which unleashes passions." Like Escobar (1995), Sachs (1999) places the origins of international development — the concept as it is generally, albeit loosely, understood today — with Harry Truman's 1949 inaugural address. This speech was not only the "starting-gun in the race for the South to catch up with the North," but it was also a defining moment in the creation of an all-encompassing economic worldview — a particularly American worldview (Sachs, 1999: 4). With a few words, Truman conferred upon a majority of the world's population the status of "underdeveloped" and thus fundamentally altered the semantic terrain of international politics. For this majority, Truman not only turned development into "a reminder of *what they are not*" but also imposed the principal goal of their lives: "to escape from the undignified condition called underdevelopment" (Esteva, 1992: 10, 7, emphasis in original).

This sweeping emphasis on the economic aspect of progress is linked to the particular "problematization of poverty" that became pervasive at the time (Escobar, 1995: 44–45). Although relative deprivation has existed since pre-history, the phenomenon of mass poverty in Asia, Latin America, and Africa was "discovered" as if it were a novel condition, the existence of which could suddenly not be tolerated. Poverty was thus "used to define whole peoples, not according to what they are and want to be, but according to what they lack and are expected to become" (Sachs, 1999: 9). This "globalization of poverty," which homogenously constructed two-thirds of the world as poor, came with its own solution that was not only obvious but also unquestionable: "That the essential trait of the Third World was its poverty and that the solution was economic growth and development became self-evident, necessary, and universal truths" (Escobar, 1995: 24).

While the discourse of development has come to be dominated by political and economic issues, particularly poverty, the importance of historical and socio-cultural features within and around the discourse should not be overlooked. Truman may have succeeded in "delinking development from colonialism" (Esteva, 1992: 17), but we should not so easily dismiss the "important connection between the decline of the colonial order and the rise of development" (Escobar, 1995: 26). In fact, the entire discourse of development can be seen, in many ways, "as a response to challenges to imperial power" (26). Consequently, despite many changes in the outward relationship between colonizer and colonized after independence, "there are very strong lines of continuity between colonial and development discourse and policy" (Biccum, 2005: 1006). Because of this continuity, many emerging countries in the South "reinterpreted the power gap" of the colonial order "as a development gap" and, in many "developed" countries, "economic disdain has thus taken the place of colonial contempt" (Sachs, 2000: 8, 1999: 9).

Even though many of the overt manifestations of colonial power have been whitewashed out of prevailing development narratives, Escobar (1995: 43) stresses the foundational influence of "patriarchy and ethnocentrism" on the configuration of the development discourse. Through this influence, "Forms of power in terms of class, gender, race, and nationality thus found their way into development theory and practice. The former do not determine the latter in a direct causal relation; rather they are development discourse's formative elements" (Escobar, 1995: 43). These "forms of power" link development to imperialism not as much through equivalent discriminatory practices — although this does happen — but through their respective "regimes of representation" (Escobar, 1995: 10). Representations are the fundamental building blocks of discourses, and because of the relationship between power and knowledge, they are often organized into those that are accepted/acceptable and those that are unaccepted/unacceptable. The resulting exclusionary effects, which help maintain the historical divisions among perceived races, are reproduced despite changes of wording or character between the discourses. In this way, critiques of international development draw on, and add to, discussions of colonial exercises of power and their relationship to the classification of individuals and populations. While the relationship between imperial motivations and development practices have a plethora of effects on the ground in the South, they have an equally important influence on perceptions in the North.

Just as the discourses surrounding "the Orient" had more to do with British, French, and American worldviews than with the actual lives of "Orientals" (Said, 1979), the discourse of development tells us as much about the way Northerners envision people in the South as it does about the vast complexity of what occurs around the world on a day-to-day basis. Many scholars writing about imperialism and development in terms of discourse have focused on the impact in the South, but we should not forget that equivalent discursive processes take place in the North. Apart from being the site where much of the world's "development knowledge" is constructed (or at least institutionalized and legitimized), the North is also a place where social and cultural perspectives on development and so-called developing peoples are reproduced (see Chouliaraki, 2006; Dogra, 2012; Hall, 1992; Jefferess,

2002a; Lutz and Collins, 1993; Moeller, 1999; Nederveen Pieterse, 1992; Smith and Yanacopulos, 2004). Whether through news media, promotional material from development-oriented charities, documentaries and feature films, magazines such as *National Geographic*, governmental development agencies, or other sources, individuals in the North are exposed to a variety of ideas and values regarding international development and the people who are seen to be principally in need of it. Besides having to interpret these representations of the world and react to them psychologically, they are often called on to respond to them externally through personal discussion, charitable donation, and political action. These responses, together with the activities of policy-makers, academics, activists, and NGO staff, shape the perspectives that determine the political and economic practices of the development industry.

As Northerners interpret and respond to representations of the South, reproducing particular perspectives of themselves and others in the process, they are commonly called on to reference historically rooted ideas of race. The racial classifications that figured so prominently in colonial discourse may have been muted or transformed — now commonly taking the guise of ethnic categories rather than biological ones (Barker, 1981) — but their legacy is starkly evident in the discourse of development. It is no coincidence that the very division of North and South that underpins the logic of international development reflects a global configuration that is equally rooted in perceived racial (and now cultural) difference as it is in economic difference. Emerging out of historical practices of colonialism and set within contemporary practices of imperialism, processes of racialization lie at the heart of the way Northern interventions in the South — in the name of development or humanitarianism — are rationalized (for example, see Razack, 2004). Stated another way, it should not be forgotten that the discourse of development is, at its heart, a racialized discourse, one that not only helps structure Northern understandings of Southerners and their problems, but that also helps constitute Northern people(s) as "legitimately" different.

The problem with child sponsorship

The analysis presented in this book privileges this view of development as discourse without claiming to map the entirety of its breadth or influence in the North. While development occupies the centre of "an incredibly powerful semantic constellation" (Esteva, 1992: 8), it should also be noted that "Within development there is and has always been a multiplicity of voices ... even if some are more powerful than others" (Grillo, 1997: 22). No attempt is made, consequently, to represent all aspects of the discourse of development, which spans an astounding range of cultural, technical, and policy-oriented texts. The goal here is to not to expose the "real" and sordid underbelly of development any more than it is to reveal the negligence of particular sponsorship agencies. Consequently, there is neither the intention to provide a comprehensive explanation around the practice of child sponsorship or its advertising nor the desire to produce a list of concrete recommendations as to how it could be improved. Instead, this project is designed to chart some specific discursive mechanisms that link some mainstream descriptions and strategies of development to the organizations, individuals, and representations involved in child sponsorship fundraising. The objective of this process, given the qualitative nature of this study, is simply to highlight that there is something noteworthy happening at the intersection between the way sponsorship is described and the way development is imagined — something that helps order the ethical landscape in the North and helps rationalize a practice whose value is questionable at best.

Child sponsorship is problematic; it is fraught with difficulty not simply because of what it might fail to do (help Southern children) but above all because of what it is actually designed to do (raise money from Northerners). The way in which child sponsorship accomplishes this fundraising task, and its remarkable success in doing so, tells us something about development and its role in the world as well as something about ethical frames of reference within contemporary liberal societies. As a fundraising strategy, child sponsorship is at least as much about satisfying the needs of Northern sponsors as it is about addressing the needs of Southern children (something sadly reminiscent of the development industry at large). It is structured around providing positive recurring feedback for donors; giving them a feel-good experience in exchange for their money (Jefferess, 2002a). This aim is perfectly understandable from a marketing perspective, and it is one of the crucial elements that make sponsorship so successful.

This orientation of child sponsorship promotion, however, depends upon and ultimately reinforces a particular vision of what it means to do (or be) good in response to problems of global poverty and inequality. Child sponsorship offers more than a fleeting feeling of compassionate warmth; it offers (predominantly white) sponsors a way to become better people — a way to develop themselves as individuals while they help develop (black) Others. Likewise, child sponsorship offers NGOs the opportunity to become better *development* organizations through being more successful *fundraising* organizations. The discursive link between personal development, organizational development, and international development is crucial in creating the space necessary to position sponsors and sponsorship organizations as "doing good" (development work) through the act of "becoming better" (people/organizations).

This articulation of international development goals with organizational and personal aspirations is problematic in that child sponsorship ceases to be (if it ever was) a means to an end and becomes an end in itself — an ethical tautology facilitated by a particular understanding of development. Far from being an abuse of prevailing ethical principles, this emphasis on doing good in the world as a by-product of personal and organizational development is a fundamental aspect of modern liberal thought and a natural extension of colonial relations. In this way, child sponsorship can be better understood as a constituent factor in the reproduction of current relations of knowledge and power in the world — and the value structures that support these relations — than as a method for transforming the status quo.

1

The "Myth" of Child Sponsorship

The notion of child sponsorship exists primarily as a marketing myth. Costly, time-consuming and hampered by the logistical difficulties posed by some of the poorest and most remote places on Earth, child sponsorship succeeds far better as a fundraising engine than it does as a vehicle for providing benefits to the children whose faces sustain it. (Anderson, 1998a: 1–9)

Child sponsorship is one of the most powerful and seductive philanthropic devices ever conceived ... For Many Americans, who donate an estimated $400 million a year to child sponsorship organizations, such appeals appear to offer a simple way of sharing their unparalleled affluence. But when the *Chicago Tribune* sponsored two young boys in the African nation of Mozambique, they found that child sponsorship as depicted by Save the Children is a myth. (Dellios, 1998: 2–8)

If the *Chicago Tribune*'s "The Miracle Merchants: The Myths of Child Sponsorship" series tried to make one thing abundantly clear, it is that child sponsorship is a "myth." According to *Tribune* reporters, it is a myth not only because sponsorship advertising regularly misrepresents the actual living standards of sponsored children and the realistic extent of sponsorship benefits, but also because there is little direct financial connection between sponsor and child:

Poor as they were, none of the *Tribune*'s sponsored children resembled

the desperately sick or malnourished boys and girls whose images are a
staple of fundraising appeals by child sponsorship organizations ... Nor,
as it turned out, were any of their lives much changed by their sponsorships. (*Chicago Tribune*, 1998: 2-2)

This allegation that sponsorship agencies often inflate claims regarding the
individuals they help and the work they accomplish was underscored by the
argument that the "'magical bond' between sponsor and child also proved to be
mostly fiction" (2-2). It is not uncommon for field staff to direct, censor, or even
compose the letters sent to sponsors or for the names of sponsors to be withheld
from sponsored children and their families. In addition to this, some of the children
sponsored by the *Tribune* "were never told that their sponsorships had ended. A
few never understood they had been sponsored at all" (2-2).

These issues of misleading marketing practices are related to another component in the "myth" of child sponsorship — the fact that "there is no guarantee
that a sponsor's dollar will ever reach that sponsor's child, and no way of knowing
whether it ever does" (Dellios, 1998: 2-8). This point, which is acknowledged by
one group of sponsorship executives (2-8), is reiterated extensively in the *Tribune*
series. The reporters noted that, in at least one case, sponsorship officials "were
unable to say how, or even whether, the money donated by the *Tribune* had directly
benefited the sponsored children" (2-8). This may sound quite alarming, but it is
not some shocking secret within the development community. The vast majority
of sponsorship programs pool money from sponsors to fund community-level
projects that (hopefully) benefit the community, but that may or may not directly
help sponsored children. Supporting development projects at the community or
regional (as opposed to the individual or national) levels is a common practice
among development NGOs and is not only accepted but also recommended by
many "development experts." Because of this, however, it is not usually possible (or
perhaps just not administratively feasible) to accurately track the direct benefits of
sponsorship on individual children in the way that sponsorship advertising implies.
This has not always been the case.

In May of 1982, an issue of *New Internationalist* magazine was published with
the title "Please do not sponsor this child: There are better ways to help." The entire
issue, which spawned follow-up articles in 1985 and 1989, dealt with the perceived
problems of child sponsorship at the time. Among the many critiques listed —
including such things as the administrative expense of maintaining sponsorship
programs, the controversial role of religion in sponsorship, and the reinforcement
of stereotypes and paternalistic sentiment — was the problem of creating disparity at the local level. This disparity was the result of sponsorship benefits going to
some children and not others, and according to the authors, it led not only to envy

and resentment within the community but also to inefficient and unsustainable development outcomes. As Stalker (1982: n.p.) writes,

> Helping an individual is divisive — and is particularly damaging in societies which are already sharply divided in all sorts of ways: rich and poor, black and white, high caste or low caste, literate or illiterate. Nor is trying to help an individual likely to succeed. Catapulting even one person out of poverty is a daunting task — especially on $20 a month. And while there will be some successes … they will be few and far between.

Before the mid to late seventies, many sponsorship programs functioned on a so-called "cheque-to-child" model, in which funds flowed (relatively) directly from the sponsor to the child. By the eighties, this practice was coming to an end, and most programs were in the process of transitioning to a primary focus on the community in the way money was spent. The criticism about sponsorship causing local disparities was likely a motivating factor in this transition, together with the relatively new and far-reaching emphasis on participatory development strategies at the community level. Despite the ending of the cheque-to-child model, the idea of *individual* child sponsorship had not fully lost its original implications, and the indictment of child sponsorship as "a sure-fire way to attract money," but "not such a good way to spend it," rang true at the time (Stalker, 1982: n.p.). Nowadays, individual child sponsorship mostly refers to collecting funds from one sponsor per child as opposed to using the image of one child to collect donations from multiple sponsors or, in some extreme cases, using a "representative child" to sell the idea of sponsorship to hundreds or thousands of donors.

Currently, funds raised from sponsorships are mostly indistinguishable from — and are often combined with — other development assistance on the ground. This is convenient and even advantageous from a community development standpoint, but it is problematic from a marketing perspective that seeks to sell the idea of individual improvement. Although sponsorship organizations have altered the way they distribute donations since the early eighties, the fundraising component of sponsorship is largely unchanged. It still emphasizes the direct personal and financial connection between sponsor and child that was the hallmark of early formulations. Consequently, the gap between sponsorship organizations' development practices and their fundraising messages has seemingly become wider over time, at least with respect to the direct benefits received by the sponsored child.

This separation between what is suggested in sponsorship advertising and what actually happens to sponsorship funds was repeatedly taken up by the *Tribune* reporters. Interestingly, the focus on providing individual aid to sponsored children that precipitated one of the strongest early criticisms of sponsorship became the missing element that makes sponsorship programs "mythical." In other words, sending money directly to children or their families, which was ridiculed years before for being the problem with sponsorship, was seen as the heart of a new critique related to false advertising.

How can this shift in the practice of child sponsorship, and the resulting critique, be accounted for? What did child sponsorship look like when it started, and what does it look like today, twenty years after the *Tribune* series? What motivated many sponsorship programs to change the way they operated, and why was this change in development practice (from the level of the individual to that of the community) not mirrored in the fundraising models of most organizations? Finally, what does this critical shift indicate about the way international development is conceived and about the organizations and individuals involved in it? These questions will be addressed in this chapter, which will set the stage for the analysis presented in the remainder of this book — an analysis that, ultimately, explores a critique of child sponsorship rooted in more than organizational problems and false advertising.

Histories of child sponsorship

If there is one "true" origin of child sponsorship, it appears to be lost in the mists of time or to the vagaries of marketing personnel. Almost every major sponsorship agency claims an original and independent foundation of the concept. While some agencies appear to have a better claim than others, such as Save the Children (Watson, 2014), what is interesting here is that the narrative surrounding this foundation is remarkably consistent across organizations. In most instances, this narrative is rooted in the personal life story of the founder who is exposed to the suffering of (distant) children, often through travel or missionary work, and is deeply affected by their plight. This experience is transformative and leads the person, a true humanitarian at heart, to start an organization to help the children in question. The initial suffering witnessed by the founder is usually a product of violent conflict and the aid to children is allotted accordingly, but the organization soon expands its mandate to encompass more children (not just those affected by the specific conflict in that specific location) and more causes of suffering (particularly deprivation related to chronic poverty as opposed to acute conflict). At some point — not necessarily from the very beginning — the idea of individual child sponsorship is "discovered" as a revolutionary means of securing funds, and it begins to define most aspects of the organization. Numerous examples of this narrative can be found among the leading child sponsorship agencies.

The oldest organization that currently offers what is understood today as child sponsorship is Save the Children. Founded in London in 1919 by the teacher and activist Eglantyne Jebb (and her sister Dorothy Buxton), this organization began as means to provide aid for the children of continental Europe in the aftermath of the First World War. The inspiration for this organization came both from her experiences during an "aid mission" to Macedonia immediately after the First Balkan War and from disturbing reports of the conditions of children in Vienna and other war-torn cities following WWI. The Save the Children Fund quickly expanded its programs and resulted in many "sister" organizations in countries outside the UK, coming to Canada in 1921 and the US in 1932. Save the Children US, which was established to help poor children in Appalachia, claims to be the first instance of a sponsorship program in 1938 — a program in which individuals could sponsor schoolhouses and provide the children who attended them with "meals, books and school supplies" (Save the Children US, 2008). Nowadays, however, some national Save the Children organizations no longer offer child sponsorship. Save the Children Canada, for example, used to have a sponsorship program but has now moved away from marketing individual child sponsorship.

In 1937, Plan came on the scene. Initially called Foster Parents Plan for Children in Spain, it was founded by John Langdon-Davies and Eric Muggeridge to help children affected by the Spanish Civil War. John Langdon-Davies, a British journalist, encountered a small boy named Jose who had a note from his father attached to his shirt. The note read: "This is Jose. I am his father. When Santander falls I shall be shot, whoever finds my son, take care of him for me" (Plan UK, 2008). Moved by this event, Langdon-Davies — along with his relief-worker friend Muggeridge — set up the organization to house, feed, and care for the displaced or orphaned children of Spain. The organization grew from this initial setting to help children all over Europe during and after the Second World War (and, consequently, came to be called Foster Parents Plan for War Children). Starting in the 1950s, Foster Parents Plan expanded into the South and into the business of development and poverty alleviation. According to Plan International (2017b), as it is now known, "Langdon-Davies conceived the idea of a personal relationship between a child and a sponsor — a model that puts the child at the centre, and today remains the core of what we do." Canada gained its own incorporated Plan office in 1968.

Christian Children's Fund (CCF), or what is now known as ChildFund in most countries, was founded by the Rev. Dr. J. Calvitt Clarke, who was also a founding member of Save the Children US a few years earlier. Clarke, influenced by his travel and relief work in Armenia as well as the reported troubles of Chinese children as a result of the Sino-Japanese War, created the China's Children Fund in 1938. Dr. Verent Mills also plays a central role in the narrative of CCF history. Mills, who was a missionary in China and became the third Executive Director of CCF, barely escaped the invading Japanese army and managed to single-handedly lead a large group of orphans out of harm's way to a new orphanage supported by CCF. Initially aiding children in China and then Asia, CCF expanded into Europe after WWII and then into other parts of the world in the 1960s and 70s. The organization changed its name from China's Children Fund to the Christian Children's Fund in 1951 to reflect this broader scope. According to the Christian Children's Fund US (now called ChildFund International),

> By 1941, Dr. Clarke had unveiled his plan for individual, person-to-person child "sponsorship," and donors began sending US$24 per year, per child. This new CCF concept enabled people to help who were willing to send smaller amounts of money on a regular basis to help an individual child — pioneering the philosophy of child sponsorship. (2008: n.p.)

In 1960, CCF Canada became the first "official international affiliate" outside of the US (Christian Children's Fund US, 2008: n.p.).

Currently the largest network of organizations to offer child sponsorship, World Vision, began with the vision of one man — Rev. Bob Pierce. While on a mission to China in 1947, Pierce was confronted by a teacher who introduced him to an abandoned little girl needing help. Piece gave "his last five dollars" to support the girl and said he would send money every month for her care; this experience was a "turning point" for Pierce, who then decided to start an organization "dedicated to helping the world's children" (World Vision International, 2017b). Once World Vision was formed in 1950, the "first child sponsorship programme began three years later" (World Vision International, 2017b). In the same year World Vision was founded in the US, Pierce came to Canada "to discuss what he had seen and learned in Asia," and a World Vision office was opened in Toronto in 1957 (World Vision Canada, 2008).

A very similar story is presented by almost every child sponsorship program (for more examples, see Children Incorporated, 2017; Compassion Canada, 2017a). The similarities between these origin narratives are not terribly surprising, however. On one hand, it is far too simple a task to meet poor children in the world. The founders' emotional reaction to such an experience is equally predictable and likely reflects the homogeneity of their backgrounds relative to the children's more than the exceptionality of the encounter. On the other hand, an easy explanation for the similarities between these stories is the value they provide in terms of the public image of the organization. It is not unusual for the public images of organizations or businesses to be built in part upon the mythologies constructed around their founding (think Henry Dunant and the Red Cross or Bill Gates and Microsoft). Not only do the origin stories of sponsorship agencies imbue the organizations with an almost romantic, heroic character, but they also provide a convenient narrative with which donors can identify, metaphorically at least. The notion of a single founder and their quest to help a particular child mirrors the donor's desire to make a real difference in the life of at least one child. The hardship endured by the founder — along with the transformative moment in which they decide to act — reflects the financial considerations faced by potential sponsors and their ultimate decision to "do the right thing." All things considered, then, one must be careful not to completely separate the historicity of origin narratives from their present use as a marketing element of the organization.

Apart from the question of their accuracy, these origin narratives highlight a number of the historical transitions that many child sponsorship programs, and by extension the practice of child sponsorship in general, have gone through. The most important of these transitions are the shifts from, first, a focus on orphans and displaced children to a broader focus on all children irrespective of their family composition; second, a focus on individual children and their particular needs to a broader focus on families, communities, or even regions and their collective needs; and third, a focus on children in a particular geographic region like Spain, the US, China, or Korea to a broader focus on children in any and all poor countries in the South. These related transitions did not occur in an easy chronological order or at an equivalent pace across all organizations, but by and large, they represent some of the major turning points in the history of child sponsorship. While there are surely many factors that influenced these organizational changes within sponsorship programs, it seems likely that both decolonization and the associated proliferation of the discourse of development in the postwar years played major roles.

Many prominent child sponsorship programs, including World Vision, Plan, Save the Children, and Christian Children's Fund, began their existence with the particular goal of helping orphaned or displaced children. Over time, this emphasis broadened to incorporate all children in need, and now very few sponsorship programs dedicated to orphans remain (SOS Children's Villages is one of the only major organization with this focus nowadays). Since the beginning of the so-called modern era, the welfare and education of orphans in the North has been seen as a distinct social problem to be dealt with through both state intervention and charitable efforts, although many early orphanages were concerned with protecting the reputation of the mother as much as the care of the child (Donzelot, 1979; see also Jacobi, 2009). Because of this long history, the care of such children in other locales was likely seen as both a natural and a worthwhile objective of a charitable organization, one that would have little difficulty garnering support from Northern individuals. During the postwar era, however, the paternalistic discourses of charity and humanitarianism that had predominated internationally during the later colonial periods shifted to incorporate the relatively new but equally paternalistic discourse of economic development. As Sachs (2000: 5) describes it, "the moral concern for people was eclipsed by the economic concern for growth." Consequently, where political, religious, and humanitarian interventions were once the prevailing models for overseas involvement, an emphasis on long-term poverty alleviation came to the fore. This emphasis would have made the transition from orphans to all impoverished children seem like a logical and necessary course of action. After all, development was initially conceived of as an economic problem at the national level, requiring solutions that would remove constraints to the "natural" progression toward economic prosperity. In this light, supporting orphans would never be regarded as such a solution, but general education among children might. Within a liberal discourse of development, the adequate preparation of children for economic life — despite supposedly inadequate material (or cultural?) backgrounds — is a truly powerful tenet.

This logical expansion to non-orphaned children, which makes perfect sense in terms of the development discourse, was and still is problematic in terms of the marketing of sponsorships. The same features that would have made fundraising for the care of orphans a relatively straightforward business — the motivation to help a lonely child with no one to care for him or her — might actually impede present-day fundraising efforts because most sponsored children have parents or guardians to care for them, making them appear less in need of support. This may help explain the elision of parents within sponsorship advertising. Even though sponsored children are often a part of supportive families living in reasonably healthy communities (how else could a development project involving them be feasibly managed?), child sponsorship still conjures up images of completely destitute and forlorn children.

The programmatic shift away from a principal focus on orphans was later accompanied by the transition away from the direct care of an individual child. Giving up the so-called cheque-to-child model mentioned earlier, many sponsorship programs began to focus their spending on projects aimed at broader groups, such as neighbourhoods and communities. This process extended over a long period and occurred at different times for different agencies. It is difficult to find child sponsorship programs nowadays that provide direct benefits to sponsored children to the exclusion of non-sponsored children in the same area (excepting the occasional birthday or Christmas gift, which in some cases is described as being sent directly to the child). That said, a few prominent sponsorship programs say they provide direct benefits to sponsored children in the form of exclusive goods and services (i.e., goods and services not offered to non-sponsored children in the same area). Chalice and SOS Children's Villages are some of the largest organizations to follow this model, through which they purport to provide specialized goods and services based on the needs of individual children or even directly send money to the families of sponsored children (for example, see SOS Children's Villages Canada, 2017; Chalice, 2017). Other programs principally fund projects at the neighborhood, municipal, or regional level, from which sponsored children are assumed to benefit. World Vision, for example, sets up and maintains what are known as Area Development Projects (ADPs) with sponsorship funds. These projects often have multi-year funding commitments to stay working in a particular area providing infrastructure, goods, or services to all individuals, not just sponsored children and their families. Compassion Canada appears to work on a hybrid model, in which the sole focus of sponsorship funds is on benefits to children rather than communities. However, Compassion still pools sponsor donations, uses local partners to administer projects, and provides services to registered but not-yet-sponsored children (Compassion Canada, 2017b; Compassion International, 2017).

As with the shift away from orphans, the transition to community-level projects was also likely related to the growing importance of the development discourse after WWII albeit a different aspect of it. Rather than the concern with a larger impact related to the ideas of development economics at the time, the impetus for a shift to a broader group focus is probably a consequence of the general movement within the development industry toward community-level participatory development strategies. This movement, which occurred throughout the 1960s and 70s, highlighted the importance of inclusive, holistic development planning and implementation processes at a level other than that of the nation-state (Rist, 2002; Turner and Hulme, 1997).

There are two important features of this transition to a community-level focus by sponsorship programs. First, it occurred quite a bit later than the shift away from orphans, and it was in all likelihood a product of pressure by experts working in the field of development at the time. A community-level emphasis, preferably involving lots of input from stakeholders, was seen as a best practice in development projects (Parpart, 2000; Rahnema, 1992). As evident from the New Internationalist's critique from the early 1980s, any direct transfer of benefits to individuals, even needy children, was seen as ineffective, inefficient, and even deleterious. Second, this revised emphasis on community-level development strategies once again strayed from what was, and still is, seen as the preferred marketing image of child sponsorship. The idea of the special bond between sponsor and child based on the sponsor's generous support to that *particular* child is not very compatible with a funding model centred on community-level projects that do not privilege sponsored children. While a community-level approach to the spending of funds makes perfect sense within the evolving discourse of development, this same approach creates tension in the principal work of child sponsorship programs — the raising of funds. Nowhere is this tension more evident than in the critique of the "myth" of sponsorship by the *Chicago Tribune*.

In addition to the use of a cheque-to-child model, most early sponsorship programs had a particular geographic area in which they worked. For example, Christian Children's Fund was originally China Children's Fund, Plan International started as Foster Parents Plan for Children in Spain, Save the Children Fund focused on Europe and Russia in the aftermath of WWI (and the nascent US branch served the Appalachian region), Children International was originally Holy Land Christian Mission, and World Vision initially offered sponsorships only in Korea. This geographic focus was mostly located at the country or regional level, but was not necessarily confined to what would now be considered poorer countries or regions. Notably, no early sponsorship programs were focused on Africa or Latin America, two areas that now receive the lion's share of attention from sponsorship programs. Instead, many organizations, such as Save the Children, Plan International, and World Vision, began their work in zones of conflict, particularly those in or related to the North. This makes sense given the time periods involved and the early focus on orphans or displaced children. Currently, the vast majority of sponsorship programs are firmly entrenched in their association with the South, although this does not mean that these organizations no longer fund projects in the US, Canada, or Europe (for example, it is possible to sponsor children from the US through Children Incorporated). This present emphasis on the South is evident in both the marketing of child sponsorship and the actual transfer of funds abroad.

Arguably, this geographic shift to the South could be attributed to the rise of the welfare state, with its accompanying increase in living standards, and to the cessation of conflict in the North. It can safely be assumed, however, that this shift in focus was related to the way in which Southern "underdevelopment" was constructed as a problem after WWII. During this period, which coincides with the end of the colonial era in Africa, a basic worldview emerged that broadly defined the North as prosperous and complete and the South as poor and lacking (Escobar, 1995). This worldview inevitably resulted in changing considerations of what were legitimate and necessary objectives for charitable institutions in the North. Consequently, the geographic transition of sponsorship programs to the South mirrored, or simply accompanied, the shift in emphasis that led away from a focus on orphans to the apparently urgent need for broad-based economic development interventions in the South.

Although not specifically a transition in organizational focus among child sponsorship programs, there is another shift in the history of sponsorship practices that deserves some mention. This shift could be described as a movement away from a focus on missionary work and the saving of souls to a focus on humanitarian or development work and the saving of lives (bodies). While many NGOs that offer child sponsorship are faith-based, these organizations now commonly state that their overseas aid involves no religious strings per se. It seems that of all the major sponsorship programs, only Compassion (2017b: n.p.) explicitly states that sponsored children will receive "Christian Teaching and Discipleship." While the notion of Christian charity still occupies a weighty role in the image and marketing of many sponsorship programs — and the faith of employees is also sometimes an issue — they do not commonly require that children are or become Christian to access benefits from sponsorship-funded development projects. The story is likely not quite as straightforward as this, a topic which will be discussed in later chapters, but the important point here is the changing way in which religion, specifically Christian evangelism, is legitimately incorporated into the work of sponsorship programs.

As with the other transitions discussed above, this point may also be related to the growing importance of the idea of development in the latter half of the twentieth century. Prior to the proliferation and acceptance of the ostensibly secular discourse of development, much of the work related to overseas aid was in the hands of churches and their missions (Bornstein, 2002). In many locations abroad, the division of labour between colonial regimes and religious representatives was quite clear despite some apparent conflicts, with the latter taking on the role of providing education and welfare services in return for support with conversion efforts (see Dirar, 2003; Pels, 1997). At "home," people aided in this process through tithing or other donations to churches and through more conspicuous acts of religiously oriented charity. For example,

> Before the Second World War in Europe one could "buy heathen children" through "slave societies" (slaafkensmaatschappijen), a practice dating back to the slave trade when missionaries could buy children and raise and baptize them in mission homes. Also when there were no more slave markets one could still purchase a heathen child for 21 DM, to whom one could give a baptismal name and as a receipt receive a photo of, for instance, an African boy in a straw skirt. (Nederveen Pieterse, 1992: 71–72)

An obvious if somewhat obscure forerunner to child sponsorship, this early practice of paying to save the souls of heathen children highlights not only the changes in aid relations between the North and South but also the curious similarities between colonial or missionary relationships and current development practices.

While some of the changes are reflected in the lack of overt and coercive proselytization by most aid agencies, including sponsorship programs, the similarities are once again evident in the promises made through sponsorship marketing. Indeed, as one prominent Christian child sponsorship spokesperson puts it in an infomercial,

> I [Jesus] am there in those children waiting to be loved, I am in those children waiting to be rescued, I am there in those children waiting to be served. Whatever you do to them, you do to me. Jesus, as St. Francis says, mystically comes through these children, and if we embrace them,

as Mother Theresa says, we are embracing Jesus. (World Vision Canada, "Heart," n.d.)

Another program words it with even less subtlety: "Compassion is passionately motivating Christians like you to become missionaries to one child — a child in need of love, encouragement, education, healthcare, and most importantly, the life-changing salvation that comes only through Jesus Christ" (Compassion Canada, "Releasing," n.d.).

As noted, the transition from an emphasis on saving souls to saving bodies reflects the secularization of international relations that occurred in conjunction with the end of the colonial period. This process of secularization may have shifted the relative importance of civilizing (read: developing) versus converting Southern people(s), but it does not seem to have significantly altered the subjects or mechanisms involved. The racialized relationships that once rationalized the ability of white Christians in Europe to purchase of the souls of black, "heathen" children in Africa are strikingly similar to those that presently allow white Northerners to purchase the lives of black, poverty-stricken children through sponsorship. It is important to keep in mind, consequently, that through all the changes in global relations over the past hundred years, the world is still starkly divided along racialized boundaries that facilitate the very conditions that seem to justify the practice of child sponsorship.

The historical transitions discussed above may be a little broad, but they still help shed light on the emergence of child sponsorship as it is commonly found today. They highlight the fact that sponsorship is the product of a number of interconnected elements, each having some association with the changing discourse of development. To summarize, the most important of these elements include the early localized efforts by non-profit organizations to provide aid to children who had no one to care for them, the rapid decolonization and redefinition of many Southern countries resulting in a starkly perceived contrast between the North and South, the discrediting of early foreign aid approaches prompting a move toward community-centred initiatives, and the maintenance of a religious or moral overtone among sponsorship organizations coupled with a need to separate themselves from the explicit paternalistic baggage of colonial-era charity. The articulation of these elements, while each making sense in their specific contexts, has formed a contemporary global practice that is generally difficult for many to understand, thus opening itself up to a history of somewhat contradictory critiques. As noted earlier, much of this confusion stems from a substantial but underappreciated separation between the raising of funds through child sponsorship and the use of those funds. However efficacious child sponsorship may be at raising money, the marketing of sponsorship is at odds with what is seen as the legitimate use of those funds abroad and, therefore, fosters the misconception that child sponsorship is much more than an extremely effective fundraising technique. In order to shed some light on this issue, it is useful to know a little more about the contemporary organizational and promotional contexts of child sponsorship.

Contexts of child sponsorship

It is important to note that the majority of child sponsorship agencies are not, in fact, entire agencies dedicated to sponsorship. Rather, they are better described as NGOs that use child sponsorship as one of their fundraising strategies. This reflects the fact that many of these organizations began their existence without the use of child sponsorship as it is known today. It also represents the reality of development spending by these organizations or their partners in the South, which is almost never focused directly on sponsored children and their individual needs but on community-wide projects that may or may not directly benefit these children. Finally, characterizing child sponsorship agencies as NGOs that fundraise partly through sponsorship takes into consideration that, in many cases, these organizations currently receive a lesser but significant portion of their revenue from sources other than child sponsorship, such as government grants. For example, Plan Canada collected only 36.8 percent of the organization's 2016 revenue from child sponsorships, while Christian Children's Fund of Canada collected 61 percent of its 2016 revenue from sponsorships (Plan Canada, 2017a; Christian Children's Fund of Canada, 2017).

Apart from this semantic issue, the separation between raising funds and spending them within child sponsorship is evident in the international and national structures of most sponsorship programs. The NGOs that run these programs are often part of an international network of differentiated and potentially autonomous organizations. These networks are most often comprised of organizations in the North that principally raise money and their partner organizations or local affiliates in the South that principally spend it. Each of these organizations often has a separate management and board with individual priorities set at the national level. Many Northern sponsorship organizations are themselves often divided up into thematically and spatially distinct groups such that those individuals who prepare televised ads may not have any regular contact with those who deal with the responses to those ads or those who prepare the mail-outs to send to newly recruited sponsors. These offices are predominantly staffed not by individuals who would be considered development professionals but by people who are educated in marketing, commerce, communications, or business administration and who were often previously employed in the private sector. This staffing arrangement is commonly reinforced through the pervasive use of a particular style of language, one that is rooted in business with its concern for market share, brand image, and the servicing of clients (sponsors, in this instance). While some of the consequences of these organizational arrangements will be discussed in Chapter 2, for now it is sufficient to note how this set-up structurally differentiates the process of fundraising from the on-the-ground development work it supports.

The organizational structures of sponsorship programs are designed to support an elaborate, extensive, and above all, effective fundraising machine. This machine draws its operating power from the wallets of "average" Northerners who provide pre-determined and ongoing monthly donations, often drawn directly from credit cards or bank accounts. According to the connotations of sponsorship promotional material, if not the fine print, these donations are earmarked for the care of a particular sponsored child. Through marketing communications, sponsors are often led to believe that their donations — and only the ongoing nature of these donations — provide the essentials for a happy and productive life for their sponsored child. Each year in Canada, for example, this personal appeal entices hundreds of thousands of people to begin and maintain sponsorships.

The actual picture is different from what many people expect, although not necessarily different from what sponsorship programs explicitly state in much of their carefully worded promotional material. As noted already, the monthly donation collected from a sponsor in Canada is, by and large, neither transferred directly to the sponsored child, nor even directly to the sponsored child's family or community. Instead, donations from all of the programs' sponsors are pooled together with any additional funds the organization has raised and sent to partner organizations in the South in support of their ongoing development projects. Because these development projects are often multi-year endeavours, sometimes with funding from multiple sources, they are financially approved in advance and guaranteed funding over the life of the project (inasmuch as anything is guaranteed within the non-profit sector). What this essentially means is that all the children who live in the project area, including those waiting to be sponsored or those who have lost their sponsors, will benefit from what the project offers. So, despite sponsorship appeals that seem to indicate that children are desperately awaiting sponsorship to receive help, this is not often the case. Furthermore, while sponsorship marketing promises to provide everything from clean water to education to medicine, the sponsorship programs that raise the funds from Northerners do not always, or even often, set the priorities of the development projects in question. As is common within development practice nowadays, project objectives are determined, in consultation with all the stakeholders, by the local people or organizations that will be carrying out the day-to-day work of the project. The overall focus of projects, however, can sometimes be set at the funding level, and this is especially true of bilateral grants funnelled through NGOs. This means that while a sponsor may think their child is getting a daily ration of food, the project in the child's community may be building a community centre or providing entrepreneurial training to local craftspeople. In most cases, sponsorship donations provide exactly the same thing as non-sponsorship donations — a source of funding for existing development projects in the South.

This model of sponsorship has produced a substantial degree of confusion among both sponsors and the public, ultimately leading the *Chicago Tribune* to criticize child sponsorship programs for not providing direct benefits some twenty years after the *New Internationalist* criticized them for doing exactly that. So, what changed in these intervening years? In aligning themselves with what came to be considered proper development practices — not fostering local disparities or providing short-lived, handout-style solutions to poverty — child sponsorship programs faced a dilemma regarding their marketing strategies. They could continue focusing on the individual connection between sponsor and child or switch to a more accurate but much less effective strategy of soliciting sponsors for communities or projects. Although some programs did try out and adopt the latter strategy, the majority of sponsorship programs opted to retain the emphasis on "individual" child sponsorship as a meaningful personal and *financial* relationship between sponsor and child. Whereas it may be understood as a personal relationship between sponsor and child, it is more realistically described as a financial relationship between sponsor and organization. At some level, however, this distinction highlights not as much the fictional nature of child sponsorship but the fundamental difference between what constitutes legitimate development practice and what produces good fundraising results.

With some notable exceptions, the largest child sponsorship programs in Canada all follow this model to some extent.[3] World Vision, Canada's largest child sponsorship program by a substantial margin, states that they "pool your monthly sponsorship donation with those from other Canadians who support kids in the same area, leveraging them for maximum effectiveness based on the needs of the community" and that they recruit sponsored children "with the understanding that the benefits will be shared by everyone in the community" (World Vision Canada, 2017a). Plan Canada, the second largest sponsorship program in Canada, makes a similar disclaimer on their website. In response to the question: "Does my sponsorship contribution go directly to one child?" they reply, "No. Sponsorship contributions are pooled centrally and used to fund programs benefiting sponsored children, their families and their communities" (Plan Canada, 2017b). The majority of smaller sponsorship agencies, such as Christian Children's Fund of Canada and Canadian Feed the Children, function on a similar model in that sponsored children do not receive special benefits above and beyond what other children in the project area can receive (except in terms of communicating with their sponsors and having the possibility, in some cases, of receiving additional monetary gifts).

Two reasonably large NGOs that offer sponsorship, Compassion Canada and Chalice, both claim to do things differently. Compassion states that they do not focus on community development projects per se and only fund partners who provide specific services to children in the form of things like health care, education, and meals (Compassion Canada, 2017b; Compassion International, 2017). As noted earlier, however, they still pool donations to fund church partners working in communities and provide outreach to non-sponsored children. Chalice (2017), a specifically Catholic NGO in Canada, says that they use a "direct family funding model." If this is accurate, it places them in a very different category than the majority of sponsorship programs. Chalice is already distinguished by its relatively small-scale marketing program (few TV ads or direct appeals outside churches), but this maintenance of a more traditional cheque-to-child model is unusual in the present climate of overseas development assistance. Before going on to discuss the implications of the community development model that most sponsorship agencies follow, it is useful to remind ourselves that, despite some significant commonalities, the field of child sponsorship is not uniform. It is also useful to remember that when most sponsorship agencies moved away from a direct funding model, they did so because this was (and still is) considered best practice in development assistance. While Compassion emphasizes the personal nature of its support and Chalice appears to pride itself on its direct funding model, these kinds of individual approaches were discarded by most sponsorship programs for very good reasons. While some might use paternalistic phrases like "fostering dependence" as a reason to avoid this practice, it is more accurate to do so due to worry about creating disparities and resentment at the local level, combining evangelism with financial support, and individualizing what is, at its heart, a broader social problem.

Child sponsorship in a neoliberal era

The general shift in development thinking toward participatory, community-level approaches may have precipitated both the *New Internationalist*'s critique and, ultimately, the change in the way sponsorship programs carried out their development work, if not their advertising, but it cannot completely explain what the *Chicago Tribune* wrote in their special edition. The *Tribune*'s concern with investigating the correlation between advertising promises and direct benefits to sponsored children highlights a different kind of logic than what motivated the *New Internationalist*'s critical appraisal. Substantive changes in the development discourse over the course of the 1980s and 90s can help illuminate the disparity between these two critiques. In particular, the revitalization and reimagining of classical liberal thought during this period likely played a role in the perception of legitimate child sponsorship practices. Commonly referred to as neoliberalism, this revival of the classical economic principles associated with liberalism places a strong emphasis on individual ability and responsibility along with privileging free-market values such as choice, competition, accountability, and efficiency (see Braedley and Luxton, 2010; Harvey, 2007; Hindess, 2002; Stein, 2002). A focus on neoliberalism, a term that is simultaneously esoteric and banal, may seem unnecessary in exploring the practice of child sponsorship and the case of the *Tribune* articles. At the heart of neoliberalism, however, lie the practices of liberal modes of government that Foucault has insightfully linked to the concepts of power, freedom, subjectivity, and consequently, ethics.

Freedom plays a crucial role in Foucault's thoughts on power in general and in his perspective of governmentality in particular. Foucault (2003 [1982a]; 1990 [1978]) discusses relations of power primarily as productive rather than repressive. Power works through production because, fundamentally, power represents the ability of individuals to choose and to act on those choices. Expressions of power are present, therefore, in all individual actions — however minor — as well as in the consequences of those actions on others. As Foucault (1990 [1978]: 93) notes, power "is produced from one moment to the next, at every point, or rather in every relation from one point to another. Power is everywhere; not because it embraces everything, but because it comes from everywhere." Because every action alters the actions of others, however, the collective actions of all individuals serve to constrain the overall possible field of actions. It can therefore be said that power allows action but also operates to delimit it. Significantly, power delimits action not by force — Foucault calls this domination — but by constraining the free choices of individuals through discursive processes of demarcating legitimate choices from illegitimate ones. According to Foucault (2003 [1978]: 139), then, freedom is "the condition for the exercise of power."

Through this understanding of power, Foucault links his thoughts on freedom and government. In part, the concept of governmentality describes the emergence of freedom as the fundamental organizing feature of power relations. While the element of freedom has always been present in power relations, it has never been more central to arts of government; "modern individuals are not merely 'free to choose' but *obliged to be free*, to understand and enact their lives in terms of choice" (Rose, 1999: 87, emphasis in original). This movement toward an understanding of government through freedom, rather than in spite of it, has been a particularly liberal undertaking whereby people "were to be 'freed' in the realms of the market, civil society, the family" only to be simultaneously subjected to "the invention of a whole series of attempts to shape and manage conduct within them in desirable ways" (Rose, 1999: 69). This shaping and management is not a top-down process but something in which individuals take an active part. Consequently, a significant facet of liberalism is the focus on improving the welfare of the population, not through force or intimidation on a broad level but through encouraging people to regulate themselves in order to reach some personal state of health, wealth, or happiness. The liberal dream was to

> produce individuals who did not need to be governed by others, who would govern themselves through introspection, foresight, calcula-tion, judgement and according to certain ethical norms. In these ideal individuals the social objective of the good citizen would be fused with the personal aspiration for a civilized life: this would be the state called freedom. (Rose, 1999: 78)

While this dream has been reoriented over time as the focus of liberal critique has shifted, it has always maintained this dual, and sometimes paradoxical, characteristic of individual freedom and collective welfare.

In this way, governmentality lies at the heart of both politics and ethics for Foucault. It represents not only the ways in which people are constrained and controlled in society but also the ways in which they are set free as individuals and invited to use this freedom to improve themselves for the supposed benefit of all. Under liberal arts of rule, individuals are simultaneously constituted as citizens of states and subjects of government, but these are not coterminous. Their role as citizens is in furtherance of their status as governed and not the other way around. This is Foucault's insight — that modern forms of power may function through the state and its institutions, but they do not predominantly stem from it. Instead, they circulate through the myriad of daily practices in which individuals, in their freedom, choose to take part. This circulation is not arbitrary or coincidental; it is the direct product of a way of thinking about the relationship between individuals and the political collectivities they form. It is through the conception of freedom within this relationship, and the specific choices that it allows, that individuals are both subjected to power and defined as ethical beings.

Two prominent examples of research that help illustrate this link between power, freedom, and the construction of ethical subjects are Samantha King's (2006) work on breast cancer survivorship and the politics of philanthropy and Barbara Cruikshank's (1996, 1999) work on poverty, self-help, and citizenship in the US. Both of these projects highlight the way in which particular modes of self-government, principally meaning self-regulation, are bound up in discourses of what it means to be a good citizen under contemporary liberal arts of govern-ment. They also both address, however, the way in which these discourses "shape identities," "cultivate political subjects," and "produce knowledges and truths" about breast cancer and the poor, respectively (King, 2003: 296). This latter emphasis on identity is valuable because it helps relocate and denaturalize the commonly accepted value of independent, "positive" action such as voluntarism, participation, and philanthropy. Instead of seeing the "Race for the Cure" or self-esteem programs as always already "good," these practices are understood as an inherent facet of neoliberalism that allows for the creation of compatible and amenable citizens.

What is important from this discussion of subjectivity and ethics is an understanding of how, in the present neoliberal context, certain individual, voluntary practices have become increasingly central to the way Northerners imagine their role in the face of social problems like poverty. While there is a great deal of academic work on the effects of neoliberalism on development in general (for example, see Comaroff and Comaroff, 2001; Chang and Grabel, 2004; Craig and Porter, 2006; Edelman and Haugerud, 2005), this element lies at the heart of the present critique of child sponsorship. Neoliberal thought tends to stress individual connections to the economy above communal bonds, which results in the legitimization of particular kinds of individual assistance and a devaluing of particular kinds of community-oriented development. Following its liberal basis, neoliberalism also puts forth a vision of childhood as a preparatory period in which the child is made ready for future economic life. Consequently, this viewpoint tends to see specific aid to children — particularly in the form of food, medicine, and above all, education — as creating (future) equality of opportunity among a class of individuals not yet deemed responsible for their economic situation (see Fendler [2001] for a discussion of how this element of neoliberalism relates to education and child development). On the other hand, community-based projects, especially those not seeking to train locals in some aspect of their livelihood, are viewed with more suspicion as potentially removing the individual incentives to attain economic independence and prosperity. In neoliberal thought, these perspectives on aid are combined with individualized rather than systemic understandings of poverty and, consequently, with a tendency to look for personal misconduct or organizational malfeasance as an explanation for continuing poverty or poor aid efficacy.

This emphasis helps explain how the reporters of the *Chicago Tribune* could present such a scathing assessment of child sponsorship programs despite the fact that, in many instances, these programs were following widely accepted development practices as well as using the most effective (albeit potentially misleading) advertising strategies they knew. It helps explain how the *Tribune* located the problems of child sponsorship in the organizations that offer it (and not in any innate nature of the practice itself) and the solution to those problems in administrative efforts to improve the advertising and reporting practices of sponsorship programs (and not in the need for some fundamental economic and representational restructuring at the global level). Ultimately, it helps explain how the "mythical" nature of child sponsorship could be presented as equally disturbing to the sponsors it supposedly deceives as it is to the children it purports to help.

For *Tribune* reporters, calling child sponsorship a "myth" seems to highlight the failed promises of sponsorship programs and the illusory character of the sponsor-child relationship. An alternative understanding of the term myth, however, highlights something very different but equally important to the critique of child sponsorship. For semioticians such as Barthes (1972 [1957]), myths are not simply fictional stories that relate to life. Instead, myths are a "type of speech" that not only represent the site of ideology but also help people make sense of cultural phenomena by structuring the connotative meanings of signs (Barthes, 1972 [1957]: 109). The result of mythical speech, then, is the perceived naturalization of essentially arbitrary (or at least artificial) meanings, such as those commonly associated with children, development, or sponsorship. What this alternative meaning of myth implies for a critique of child sponsorship is that, rather than sponsorship being seen as a fiction that deceives sponsors, it can be understood as a form of communicating information about the world that naturalizes particular explanations of global poverty, its causes, and its solutions.

Taken one step further, this alternative understanding of the mythical nature of sponsorship helps explains the reason why the articles comprising the *Chicago Tribune* series on child sponsorship are so relevant to this book. While these articles provide a useful, if somewhat dated, description of common sponsorship criticisms that serve to introduce each chapter, they represent more than a simple counterpoint to the analyses presented in this study. The explanations and recriminations contained within these articles also represent a mythology of sponsorship critique, a naturalization of particular ideas of what is wrong with sponsorship, and by extension, what can be done to improve it. By unpacking some of the narratives within these articles and highlighting the logic of their critique, this mythology is exposed. Uncovering this mythology, at least in theory, is an essential first step to begin reimagining a critique of sponsorship that does not start and end with false advertising and individual or organizational error.

In explaining how child sponsorship operates as a fundraising practice in the North, the preceding discussion highlights the political and economic contexts within which sponsorship presently operates. Additionally, it sets the stage for an analysis in the following chapters that focuses largely on the (mediated) relationship between sponsorship programs and sponsors.

2

Child Sponsorship as a Fundraising Technique

"I am not a missionary, I am a businessman." According to Jackson and Tackett (1998: 2-4) of the *Chicago Tribune*, this phrase was often used by Joseph Gripkey, a former CEO of Children International (CI). Gripkey took over the American organization, then known as Holy Land Christian Mission, in 1973. With the help of Jerry Huntsinger, an experienced child sponsorship marketer, Gripkey transitioned the organization from a small operation providing "love baskets" to widows and orphans in Bethlehem to a "philanthropic powerhouse" (Jackson and Tackett, 1998a: 2-3, 1998b: 2-4). Pursuing a low-price, no-money-down version of child sponsorship, CI ended up collecting some US$65 million in donations from more than 200,000 sponsors in 1996 (Jackson and Tackett, 1998b: 2-4). In return for his services, Gripkey earned more than US$190,000 in 1992 alone, so much that the charity had an external company process the payroll for its executives because it "did not want other workers to know what they were earning" (2-4). Despite noting this concern, the *Tribune* reporters were not expressly critical of the amount of Gripkey's compensation.[4] Instead, they discussed the discrepancy between the publicized amount of Gripkey's salary, about US$120,000 plus an US$18,000 expense allowance, and the amount listed on internal records, some US$50,000 more (2-4). For the *Tribune*, this discrepancy appeared to underscore some of the central problems of child sponsorship, namely a lack of adequate transparency regarding sponsorship costs and benefits, insufficient oversight of donated funds, and inefficient or inappropriate use of those funds.

These problems with child sponsorship, which are largely perceived to be organizational in nature, were highlighted again and again throughout the *Tribune* series. For example, the reporters found that Children International's claims regarding the benefits of sponsorship were often "overstated," with none of the children they met having experienced any extraordinary transformations in their daily lives as a result of the sponsorship (Tackett and Jackson, 1998a: 2-3). While the children did receive some useful goods and services for their participation in the sponsorship program, these were far from the miraculous and life-altering benefits advertised by CI (2-4). In some cases, the goods and services provided were redundant, unusable, or simply inappropriate for children, such as jeans or shoes several sizes too big, sheets and blankets in a tropical area where no one uses them, a "barefoot doctor" with no training and no supplies, plastic dinnerware when the family already had a set given by CI the previous year, or some nails and plywood sent as a child's birthday gift (Schmetzer and Crewdson, 1998: 2-8).

Added to these concerns about what constitutes a "benefit" of sponsorship, and how this differs from the ideas conjured up in promotional material, was the problem of costs. According to the experiences of *Tribune* reporters, many of the goods and services provided by CI did not seem to come close to the amount donated by sponsors. For example, after receiving an extra $25 gift from a *Tribune* sponsor, CI gave the sponsored child a jogging suit worth $13 in local stores (Tackett and Goering, 1998: 2-5). This is in line with what was stated by a local head of CI that "between $70 and $80 of each $144 annual sponsorship fee reaches the Philippines" (Schmetzer and Crewdson, 1998: 2-9). Unfortunately, this was significantly less than the circa 80 percent that CI says goes to "worldwide charitable programs" and, at the time, CI was unwilling to open their books to the *Tribune* in order to explain the discrepancy (2-9).

From these and other examples in the *Tribune* series, one is seemingly led to the conclusion that the "mythical" nature of child sponsorship is largely an organizational problem. Administrative malfeasance or ineptitude is seen not only to underlie the disconnect between advertising messages and project spending but also to result in a dearth of positive outcomes. However, if organizational environments and their failures are seen to be at the heart of the problems with child sponsorship, then the stage is already set for a discussion of the solution — greater transparency, better oversight, and more targeted development assistance. While this discussion is undoubtedly necessary, such a formulation of problem and solution leaves out many important questions about how child sponsorship functions, particularly those questions related to the broader contexts of international development work and neoliberal conceptions of society. Consequently, this chapter and the next attempt to go beyond the normative critique of sponsorship presented in the *Tribune* series.

Using the lens of developmentality introduced previously, these two chapters

explore the relationship among the structures and practices of these organizations, the specific understandings of development that inform these structures and practices, and the ethical framework within which these understandings operate. Through investigating how child sponsorship staff employ the discourse of development in their work, it is possible to highlight how sponsorship programs position and justify their efforts to address global poverty. This analysis of the development discourse within the everyday work of sponsorship agencies allows for a critique of these organizations that focuses more on problems with the broader context of development rather than things like duplicity or negligence. The present chapter begins this analysis by looking at how child sponsorship programs are structured nationally and internationally as fundraising machines. This simple but important argument lays the groundwork for the discussion in the next chapter, which looks at the organizational and ethical implications of this reality.

To help explore these issues, both this chapter and the next draw on in-depth interviews with fourteen current and two former staff members of child sponsorship programs. Between one and four staff members were interviewed at each of the following organizations: World Vision Canada, Plan Canada, Christian Children's Fund of Canada, Compassion Canada, Canadian Feed the Children, and Food for the Hungry Canada. At the time of the interviews, staff members worked in the following areas: three in senior management positions that directly or indirectly monitor the production of promotional material, five in marketing or communications positions, three in donor relations positions, and three in program positions (dealing directly with the partner agencies overseas). Interviews lasted between one and two hours and were loosely structured around a set of open-ended questions dealing with participants' roles at the organization, their thoughts on the benefits and challenges of child sponsorship, and their perceptions of the world in general. Throughout these chapters, pseudonyms and non-specific job descriptions are the only distinguishing features to differentiate participant responses. Any quotations that suggest a participant's organizational affiliation are altered to protect the identity of the participant.

Child sponsorship as a fundraising tool

There are many reasons to see child sponsorship as a type of fundraising approach rather than, or at least in addition to, a specific way of addressing long-term poverty and its consequences. The most important of these reasons is something that has been brought up several times before and is supposedly at the heart of the "mythical" nature of sponsorship — the disconnect within contemporary sponsorship models between fundraising efforts in the North and development efforts in the South. This disconnect resides in the incongruence between sponsorship promotional messages, which often imply a one-on-one financial relationship between sponsor and child mediated by a single organization, and the use of sponsorship donations, which most often support community or regional-level development projects that do not privilege sponsored children and that are carried out by local partners. Related to this disconnect is the way in which organizations are structured, both nationally and internationally, and the way in which organizational culture, language, and staffing manifest themselves within these structures. Before fleshing out these issues, it should be noted that, contrary to the *Tribune* critique, this disconnect should not be seen as rendering sponsorship "mythical" (in the sense of being fictional or deceptive). Despite any incongruence between fundraising messages and project outcomes, child sponsorship cannot be seen as a myth if it is understood as primarily a fundraising mechanism. In this case, it is true to itself inasmuch as its purpose is seen to be fulfilled by the raising of funds. The myth, if there is any, lies in seeing sponsorship as much more than a fundraising tool. That is to say, the myth of sponsorship is not about what it might fail to accomplish in terms of its promises but what it actually accomplishes in terms of its effects on individuals in the North.

An understanding of child sponsorship as a fundraising mechanism is not a terribly controversial claim among many sponsorship staff members. As one marketing and communications specialist (Gina) noted, "the reality is that sponsorship is one tool to bring money in to achieve our mission to lessen the impact of poverty on children and families." Margaret, a program management specialist, explained this notion in slightly more detail:

> For us, sponsorship is more of a tool for fundraising rather than an implementation tool in the field. Our programs vary dramatically; we do not have a cookie-cutter approach to a sponsored program in the field. Some in [one country] are very different than others in [another country], so the programs are implemented according to the need as opposed to a boxed-in "this is what sponsorship must be." We basically eliminate that, but funds are raised based on sponsorship.

This description of sponsorship as a fundraising tool, technique, or mechanism was not uncommon in many of the staff interviews, and it is reiterated in a prominent report sponsored by Plan International. The researchers at the Institute of Development Studies at the University of Sussex, who were contracted to produce this report and who interviewed staff at eight different Plan locations, concluded that sponsorship "is perceived by most operational staff and volunteers [at Plan] as a fundraising rather than a development activity" (Plan International, 2008: 8). In other words, most operational staff "perceive sponsorship mainly as an effective fundraising approach" (5). The report also noted that Plan's offices in wealthy countries (known as National Offices, National Organizations, or simply NOs) "have been undergoing a transition from being primarily focused on sponsorship and fundraising, to becoming development organisations with staff capacity and knowledge of programmes. NOs vary in how far they have come and how committed they are to this transition" (10).

While the Sussex research found that "Senior level staff are more likely to articulate the developmental benefits than operational staff" (Plan International, 2008: 5), this was not always the case among this book's sample of participants. Brian, a senior manager, summed up his view concisely, saying that "sponsorship is a funding model." Speaking candidly, he explained that he had "come to the conclusion that most attempts at child sponsorship were clever marketing." He added,

> child sponsorship tells me nothing; it is just fundraising, just marketing … to say I am a believer in sponsorship from a marketing perspective, yeah, it is a great marketing tool, but from a helping the poor perspective, [I am] not that much of a believer.

These statements seem perplexing given the source, except that he was specifically referring to the way that other programs address sponsorship. While he stated that his organization's "marketing message is not much different than the marketing message of many organizations in Canada," he also said,

> I am convinced that if you went and saw what we do, you would come back and say, "your marketing message is pretty accurate." I am also as convinced that if you did the same thing with other organizations, you would come back and say, "Woah, woah, woah. You need to change your marketing message, or you need to change your programming because there is no match."

This dual admission and admonition on the part of one senior staff member not only illustrates the common understanding among many such insiders that sponsorship is primarily a funding tool, but it once again highlights the inconsistencies that plague, but strangely do not disrupt, discussions of child sponsorship. Leaving aside the question of whether or not the way his organization and its partners operate is somehow more legitimate than other organizations, it is important to point out that the recognition of sponsorship as a marketing tool by many interviewed staff occurred alongside the aforementioned descriptions of sponsorship as a solution to development problems. The obvious explanation for this contradiction is that sponsorship is commonly understood to be simultaneously a fundraising practice and a development practice. It is seen to bridge this divide by being the means through which the perceived work of development is accomplished.

Acknowledging the marketing effectiveness of child sponsorship, Jacqueline noted that it is "a wonderful way to make a connection and to motivate donors to give monthly." She subsequently divulged the role of her organization in relationship to this as one of facilitating development work through fundraising. In her words, "Our mission and our goal is to be a bridge and provide the resources to people in need and to give people in Canada the opportunity to help and to make a difference." This point both introduces the question of what really counts as the work of development (or what the work of development is, to begin with) and foreshadows the discussion of how the problem of development is constructed in relationship to child sponsorship. Before moving on to this discussion, however, it is still necessary to examine the evidence for understanding sponsorship as, first and foremost, a fundraising technique.

International divisions

At an international level, there are two main aspects of child sponsorship that encourage an understanding of sponsorship as a fundraising technique. The first relates to the structure of NGOs that use child sponsorship and the second relates to the way funds from sponsorship are used. As noted in previous chapters, sponsorship programs are almost invariably housed in organizations that are both independent of, and functionally differentiated from, the organizations that carry out the projects funded by sponsorship dollars. The vast majority of Northern sponsorship programs, including all those interviewed for this project, are part of international networks of nationally run organizations that (almost exclusively) raise money and then transfer that money to national or local partners in the South so that they can carry out development projects. James, a senior manager, stated it quite succinctly: "we in Canada and other national offices do not tend to be program deliverers." Jennifer, a marketer, explained, "we make a pledge to the field office. So, our offices are all kind of autonomous, like our office in [an African country] ... and we send them money, but they run themselves." With a slightly different structure, Petra's organization has

> what are called country offices, and those house staff that are paid by [our organization], and they are responsible for overseeing the partners. So, what we call a sponsorship program — a partner is responsible for that program. [Interviewer: So, a local NGO maybe?] A local NGO, okay, yeah ... so we do not implement those programs; they are partner programs.

Within this framework, the amount of direct project oversight by Northern

NGOs seems to vary. Some organizations simply check annual accounts while others monitor or evaluate project sites and train local staff. However, the actual planning and running of projects by the Northern staff of these organizations is exceedingly rare. Margaret, who works in programs, described the situation in her organization:

> We do not have overseas staff for the most part … so, with that in mind, we have to be able to trust our partners that we affiliate with because, for the most part, we do not have day-to-day contact with them. So, we have to be able to trust they are going to manage a sponsorship program, or any other program, adequately. Our reporting ensures that — the fact that they have to send financial statements on an annual basis; we do random audits as well.

Margaret went on to clarify that it is the partners who produce the "development plans," and "we fund it based on a child sponsorship model." This organizational division of labour leaves many such Northern NGOs with little to do except raise funds and account for the reasonable use of these funds.

A key to understanding the organizational nature of child sponsorship is to understand how sponsorship money is used, and in many ways, this is a direct consequence of the structural arrangement noted above. So, how are sponsorship funds used? They are spent in the same way as other private donations and, often, in the same way as other sources of funding, such as bilateral grants, that are targeted at child-centred community development. A senior manager, Paul, explained "this is just an integrated funding model that we have got, and we will bring together all these different sources of funds. Sponsorship is the most important one, but we are able to bring that together with our other funding sources including government grants as well." This means that development projects funded, in whole or in part, by sponsorship often look exactly like other such development projects; it also means that there is often no differentiation on the ground between sponsorship funding and other funding within any particular project. "Our programming" said Tamara, a program specialist, "is very linked on the ground with sponsorship. For a field office, there is no difference between Canadian CIDA money and sponsorship or USAID money. For them, it all goes into one program." In fact, when a Northern NGO using child sponsorship sends money to its overseas partners, there is not usually any separation of sponsorship funds from other sources of revenue. Commonly, the only distinguishing influence that sponsorship has is in determining the geographic destination of the funds. As Jennifer noted,

> our child sponsorship programs are, for the most part, very much integrated with other community programs, and it is not just working with the child. You are also doing agriculture and other education and health

care, leadership training in the whole community, and that is part of our other programs we run as well.

This last point by Jennifer highlights something else that has been mentioned numerous times already, that sponsorship funds are used by and large to support long-term, community-level development projects.

These projects are intended to benefit the entire community or region by gradually increasing the area's perceived level of development. Through this "developmental" increase, children in the area, whether sponsored or not, are expected to indirectly benefit (and sometimes do directly benefit through the payment of school fees or the purchase of school supplies, for example). With respect to the basic sponsorship contributions by sponsors, sponsored children cannot generally expect to receive specific benefits denied to their non-sponsored siblings or peers. Once again, this is not something that is in any way denied by organizations or their staff; rather, it is often offered as a sign of good development practice. Paul stated it clearly when he said,

> we are an organization that is focused on children, but we do not work at it in terms of individual children. We take a community-based approach to our development. So, with child sponsorship, when you are sponsoring a child, it is not that you are just providing a handout to a particular child. [It is] more that we are working with the whole community, and sponsorship is a funding mechanism for supporting our development work in that community.

Petra, a donor services manager, explained this same idea with a simple example: "if there is a dentist going to the community, say, twice a year, the dentist will not only see sponsored children but other children in the community that need dental assistance." Tamara echoed these statements, declaring

> the beauty is, again, [in] this new trend in sponsorship, it is not going to one child; it is going to the community. So, it is not the one child [who] is benefiting from the program and the next-door neighbour who is not. They are equally poor. I mean the whole community is poor in these communities ... The health worker is not going to say, "okay, you are not in the [project] community you do not get services" ... That is the whole beauty of sponsorship now.

Susan, who also works in donor services but with a different organization, even commented that her organization is "moving away from just saying child sponsorship; we are saying child-centred community development program."

There are a couple of implications of this community-centred approach that relate to the fundraising nature of child sponsorship. Two comments serve to illustrate these implications. The first deals with the lack of correspondence in terms of timing and budget between ongoing projects and sponsor donations. In discussing the role of local partners, Jennifer noted that

> they pick a community, and so *the money that we pledge based on the number of kids we think we can get sponsored* goes to help all the kids in that community. But the ones that are actually sponsored are the ones that get to write the letters back and forth to the donors and things like that, but we really try to as much as possible make sure that it is not half the kids are allowed to go to school and the other half are not (emphasis added).

What this discussion of pledging expresses is that, in most cases, local partners create project plans, usually spanning many years, for which they require stable funding. Northern NGOs then agree to fund these long-term projects using their revenue, most of which is derived from sponsorship, creating a commitment that they try to fulfill. Logically speaking, this implies that the overseas funding commitments of sponsorship programs are only loosely tied to the sponsorship of actual children in the South — children, by the way, who benefit equally under this model whether or not they are currently sponsored, up for sponsorship, recently unsponsored, or not even considered for sponsorship. How could it be otherwise, in truth, given the administrative hurdles involved and the ethics of project work in the South? Could projects operate on a monthly budget corresponding to variations in the number of sponsors who either begin or end a sponsorship of a child from that area? Could Northern organizations even track or transfer funds based on such variation? Should the projects of all local partners or, even worse, the lives of individual children be subject to the volatility of sponsor lapses? This aspect of sponsorship makes perfect sense; however, it also highlights the distance between the act of sponsorship as seen from the sponsor's perspective and the actual use of the donations in relation to the sponsored child.

The second comment addresses the issue at the heart of the disconnect between the fundraising messages of sponsorship programs and the development practices of local partners — the fact that many sponsors assume their donations go, in some way or another, directly to the child or their family even though this is largely not the case. It also reiterates the idea that the community-centred development approach is the best method of doing development work. Irving, a staff member working in communications, made the following comments:

> A lot of people think that their $33 or $35 is going directly to the child in an envelope. We try to help people understand that, if you did that, it

is probably not the best use of the money because the kid [or] the family would blow it on who knows what. And to give a family money does not do anything to change the circumstances in the world. All you are doing is driving up the inflation in the community, so it is actually not that good of an idea. So, the mechanics are that you pool that money together, and then you create a fund to help develop that entire community in an equal way ... A lot of things people are interested to learn is that it is not just the sponsored children who are graduating, it is the whole community. So, one child in the family might be sponsored ... but then their five or six brothers and sisters are all going to benefit from the advancements that the household is making.

Funding community-level projects rather than dispensing money directly to sponsored children (or creating programs that solely benefit sponsored children) does not necessarily make sponsorship solely a fundraising tool. However, combining this approach with promotional material that emphasizes the personal connection between sponsor and child does widen the space between what child sponsorship is for sponsors in the North and what it supports in the South. This gap, in turn, highlights how the financial and administrative components of sponsorship are only a very small part of what happens in the South.

While sponsorship programs are careful not to be expressly fraudulent in their marketing messages, and therefore never state that the money goes directly to the child or that the child will receive any specific benefits, their staff understand the need to focus on individual children. Beatrice, a communications specialist, explained that the "child is always a starting point and a way of simplifying the complexity and interdependence of all the projects that [our organization] is doing." One must remember, though, that "you have to be careful not to suggest that a particular child will receive any particular direct benefit as a result of having been sponsored." Beatrice ended this point with the thought that "sponsorship organizations are a victim of their own success." By this she implied that the individual emphasis of sponsorship marketing, that which makes it effective, works too well in that many of their sponsors believe sponsorship donations go directly to the child. Pascal, who works in marketing for a different organization, confirmed this dilemma when he said,

I would pose to you that over 90 percent of our donors suspect that the $35 a month goes directly to the child despite all our efforts to inform them through monthly email, through [newsletters], even through my appeals, that it is pooled at the community level and used to satisfy the needs of the community.

Jennifer also discussed this issue and summed it up very well, proclaiming

> I think that more transparency would be good, and I think that we prob-ably would, as an industry as a whole, take a hit as far as numbers if we were obvious about that this is helping the child's community. But I think that we would be able to do better work overseas then, and just that we would have more integrity within ourselves because what we do not want is for child sponsorship to get a bad rap, right? And that is what is hap-pening when we are telling donors one thing and doing another. I think we really just need to be up front about what we do, and part of that is maybe doing a bit more push in educating our donors in showing them why it is better to help a child's family and a child's community.

This leaves sponsorship programs with a difficult challenge: having to educate their sponsors and potential sponsors about how their donations are used while not undermining one of the elements that makes sponsorship effective.

It seems that sponsorship programs try to accomplish this by simultaneously stressing the legitimate, beneficial nature of community-centred development rather than by playing down the individual component of sponsorship. In some cases, there is a recognition that this balance has not been done as well as it could be. For instance, Tamara proclaimed that her organization (or, more accurately, its partners) "is doing a way better job than many other NGOs. Because of the sponsorship money, we usually remain in a community for ten or fifteen years. You can do a lot of things [in that time]"; however, she also noted that "the bad thing" they have done is "not convey these messages [about the way donations are spent] to the public."

In other instances, educating sponsors about sponsorship is described as being a constant challenge both because of what is implied by sponsorship promotional material and because many sponsors apparently want their money to go directly to the child. As Susan commented,

> when we tell [sponsors that] this money is pooled together and benefits everybody else, some sponsors say, "no, this is my child; I want the $33 to be given to him." We say, "no, no, no. The money is not given to him it is kind of pooled together; the benefits are spread out" … So, it is constant educating.

Paul echoed this, stating that

> some people do have that expectation that they can send their money directly to their child, and they are disappointed when they find that

they cannot, but … we are not going to be able to provide access to clean water and to invest in bore holes and that kind of thing if we are providing individual handouts. It is just not going to happen.

Whatever the case of sponsor expectations and whatever the actual situation is regarding the best method of development assistance, the simple fact that there is a substantial disparity between what many sponsors think happens to the money and what actually happens is indicative of the aforementioned disconnect. This lends support to the idea that most of the day-to-day practices that occupy child sponsorship programs are more related to fundraising than to "development," inasmuch as the two can be separated. What it does not mean is that sponsorship donations are poorly spent.

As mentioned in Chapter 1, a focus on long-term community-level projects that are locally planned and directed rather than on short-term, top-down, or individualistic interventions is presently understood to be the most effective international development approach (for example, see United Nations Development Programme, 2010). While this begs the question of what a development intervention is and how useful these are in dealing with problems of global poverty and inequality, it is important to note for now that an argument to understand child sponsorship as primarily a fundraising tool is not the same as an argument to see sponsorship funding handled or spent differently. In other words, this chapter is not intended to put forward a critique aimed at necessarily changing the funding practices of sponsorship programs, and it is especially not asking to increase their involvement in the running of overseas projects or act more in line with sponsorship advertising (that is, have funds go more directly to the child). Instead, it seeks to explore the irony embedded in a situation in which, by following what they believe to be the best development practices, sponsorship programs and their staff end up distancing themselves from the very development work they purport to do. All of these points are well summed up in a statement by Jennifer:

In reality, in most organizations, the money does not go to that particular child. It goes to help the community as a whole, which we in the field or on the development side of things know is the best way of helping that child. But from the average Joe Blow donor [sic] … what they would prefer usually is for a cheque to be written in that child's name to that child, which we know would be the absolute worst thing that you could possibly do. But the best way of selling the child sponsorship program is by focusing on that one individual child, saying help this child rather than help this community of nameless, faceless children, right? So, there has been some bad press about that, just about the way the relationship between the way child sponsorship is often marketed and the way that the program is actually run.

It is hard to imagine a clearer description of this core challenge of sponsorship than Jennifer's candid outline. Less clear, however, is the response of sponsorship programs to this challenge apart from trying to avoid "bad press."

National divisions

In addition to the international division of labour within child sponsorship, a number of elements within the offices of Northern sponsorship programs point to an understanding of sponsorship as a fundraising tool. The first of these elements relates to the organizational structures within many Canadian NGOs that offer child sponsorship. These structures reflect a division of roles and staffing that were, for the most part, not represented as unusual or problematic by the interviewed staff. Depending on the size of the organization, sponsorship programs usually consist of several people or groups of people that are differentiated by their responsibilities. There are those individuals or groups, often referred to as marketing personnel, who are responsible for the production of promotional material designed for potential sponsors, such as TV spots, magazine inserts, or direct mail appeals (although this is itself sometimes subcontracted to for-profit advertising agencies). In larger sponsorship programs, these people are often separated from those who are responsible for the production of correspondence to current sponsors. They are also sometimes separated from those people who target corporate donors or major gifts. In James's organization, he explained that

we create our own marketing and [organizational] development strategy [independent of partner organizations]. Interestingly enough, it actually operates as two different business plans combined within the organization. [Interviewer: Two? You mean marketing and development?] Yup, two different business plans. Two different directors, one for each area. And those business plans reflect a three-year strategic plan, but that strategic plan is entirely [for] the Canadian operations ... The marketing team's responsibility is to go after a large number of donations. So, they are going after large volumes of donations — large quantity of donations. [Interviewer: The regular sponsorship program would fit into that?] That would be part of it, but not the only part. But just when you think of the marketing department, think large volumes of contributions. When you think of the development department, think of large value of contribution [Interviewer: So, corporate donations or major gifts?] Corporate, major gifts, planned giving, exactly.

In many cases, there is another distinct person or group of people who are responsible for communications, which can mean anything from media relations to website content to "ensuring brand consistency," as Beatrice phrased it. All of these types of staff are usually separated from those divisions referred to as donor services, client services, supporter services, sponsor relations, etc. These individuals, who mainly work in in-house call centres, can themselves be divided into those who deal with the questions, requests, or data-gathering of sponsors, potential sponsors, or other kinds of donors (such as those who buy from the gift catalogue). No matter the size of the organization, all of these kinds of staff are separated from, and usually independent of, those who work in programs. The work of those individuals referred to as program staff varies from organization to organization, but in general, these people do such things as represent the organization to other NGOs or government bodies and communicate with field offices or local partners (to select new projects or project areas to fund, to monitor and evaluate projects or project budgets, and quite often, to ensure the transfer of information and correspondence between sponsors and sponsored children).

On an important aside, this separation between program staff and other sponsorship staff does not necessarily mirror the breakdown of organization expenditures found on websites and in annual reports. These expenditures are normally divided into fundraising expenses, administration expenses, and program expenses (i.e. services that are supposed to help children). Almost all child sponsorship programs follow what is referred to as the 80:20 ratio; that is, about 80 percent of revenue is supposed to go to program expenses and no more than about 20 percent should be spent on administrative and fundraising expenses. Because of the way child sponsorship is set up and because of reticence to divulge financial information, however, it is often difficult to confirm how much money makes it to a sponsored child (or, more accurately, the project in their area). What can be said is that there is no common definition of "program" expenses and no regulatory body that checks on this statistic.

While charities must summarize the amount spent on fundraising, administration, worker compensation and the like for the Canada Revenue Agency, these figures rarely match up exactly with the ones presented in promotional material or even annual public financial statements (see Maren, 1997 for a critique of Save the Children US's "pie chart"). Brian confirmed this, saying "there is no one policing that ... and it is a nightmare to try and find out the accuracy of that." In fact, many of those services listed as program expenditures either still occur in the home office, such as telephone support staff for sponsors, or are used to pay for salaries, travel, and office expenses abroad (something most people would still consider to be administration). Susan, who works in sponsor relations (and not in any development project capacity), is candid in spelling it out:

Can I be totally honest? Okay, 80 percent, no 80 percent, yes, we tell sponsors we spend 80 percent, but that includes actual overheads if you know what I mean, but that is not what the sponsor perceives, right? The way it is worded is, it is not a lie, but it is not an outright truth … It is the way you say [it], okay, it is true our department comes under programs, you know, so that is put under program expenditures, not under administration. So, that way it is 80:20, but that is what all organizations do … So, now do I explain that to a sponsor? I do not. I cannot explain because technically that is under program. We are not covering [up] anything even when we do our financial audits and year-end statements. It comes under it, but you need to be an extremely good financial person to know exactly what those terms mean. Most people do not.

It should be noted that the issue of transparency around administrative expenses versus program expenses is not solely a problem for child sponsorship programs; this is something that affects the entire charitable sector. Not only are there challenges in accurately assessing what are appropriate or inappropriate program expenses, but there is also disagreement around how much money should be used to run the administrative and fundraising aspects of a charity. Donors are increasingly, and perhaps rightly, concerned with the breakdown of charity spending (Imagine Canada, 2014). However, this concern should not cause us to forget that there are other, and perhaps more important, criteria that should be used to evaluate a charity than simply the amount they spend on administration and fundraising, such as their relationship to the actual or imagined aspects of the problem in response to which they were founded (Imagine Canada, 2014).

Apart from the relationship to organizational expenditures, the divisions within sponsorship staffing are important for a number of reasons. While it may seem natural and necessary to separate staff according to particular responsibilities, these separations tell us about how organizations conceptualize and prioritize what they do day to day. Not only does staff differentiation indicate something about how management understands the purpose of the agency, but it also commonly separates them physically into different offices, different areas, or different floors. This is important because, in many Northern NGOs offering sponsorship, the people who work in marketing, communications, and donor services are people who seem to come predominantly from backgrounds in marketing, communications, and the service sector, and these people far outnumber program staff, who occasionally but not always come from backgrounds in development studies. This means that many organizations offering sponsorship are stuffed to the brim with staff trained in and aimed at raising as much money as possible from Northern donors, and these individuals are functionally and spatially separated from those few individuals who have a good grasp of development work in the field.

James summed up the situation in his organization, noting simply that "the professional development expertise does not reside within the marketing or the development fundraising area." Explaining the situation in greater detail, Beatrice admitted that her organization struggled with this separation but, because of its size, could often overcome it. However, she also noted that

> from what I know from other organizations, there is actually an over-tendency to separate [marketing] out. You end up with people operating in silos, you know what I mean. Your youth program has this objective and this objective, and they would never talk to someone in marketing. And marketing's objective is raise this much money. The only time they would ever talk is if there is a youth event designed to raise money.

More to the point, Beatrice also talked about her personal history and how she came to manage communications at a Canadian NGO offering sponsorship. Like many such people working in the marketing, communications, and donor services branches of these organizations, she had no formal education or experience in international development issues. Instead, she was hired because of her communications experience within the for-profit community. She said,

> I do not come from a development background by any stretch of the imagination. I spent ten years working for a [business] and ended up doing a lot of communication but learning a lot about client service and customer service. So, very weird kind of split, and at the time I joined here, there was a position that was looking at both. The customer service side was useful because we were looking at communication and retention of our donors, and the communication side was valuable because what is the very biggest key to that, the single most important thing, is communication. So that is how I joined the organization ... So, I do not come from a development background at all, and when I first made the decision to come to work here, it was based on wanting to get into not-for-profit, and it was based on a fit with my skill set that could get me in there.

Beatrice's story is indicative of how people come to work for sponsorship programs. Paul, for example, came to manage marketing and donor services at a sponsorship program after working in the for-profit sector with a degree in business. Responding to the question of how he came to work there, he said, "I felt that I liked being in a professional environment, but I also wanted to be in an environment where I could make a difference."

A business background is not limited to the marketers and communications experts at sponsorship programs. In 2009, Christian Children's Fund of Canada installed Mark Lukowski as Chief Executive Officer. Apparently, Lukowski was a good choice because of his "corporate background of innovation and process improvements at industry giants Motorola Cellular and Hewlett-Packard" (Christian Children's Fund of Canada, 2010). The importance of fundraising to the organization was made even more clear: "Lukowski's track record of increasing revenue and reducing operating costs will contribute to a new era of growth for CCFC's child focused programs." While Christian Children's Fund has recently shifted to a CEO with a background in human rights, it has not been the only agency to hire long-term top executives with business backgrounds. Plan Canada's previous CEO, Rosemary McCarney, is a lawyer with an MBA who has had extensive business experience. The new CEO of World Vision Canada, Michael Messenger, is also a lawyer, and the new CEO of Plan Canada, Caroline Riseboro, has a background in marketing and fundraising.

At first glance, this organizational division of labour does not seem to be too problematic, and one cannot fault someone working in business for wanting to "make a difference." The Plan International (2008) report mentioned earlier, however, highlighted this issue as a major difficulty. The researchers revealed that

> Some NO [National Office] staff, particularly those involved in marketing and supporter relations, have limited exposure to programme realities and CCCD [Child-Centred Community Development] approaches, and this affects their ability to link sponsor engagement with CCCD and development education. Sponsorship and programmes in NOs are managed separately, although Plan's continued evolution means NOs are making efforts to broaden staff exposure to programmes.

Not only does the background and experience of marketing, communications, and donor services staff make it more difficult for them to produce promotional material that is educationally beneficial, but it also says something about the immediate goals of the organization and its programs. The fact that the marketing, communications, and donor services staff who make up the majority of Northern offices are not "development experts" (and need not be development experts, from the eyes of management) only makes sense from the perspective that these organizations are principally focused on the work of raising funds and not the work of development per se.

It should be noted that not all NGOs offering sponsorship in Canada are equivalent in this regard. For example, Tamara agreed that "fundraising and communications and media are totally separate and advocacy teams are separate … we have a separate media relations person here and that person was independent. I mean it is not a part of the marketing team." However, she also stated that "we have a communications team here and they do media relations work and raising public awareness and most of this work is done by program people not by marketing people." While it is important to recognize the variability within sponsorship programs, the difficulty with Tamara's statement is that the program staff she is referring to are not, in fact, people with any specific background in development studies (they are simply hired as communications personnel rather than marketing personnel).

This understanding of national organizational division is reinforced through the type of language that seems to predominate in sponsorship offices. Just as development studies has its own language, with terms such as participatory, sustainability, and multilateral, so too does business, with expressions like market share, revenue stream, and customer care. There is no easy way, however, to analyze the language use of an entire organization, and as with the often-oversimplified concept of organizational culture, one must be careful not to assume any unified language practices or specific effects. That said, many of the interviewed staff repeatedly employed terms and concepts in their discussion of sponsorship that seem to be more at home in a business environment than in any kind of international development context. In particular, this use of business or marketing language was evident in the often-blurred boundary between sponsorship as a way of supposedly linking sponsors to children and sponsorship as a product produced by the organizations and sold to customers.

In several instances, James expressly referred to sponsorship as a "product," and Irving made reference to donations as "investments." In discussing the future of sponsorship, Irving also made the comment, "I know a lot of other organizations are committed to diversifying the product offerings when it comes to international development." In an example of the odd but frequent substitution of the term customer for donor/sponsor, Susan expressed the need to "try to keep customers satisfied and keep them hooked into the child sponsorship program." Pascal, however, provided some of the best exemplars of how a particular kind of marketing rhetoric so often pervades the work of child sponsorship in Canada. Using phrases such as "to maximize our spend" and "our spots are stale-dated," Pascal's language exposes the way sponsorship is considered and presented by staff, outside of the promotional content itself. In explaining his daily job, apart from overseeing the production of ads, Pascal said he focuses on "how we drive a supporter through the giving lifecycle, if you will — so what we do in terms of acquisition, how we maintain or convert them, how we direct them to other giving programs." Referring to another sponsorship program, he also said,

I know that they are, that they appear to be, very sophisticated in terms of their database marketing techniques. So, they can target their "gift for child" programs more easily than us. At least, that is my impression. They also have what appear to be more expensive packages. Where we will usually use a postcard or a card of some sort, they will have seeds or a ruler or an eraser or something to that effect. In my previous life, we referred to that as trinkets and trash.

Use of such language that is heavily influenced by business and marketing is not necessarily unusual among large non-profits, especially when several interviewees noted the benefits that corporate experience has for being hired in the fundraising sector. Its prevalence, however, does suggest particular ways of viewing one's work and the work of one's organization, once again betraying an emphasis on the centrality of fundraising. It could also be expected to influence the day-to-day activities and interactions of staff.

Program staff trained or experienced in international development and spending more time in communication with field partners do not always seem to see eye to eye with the other staff in sponsorship programs. Gabrielle, a former program staff member at a large Canadian child sponsorship program, talked about how there are not only differences internationally between organizations that raise money and those that spend, but these differences also exist "in the same office. For example, there was always a constant, I would say heated, discussion between the group that raised money and the group that spends money." In particular, she commented that these discussions revolved around the portrayal of children in ads, where marketers "would always say 'sound bite' and 'in this kind of sound bite you cannot give them the history of what is happening.'" This disagreement over the amount, tone, and relevance of included information is likely related to more than simply different backgrounds. Because the different staff groupings appear to have different written and unwritten objectives to their daily work, there is both a natural cooperation as well as a natural tension between these staff members.

The cooperation comes from what seems to be the logical differentiation of labour involved in the daily activities of sponsorship. Pascal explained one aspect of this cooperation when he said, "what [my communications colleague] does is he will go in and soften the ground for me, and then I go in and ask for money." Jacqueline highlighted her "programmatic" role of keeping her marketing and communications colleagues informed about the status of projects and sponsored children. The tension seems to come from the fact that marketing and communications staff, who are in the majority, are primarily tasked with the job of maintaining and increasing revenues, while a few program staff are there to ensure an effective transitioning of funds to partners.

Moreover, despite there being a concern from management and some program staff about the portrayal of children in promotional material — a concern augmented by media criticism — marketers are still expected to bring in the funds necessary to meet the organization's overseas commitments. Irving commented on the result of these competing dilemmas:

> generally, I would say the bottom line wins. We start out with these grand ideas wanting to change the whole conversation [about sponsorship], and as we get down to the process, we realize this is not working, we got to pull it off the air.

Talking about the need to compete with other sponsorship programs to bring in the donations, he described the personal dilemma involved, remarking that "at the end of the day it comes down to our job performance." Pascal also mentioned the personal aspect of having one's job centred on fundraising, saying "it is always stressful the first two weeks after an appeal is dropped, where the response is 'how come we are not raising the money, what is going on?'" Talking about the high marketing costs involved in sponsorship, he went on to complain: "I can spend two dollars, but I have to raise ten, okay. And if I do not, then within a year or two I am looking for a new job." Tamara, a program manager, highlighted this issue by referring to the oft-discussed need by program staff to

> bring more reality into what [sponsored children] are getting out of [sponsorship], and [marketing people] are scared. We have had ten or twelve meetings, and you can see the marketing [staff] just sitting on their edge. And I understand because we are all dependent on their money. If today they did not bring [enough funds], the field offices are waiting there, so you see it is a very nerve-wracking thing.

Tamara went on to say that "the marketing fear is that if they put too much global education into their messaging, their donor will not fund. And maybe they are right, maybe not. Who is going to test?" Through these comments, Tamara brings together the issues of the functional division of staff, and what are often seen as the negative marketing practices of sponsorship — too much desolation and not enough education. Irving also referred to the use of controversial imagery, admitting that

> it is a perpetual problem we have not solved it in sixty years ... [Audiences] say that the images they have seen on TV for the last forty-five years have not changed at all — it is flies-in-the-eyes-and-bloated-bellies. Well, the problem for us is, especially with our development people, we know that is not the reality. We know we are making a difference. We know people

want to see the difference, but when you put on those sorts of more posi-tive, more "here is the change" sort of stories, they do not drive results. So, to meet your bottom line, you have got to perpetuate your own problem. And by perpetuating your own problem, you are excluding people who might otherwise buy from you. So, it is a big circle, and we are not sure the way out.

This need to raise money as a priority, even in the face of using disagreeable or damaging content, draws attention to the unquestioned link between what are seen to be effective marketing strategies and those that generate the highest revenue.

This formulation of the objective of sponsorship marketing tells us, once again, about how the problem of "underdevelopment" is constructed in relation to child sponsorship. As with other realities within sponsorship programs, it highlights the central and almost exclusive role that raising funds plays in the day-to-day practices of sponsorship in Canada. What is important here is not simply an emphasis on fundraising, however. As stated before, this would not be terribly controversial, or even troubling, if not for the ethical implications of this dynamic. The difficulty comes not from the desire to raise as much money as possible for perceived devel-opment work but from the misconception of child sponsorship as development work itself. This argument is detailed in the next chapter, which forms the second half of the analysis of sponsorship organizations.

3

Organizational Development within Development Organizations

Lack of adequate transparency and oversight has been a problem for the American branch of Christian Children's Fund (CCF), at least according to the *Chicago Tribune*. In one article, *Tribune* reporters discussed how difficulties with poor management and fraud at a South Texas project site "raises questions about how Christian Children's Fund monitors funds and sets priorities" (Jackson, 1998: 2-11). In addition to infighting and misuse of funds by the local CCF affiliate, which resulted in its collapse and the suspension of any kind of benefits for the child the *Tribune* had sponsored, CCF almost found itself in court in 1996 because one of its managers in the same area had funnelled sponsorship monies into his own development company (2-11, 2-12). Rather than following up with an open investigation, however, "CCF pushed to settle the South Texas matter quietly" (2-12).

The *Tribune* report also told the story of Maria Cleidiane, an eight-year-old Brazilian girl who was sponsored by one of the reporters. When the reporter arrived to visit Maria, she was ill with multiple bacterial infections and remained severely malnourished despite the fact that the local Brazilian project that oversaw Maria's sponsorship received more than US$21 per month on her behalf (Crewdson and Goering, 1998: 2-14). Rather than providing local children with food and health care as CCF claimed in correspondence with sponsors, the project used sponsorship funds to buy computers, a telephone line for Internet access, and lessons for teens in computer use (2-14). It seemed obvious to the *Tribune* reporters that something was wrong with the case of Maria; after all, CCF assured her sponsor that she would get hot meals and health checkups, neither of which occurred. CCF's head of foreign operations did not think there was anything really amiss with the project, however, stating that CCF and its affiliate "did not fail Maria by any stretch of the imagination" (2-15). Apparently, he had been (incorrectly) told that the project did provide meals and that it ensured medical care (at least for children under six). He admitted that he had not seen or approved any kind of budget, though. According to him, CCF is a "decentralized system" and project budgets are something for which each "national office" is responsible.

With these stories, the *Tribune* critique of child sponsorship once again placed organizational impropriety and negligence at the forefront. While we should not dismiss dramatic issues such as these, of course, they can draw us away from some more commonplace, but also more fundamental, challenges to the sponsorship model. Building on the discussion from the preceding chapter, which examined the way sponsorship programs are commonly structured and run, this chapter expands on the argument that sponsorship is first and foremost a fundraising technique. Using the same set of interviews with sponsorship staff members, this chapter explores the implications of the fact that sponsorship is overwhelmingly grounded in the raising of funds and yet is routinely presented and discussed as something more than that.

As a point of departure to introduce this argument, let us begin with a question inspired by Foucault's (2003 [1984b]) concept of problematization. What is the problem to which child sponsorship is most commonly presented as a solution? At first glance, this seems to be an easy question to answer. The problem sponsorship is supposed to address is the poverty of the child and their community, or more specifically, the lack of development that is supposedly at the heart of this poverty. In sponsorship advertising, children are generally portrayed as malnourished, sick, undereducated, and in desperate need of external support. Sponsorship organizations offer to provide what these children are missing for a relatively small monthly sum. Consequently, the problem of "underdevelopment" is supposedly solved, or at least mitigated, through the provision of the funds that sponsorship delivers.

This understanding of sponsorship is reiterated by staff members, who commonly describe sponsorship in terms of what the funds can purchase for the child and their community. However, if sponsorship funds are used in the same manner to accomplish the same things as other sources of development funding and are, in fact, often indistinguishable from this funding in the field, then it seems to be the provision of funds that is understood to be the solution to "underdevelopment" and child sponsorship is simply an effective means to secure those funds. Seen in this way, child sponsorship is a response to a fundraising challenge and not a development problem. In fact, the *direct* problem to which child sponsorship is a solution is not that of "underdevelopment" in the South, it is the problem of how to effectively raise money from a Northern audience for a cause that appears remote geographically and personally.

Before going on to discuss the implications of this point, it is important to note that the assessment of child sponsorship as primarily a fundraising practice necessarily excludes two commonly cited aspects of sponsorship: one, the supposed benefits to the sponsored child related to the relationship itself (i.e. getting letters and extra gifts from your sponsor or knowing that someone far away wants to help you), and two, the supposedly awareness-raising properties of sponsoring a child that might lead to a better informed and more compassionate Northern population. While neither of these aspects should be discounted, there is little evidence to suggest that these are anything but peripheral to the fundraising purposes of sponsorship. In addition to the problems of disparity at the local level that initially led sponsorship programs away from a more direct funding approach, the first aspect is not likely a significant factor for many sponsored children. While some may receive positive benefits from this direct relationship, this is apparently not the norm. A Plan International study (2008: 6) concludes that

> claims (e.g. in materials for sponsors) about the positive effects of sponsorship on children's growth, self-esteem and ability to communicate and participate in community development cannot be generalized. Despite the care taken by some NOs [National Offices] to qualify these claims, the use of such messages should be re-assessed.

As for the awareness-raising or global education aspect of sponsoring a child, this outcome is only as accurate and productive as the messages themselves.

Sponsorship promotional material is the topic of the next chapter, but even without an in-depth analysis, it is possible to illustrate one of the key messages of sponsorship advertising — that sponsoring a child is a way of alleviating poverty and helping children and communities develop. Using carefully worded appeals, sponsorship programs commonly describe the bleak situation of some children in the South and then offer sponsorship as the "best way to help" these children or children like them (Plan Canada, "Susan," n.d.). Though not all material follows this format, it is such a common theme that examples are easy to provide. In a televised segment entitled "Heart of a Child" (n.d.), a Plan Canada spokesperson clearly describes what the expected result of sponsorship will be — freedom from poverty:

> Now is your chance to be part of something extraordinary. Plan is here now ready to help, but we cannot do it without you. That is the simple truth. You have met the children. You have seen how desperate their situation really is, but you have also seen how, through sponsorship, you can help a child and their family free themselves from the crushing grip of poverty.

This sentiment is spelled out in more depth in a Plan Canada ("Susan," n.d.) brochure:

> Your gift of $33 a month — about a dollar a day — will mean so much! It means preventing diseases like malaria. It means new wells, and water that is safe to drink. It means more schools where children can learn to read and write. Most of all, your sponsorship means a better future for one special child — your sponsored child! ... By sponsoring a child through Foster Parent's Plan, you will help ensure that their community is strengthened to provide access to basics, such as clean water, healthcare, an education, and protection against life-threatening diseases.

In discussing the sponsorship and poverty, World Vision Canada does not shy away from using the term "solution." In one brochure provided to new sponsors, World Vision ("You," n.d.) makes reference not only to the community-level nature of the work being funded but also to the way this work links sponsorship with the solutions to poverty:

> By becoming a child sponsor, you have stepped forward to show you care. Your commitment, along with other Canadian sponsors, is a partnership with World Vision and your sponsored child's entire community. Together, we help provide long-term solutions to poverty that will enrich your sponsored child's life — and touch your own life as well. Thanks to you, your sponsored child will receive essentials of life, including things like: Health and Nutrition ... Food and Agriculture ... Education ... Clean, Safe Water.

One of the organization's previous spokespersons, Alex Trebek, states it more directly in an introduction to the infomercial "Sponsor a Child, Change a Life" (World Vision Canada, n.d.):

> If you had a chance to make a lasting difference in the world, to do something extraordinary, would you do it? Well, today you are going to have that chance, the chance to personally rescue one boy or girl and give them health, hope, and a future. Right now, there are kids living in horrific situations that you cannot even begin to imagine. They are hungry, sick, neglected, and yes, sometimes abused. Each day is a tremendous fight for survival, but there is a proven solution and it is World Vision child sponsorship.

Although not all advertisements state so baldly that child sponsorship is a "proven solution" to the difficulties that many poor people in the South face, the implication in most promotional material is clear enough. It does not seem terribly controversial, however, to suggest that this is the message of many, if not all, sponsorship ads. After all, sponsorship was commonly explained by staff members as a particular way of dealing with poverty in the South.

Although the interviews conducted for this study were semi-structured, and therefore somewhat informal, one question was consistently asked all of participants at the outset: "How would you describe child sponsorship to someone who does not know anything about it?" The purpose of asking this question was to establish a baseline indicator of how sponsorship is perceived by the individuals who promote it. What participant responses revealed, however, was an interesting disconnect between general descriptions of what child sponsorship is and specific explanations of what sponsorship staff actually do on a daily basis.

In many instances, the responses to this question reiterated what is found in sponsorship promotional material. Irving summed up this idea that child sponsorship is a program designed to address problems of development in the South:

> Child sponsorship is basically the idea that people in Canada can help change the lives of children in other countries through a reasonably small donation every month ... We take that money and then what we do to create efficiencies is we pool that money together with other sponsors' money and we target specific communities in developing countries that are in very bad situations ... and we try to change the circumstance of that one community by educating people, giving them opportunities, providing them with nutrition, their food, all that sort of stuff, and we target the children there because they are the best investment you can make ... they are going to continue to grow up and change their community, and our goal is that by changing the lives of these children we are going to change the lives of the community.

Jacqueline, who deals with communication between overseas partners and the organization, explained child sponsorship in a similar manner:

> When you sponsor a child, you are making a monthly commitment to, and we link you with, a child and will update you on their progress each year. Basically, your funds are pooled at the community level with those of other child sponsors, and we are implementing a community development program so every child will benefit with educational support, with either their school fees being paid or receiving educational materials, also health care and nutrition.

The same descriptive format — starting with the Northern donor, outlining the path of funding, and then listing the possible benefits to the sponsorship child — was employed by many staff members, as in the following account by Gina, another marketing and communications specialist:

> It is an opportunity for a Canadian individual or family to support people in developing countries through the act of embracing one child or one child's needs ... We tend to focus more on how that child's community can improve around that child so that they individually benefit; they get healthier; they have more opportunities. So, the sponsorship process allows that child in particular ... to have improved health and well-being because this individual or family in Canada has chosen to give money in that way. So, to me, it is more of a focused way of donating.

These general descriptions of child sponsorship, which are largely similar to those of other interviewed staff, have several things in common. First of all, while they begin with a brief focus on sponsors and their financial commitment, they quickly go on to emphasize the possible benefits of sponsorship for the community and child. These benefits are enumerated with broad terms like nutrition, education, and health care and are presented as concrete solutions to the lack of these "basics" and appropriate responses to the lack of development. Although it will be evident later that much of the communication about sponsorship revolves around the sponsor and not the child, basic descriptions of sponsorship seem to point unerringly to the (perceived) outcomes for the child. In this way, child sponsorship is consistently, although indistinctly, tied to the Southern development projects it funds.

This connection seems logical, and it supports the idea that sponsorship is presented as a solution to poverty and "underdevelopment." However, this point also highlights a second commonality among staff answers, one that will be mentioned here but discussed in more detail further on. Within many staff descriptions of sponsorship, there is a curious mix of specificity and generality. What is particularly noteworthy about the answers is not only the apparent difficulty many staff members had in summarizing child sponsorship, but also the way they stress the possibility of many specific benefits without specifying anything at all. There is a strange oxymoronic quality to how staff detail the minor steps involved in sponsorship while simultaneously remaining vague on what happens (or might happen) in faraway communities because of a sponsor's commitment. This ambiguity is not that puzzling; the interviewed staff members are all working for Northern sponsorship programs and, therefore, have little if any day-to-day contact with the projects being conducted in the South. What specific knowledge would they have of projects when their job is not to plan and execute development interventions but to acquire and retain sponsors? This aspect highlights a critical proposition for this study, that child sponsorship is primarily a fundraising tool *even though* it is routinely described as something else — a type of development intervention. It is within this discrepancy that one of the most important aspects about sponsorship organizations can be found: sponsorship organizations can position themselves as doing good international development work primarily through the raising of funds nationally.

The misrecognition of sponsorship

The practice of sponsorship appears to revolve around the effective raising of funds even as it is commonly conceived of by organizations and their staff to be a direct solution to the problem of "underdevelopment." This implies that Northern sponsorship programs are necessarily focused on raising money, and from their perspective, this money is the solution, or funds the solution, to the problem of global poverty. These two factors go together to create the perceived situation in which the more funds raised, the more "development" done. While this relationship appears to be natural (and not very controversial), what it accomplishes is to transfer the ethical value accorded to on-the-ground project work to the raising of money for such work. In other words, it fosters a state of affairs in which the work of international development in the South, i.e. helping the world's poor to "progress," is completely aligned with the work of organizational development in the North, i.e. increasing the size, the scope, and most importantly, the revenue of an organization. This circumstance has a substantial ends-justify-the-means impact on the content of sponsorship promotional material; it also generates legitimacy for the entire practice of child sponsorship not because of what it actually is — a fundraising tool — but what it is misunderstood to be — a development method.

As with Derrida's (1992) gift or Bourdieu's (1986) symbolic capital, the ethical value of child sponsorship comes disproportionately from its misrecognition as something other than an effective way to raise money. This misrecognition is facilitated by a discourse of development that consistently distances the perceived causes of global poverty and inequality while simultaneously individualizing the supposed solution. The real difficulty with child sponsorship becomes apparent, however, when the so-called problem of underdevelopment — the problem of global poverty and inequality — cannot be addressed through straightforward injections of money or the projects these dollars support. In this case, the funding that sponsorship provides is not the solution it is thought to be, and sponsorship as a practice ends up having far greater ethical value than practical value.

Child sponsorship is a fundraising technique, and the organizations that offer it are focused on raising funds above all else. They are simply designed and staffed primarily for this purpose. This is not necessarily a recrimination, however; it is simply an explanation of the role that sponsorship plays in the development industry. When she first started working for a sponsorship program, Tamara said that she had little respect for sponsorship. "How can they talk about a child as a product?" she wondered. However, as time went on and she saw how effective sponsorship was and how other agencies were continually threatened by lack of funding, she said that she changed her mind about sponsorship. The situation was straightforward, she said, "we need money … somewhere somebody needs the money." Despite the telling incongruence between pronouns, this statement does reiterate the idea that so far as development projects are essential to the short and long-term welfare of poor people in the South, funding these projects is equally important. As Brian plainly noted, "money drives development," but we need to keep in mind that

> Money is not the important thing; everybody knows it takes money to do anything … What is going to help them out of poverty, what is going to make them a fulfilled adult, is not the money but what that money provides for them.

This statement by Brian highlights the two issues at stake: one, the conceptual linkage yet practical separation between funds that are raised and solutions enacted, and two, the (developmental) rationality within which these solutions (and therefore the funds that support them) are perceived to be both legitimate and valuable.

There is a recurring misrecognition, or perhaps what could be called a slippage, in the discourse around child sponsorship that pervades not only promotional material but also staff discussions of sponsorship. This slippage seems to be a particular feature of sponsorship related to the conceptual overlap between raising money in the North and the development that it is supposed to produce in the South. To understand this slippage, it is useful to look back to the descriptions of sponsorship covered near the beginning of this chapter. These descriptions highlighted the way in which the supposed developmental benefits of sponsorship were seamlessly intertwined with understandings of sponsorship as a fundraising tool. A few examples will serve to underline this point.

Jacqueline told a story about a poor child she met while visiting a project abroad. After seeing the child, she said that she knew she wanted to sponsor him, but she followed this up with admitting to herself, "'you are silly' because I understand very clearly how it works, but you still feel that emotionally, 'I am going to sponsor [him].'" The little boy in question was already in the project area and would not get anything extra out of her sponsorship. Despite knowing this, she wanted to sponsor the boy anyway. This does not appear to make sense; she knew that she could "help" the boy in the same manner if she were to just give the money to her organization (possibly more so if the boy were sponsored by someone else as well). So, was this desire to sponsor solely related to an emotional reaction, or was there something else involved? Jacqueline notes that Plan markets sponsorship in the way it does "so that people feel that commitment to continue." Consequently, it is likely that her reaction was fuelled in part by the illusion of direct connection that makes sponsorship such an effective tool in the first place.

Jennifer's very clear but ultimately inconsistent discussion of sponsorship also demonstrates this possibility. Jennifer proclaimed that sponsoring a child

> is the best way of breaking that cycle of chronic poverty because they are the ones who are going to be growing up and running the countries or running the communities. So, if they have the proper education and nutrition and training and support, family support, community support, then that in itself will break that cycle whereas if they just grow up as their parents grew up, chances are they will end up in the same kind of rut as their parents are in.

Shortly after this statement and in the context of a discussion around the community-level nature of the projects funded by sponsorship, she noted that we

> know children do not exist in isolation, right? They exist as part of a family and as part of a community. So, in order to best help them, we have got to help the community and the family to raise their own children.

Although not directly contradictory, Jennifer's comments exemplify the incoherence that often exists around the structure of sponsorship, the benefits for sponsored children, and the perceived developmental needs of the child or community. This confusion often leads to the conceptual equation between Northern sponsorship and Southern development. Jennifer even summed this up at the end of the interview, effectively linking acquiring donors with "doing development." She said,

> Child sponsorship is really the way to get donors in the door, and it is a good way. I mean because, like I said, it is not like it is just a marketing tool. It is not at all. It is really what we believe is the most effective way of doing development.

This slippage in the expression of child sponsorship was shared by Gina, who declared that "the reality is that sponsorship is one tool to bring money in to achieve our mission" and that the sponsored "child is a symbol of potential in the growth that a community can experience when there is targeted support offered." As she later admitted, however,

> I do not know enough about what actually goes on in each community where there is sponsored children, but I can pretty much assume that … the children that are sponsored are in fact getting greater benefits and having more opportunities for improved health.

This assumption of "benefits" despite a lack of direct experience regarding specific, or even general, project goals and accomplishments was a common feature of staff discussions of sponsorship.

Placed alongside a disclosure of sponsorship as "one tool" and the sponsored child as a "symbol" rather than a target of aid, the understanding of child sponsorship as directly equating to improvements in the child's life is a misrecognition of how sponsorship works. Even though sponsorship is simply a financial relationship between the sponsor and the Northern organization (and not between sponsor and child or even sponsor and project) and there can be no guarantee to sponsors about the particular progress of any specific child, there is a tendency to "assume" that the means (funding) are equivalent to an unspecified or generic end (development). In other words, because of the structures and practices of the child sponsorship model, it seems that the goal of fundraising is misrecognized by organizations and their staff as essentially the same as that of development (reduction of poverty, improved life, etc.). Once again, this misrecognition does not mean that sponsorship monies are poorly spent; it simply means that the promise of sponsorship is often unrelated to, and therefore potentially undone by, the very practice of sponsorship itself.

If this situation is made possible through the disconnect between promotional messages and funding practices, it is made understandable (to those involved) through the circulation of a particular discourse of development. Despite the wide variety of staff perceptions around the causes of poverty and inequality in the South and the possibilities of dealing with these issues, a few things seem to be held in common. The first significant point relates to the variety of responses itself. While staff members were fairly uniform in describing the imagined benefits of sponsorship to the child and community, there was a diversity of responses around the question of why there are so many poor people and countries in the South. Apart from the kinds of projects their organizations funded, there was also little agreement among the participants on what should or could be done to rectify this situation. This was the case even among staff at the same organization, which leads to the suspicion that not only is there a separation among staff, as previously noted, but that there is also little in the way of a unified philosophy around development at these organizations. This difficulty echoes a statement made by Shelby

Miller, a child development expert and someone who produced a report for Save the Children US. She notes that Save did not have "a commonly accepted and understood theoretical perspective" (as cited in Maren, 1997: 143). This point is in line with the argument that sponsorship programs and the NGOs that host them are primarily fundraising organizations, and it highlights the amorphous nature of the development discourse that circulates within these institutions.

The discourse of development revisited

As noted earlier, there was a certain vagueness or generality surrounding staff discussions of what goes on in project communities in the South. Holding tight to key terms such as "education," "opportunity," or "capacity-building," this generality was able to address specific imagined deficiencies, or to encompass specific ideas of "progress," without actually specifying anything at all. At first glance, this could be mistaken for wilful ignorance, but that does not seem to mesh with the complexity of many of the participants' responses. On the other hand, this generality could easily be seen as a feature of the discourse of development itself. Sachs (2000: 9) explains that development means "everything and nothing"; as a concept, it has ceased to signify anything in particular except "good intentions." This is despite the fact that it can be understood as nothing less than "a secular salvation story," which for fifty years "has been much more than just a socio-economic endeavour; it has been a perception which models reality, a myth which comforts societies, and a fantasy which unleashes passions" (7, 13). Esteva (1992: 8) echoes this point by Sachs, noting that

> there is nothing in modern mentality comparable to it [development] as
> a force guiding thought and behaviour. At the same time, very few words
> are as feeble, as fragile and as incapable of giving substance and meaning
> to thought and behaviour as this one.

If this is the case, then the ambiguity about the precise developmental benefits of sponsorship is not merely related to organizational structure or personal background; instead, it is built into the way development is imagined and represented. From this perspective, expressing the precise use of funds becomes immaterial, as what actually occurs on the ground is swept away in a cloud of "good intentions."

This capacity of the concept of development to mean "everything and nothing" is facilitated by another feature of its discourse, one that was repeatedly evident in the staff interviews: the separation of the problems of "underdevelopment" and, therefore, the work of development from the lives of people in the North. This separation takes the form of understanding the causes of poverty of people in the South to be uniquely associated with some aspect of their lives, be it violence, corruption, improper economic or agricultural practices, cultural viewpoints, etc. Similarly, the mechanism to deal with these problems is also to be found in the South, be it improving education or health levels, creating local economic opportunities, building social capital, etc. In discussing these issues, Jennifer explained that "we also believe that there are lots of wrong ideas [in the South] … Because of their false ideas, that is what causes the poverty in their community." She went on to say, "we always go in to empower them to make the change … Once you can change the way that they think about themselves and their world, then it is a completely different thing." This perspective was mirrored by Dorothy, who stated that

> it is not a matter of not enough resources or not enough food per se. It is their mindset, and their mindset is that we have always been poor, we always will be, how are we ever going to get out of this, and then they wait for the rest of the world to come in and hand out stuff to them.

The solution, then, lies in

> educating them. It is not about "how to fish" or that they need to fish. It is "why do you need to fish." Figure it out; "why do you think you need to do this" because we can show you how, but then we will leave and you will forget. So, you need to actually teach them, and they have to get it. They have to embrace it, and they have to get it. Otherwise, there is no transformation. It does not happen.

From a different perspective, Brian argued that the "root cause of poverty is due to lack of opportunity" and added that "most poor people are born with an entrepreneurial spirit." His idea for a solution, however, sounded very similar to those of Jennifer and Dorothy. He said,

> Poverty is a cycle … That cycle breeds fatalism. It breeds a lack of self-esteem, of self-respect. So, even though you might have within you an entrepreneurial spirit, you have lost the drive because you see no way out. And so, someone comes along in some mechanism, i.e. sponsorship or the like, and takes you out of that cycle and shows you the opportunity to change your environment. Not changing it for you, but just introduces you to a different thinking. You are not lazy, you have just lost the drive.

Despite the paternalism embedded in common statements like these, this separation of the lives of those in the North from poverty in the South does not necessarily involve ethnocentrism or ignorance. Margaret said that it was not her organization's place "to be the great white gods," and that the local partners knew what was best for them. This may well be true, but it does not acknowledge any *connection* between the perceived "underdevelopment" in the South and what goes on in the North. This lack of acknowledgment may not be extraordinary, but it is central to the way development is discussed and the way sponsorship is structured. It is also central to the reason why Northern sponsorship programs, which are basically fundraising machines, can understand (and represent) themselves as being directly responsible for so much good in the world.

The separation, or what might be more descriptively referred to as the "Othering" of poverty, that is commonly part of the discourse of development not only compartmentalizes so-called poverty reduction strategies so that they appear "naturally" confined to the South but also establishes the seemingly legitimate role of people in the North. Because the causes and direct solutions to problems of global poverty are disconnected from the North, the role of Northerners is logically limited to charitable donations that are typically assumed to be generous for this very reason. Remember that it is the quality of not being required which makes something charitable; what is obligatory is not usually seen as generous (such as paying income tax even when it is used to support the same kinds of things that charitable donations do). Consequently, for charitable donations to be charitable there is often assumed to be no connection between, for example, one person's poverty and another's wealth.

When combined with the slippage in expressions of sponsorship noted above, this limitation reinforces the idea that the funding provided by sponsorship is the best means of aiding in the development of Southern peoples. This notion — that economic growth facilitated through foreign aid is the key to development — is as old as the concept of international development itself (Escobar, 1995). Even when developmental priorities broadened to include the essential improvement of social contexts, the idea that this was something accomplished in the South through financial support from the North remained pervasive. Gabrielle, however, spelled out one problem with this line of thought. She said,

> some people think that they can make all the change with this money, and I think it is very misleading ... development is not that easy ... We have to live in a different way if we want to make change in the world.

By highlighting the inadequacy of simple monetary solutions to the problem, Gabrielle brings to the fore the complex relationship between Southern poverty and Northern lifestyles.

The idea that the historical roots and current manifestations of global poverty are inextricably linked to exploitative practices, and rationalizations of these practices, is not new to the literature on poverty and development (for diverse examples, see Escobar 1995; Frank 1996; Sachs 1992; Wallerstein, 2004). Systemic explanations of global poverty, which focus largely on power relations between wealthier countries and poorer countries (or, increasingly, between wealthier people and poorer people), highlight such things as unfair trade relationships, aid that is tied to reductions in social spending, restrictive intellectual property guidelines, deregulation of governmental oversight on working conditions, and even military interventions to secure scarce resources or bolster politically aligned regimes. It is the sustained exclusion of these practices from the mainstream discourse on development that ensures fundraising is perceived as an appropriate and *sufficient* Northern response to global poverty. For example, the common elision of colonial histories — including such things as resource extraction or even slavery — from many contemporary explanations of global poverty helps make possible a view of the world in which the difficulties faced by ex-colonies can be attributed solely to internal factors and not a legacy of interference and abuse.

Even when a connection between Southern poverty and Northern political and economic arrangements is acknowledged, this connection can be trumped by the way sponsorship is organized. Neither Pascal nor Irving come from backgrounds in development work, yet both explained poverty as a systemic problem related to the historical actions of "the West" and its present relationship to poorer regions. Irving noted that

> the reason poverty still exists is because the West is not willing to sacri-fice its position in the world — our society is built on the backs of these countries … I think that is the thing no one will articulate and no one wants to acknowledge.

Discussing such things as unfair trade relations, Pascal echoed this statement, saying that "the rich West has allowed a number of countries to remain poor." However, neither he nor Irving felt they could express these thoughts in their professional capacity as marketing and communications staff. Pascal explained, "at this time, I have not seen any organization that is courageous enough to go out with that message for any length of time." Irving simply stated that there was no budget for material that presented these kinds of messages. He said, "advocacy is not what our core business is."

The issue of advocacy with Northern NGOs in general and sponsorship programs in particular is illuminating. While some NGOs offering sponsorship engage in advocacy work in Canada — which often takes the form of lobbying the federal government on various elements of multilateral agreements, fairer trade policies, amount and distribution of official development assistance, and so on — it is a very small proportion of what they do. As noted, this situation is due in part to the association of advocacy work with politics and, therefore, something to be avoided in order to reach the widest donor base possible and to maintain charitable status in Canada. This is especially pertinent since 2012, when the Canada Revenue Agency received a renewed mandate to follow up on the political activities of charities and revoke charitable status for infringing on the limits of so-called political activity (which are generally set at 10 percent of revenue).

This link between charity and political neutrality is another discursive feature that influences the formation and function of sponsorship programs. Many staff indicated that advocacy work has been an increasing priority in their organizations, even though it still remains a very small part of their objective. As Pascal stated, "the reality is that we are all playing with an 80:20 fundraising [ratio]; really ... of that 20 percent, how much of that is the organization going to dedicate to advocacy?" What is interesting about this statement is not simply the small amount thought to be available for advocacy if the will were there, but also that advocacy was assumed to fall under the 20 percent commonly reserved for administration and fundraising.

The exclusion of advocacy from the "business" model of sponsorship (often represented as a desire for political neutrality) goes hand in hand with the idea that something meaningful in terms of poverty reduction can be accomplished without it. As global poverty and its contexts are distanced from sponsorship programs and their supporters, fundraising comes to be seen as more closely linked to the "real" work of development than political interventions such as advocacy. Fundraising is thus granted a greater priority and legitimacy in Northern NGOs. In this way, the peculiarities of the discourse around sponsorship and development work together to create a situation in which the (imagined) work of international development coincides with the (practical) work of organizational development. This is, of course, not unique to NGOs offering child sponsorship, but these agencies provide a particularly relevant example of this phenomenon.

The developmentality of child sponsorship programs

In physics, the concept of inertia is slightly different from its colloquial usage. Instead of simply referring to inaction or sluggishness, inertia refers to the tendency of an object to continue moving along its trajectory, resisting changes in direction and velocity. It is not unusual for large organizations, especially non-profit ones, to develop this form of inertia. Gabrielle expressed it clearly:

> I think when organizations start to get bigger and bigger, at some point they kind of definitely take a leave of why they began in the first place and a certain amount of wanting to exist for their own sake happens.

Recognition of the fact that some organizations seem to "exist for their own sake" is not uncommon, but the interaction between the development discourse and the practice of child sponsorship adds a new dimension to this. It is relatively understandable to be driven to maintain the security of one's position by assuring the continuing need for one's work; however, this takes on a different tenor when one's ultimate objective (i.e. international development) is poorly defined and the supposed means of securing this objective (i.e. development projects) is in the hands of other people. Combine this with a recurring misrecognition of child sponsorship as the direct means of securing this (interminable) objective, and raising money through sponsorship becomes tantamount to the "real" work of development in the South. Through these processes, the development of Southern peoples and their communities becomes ethically synonymous with the development of the sponsorship program itself.

This process means that the Northern organizations offering sponsorship are both the funnel through which funds are seen to be effectively reaching their goal (to foster development in the South) and the goal itself. Jacqueline clarified the role of her organization:

> As an organization, we are simply providing that link giving the donors the opportunity to say, "yeah, I see that need, and I want to do something to support that." And we are saying, "well, support us, and we will make sure your funds are used to do that."

Susan, on the other hand, discussed her organization's role in a slightly different manner. Commenting on how to attract donors, she noted, "the secret is showing how we have progressed — what we have achieved — and saying, this is what you can help us achieve." These disparate statements highlight the flexible understanding of sponsorship programs made possible by the shifting representations of sponsorship and development.

This ethical alignment of international development and organizational development also creates a situation in which the limitless raising of funds (and, consequently, growth of the organization) is rationalized, the competition that exists between sponsorship programs is validated, and more importantly, almost any technique that brings in revenue is considered justifiable. Irving proclaimed the first point clearly, saying "everyone wants to grow." He did qualify this statement, however, with an aside about needing to branch out past sponsorship. "We're not going to jump to double digit growth rates in sponsorship," he commented. "Because risk management and growth are so important to charities in this sector, we do need to look to diversifying our revenue sources." A perfect example of the type of language often used to discuss sponsorship programs, this statement hints at the overarching need not to maintain sponsorship because it is the best strategy for the children involved but to use sponsorship as one tool among many in the pursuit of more funding (both for the organization's overseas commitments and for the maintenance of the organization itself). On the whole, however, child sponsorship is acknowledged as "a win-win situation for both the children in the field and also *for us as an organization*" (Jennifer, emphasis added). In a similar vein, addressing the need for the organization to "win," Irving spoke about competition between programs:

> There is this chunk of the world that is interested in child sponsorship, and we are just fighting over this one little part. And how do I make [our organization] seem more appealing than [that organization]. And when [another organization] does something, we have got to steal the idea and be second in the market with it. Or we do something and [that organization] has to follow us in. So, we spend a lot of time and energy worrying too much about each other, which is a little bit ridiculous … At the end of the day, we are all doing the same thing, so why are we competing with each other.

While some participants asserted that as long as people gave to the cause it did not matter to whom the money went, there was still a widespread understanding of competition between sponsorship programs. The recognition of similarity between the "products" offered often led to a situation wherein programs had to differentiate themselves in the form and intensity of their appeals. James reiterated this point (also found in Irving's statement above):

> If I am a Canadian consumer, there is a huge challenge for me trying to figure out what is the difference between all you guys. You look, feel, sound exactly the same, but why should I work with you versus that organization over there. And when they all look the same, then there is no decision point. It is whoever makes the loudest noise.

This implies that the content of the promotional material is not only determined by the situation in the communities where sponsored children live and the need to create a product that grabs donors' attention, but it is also influenced by the desire to stand out from competitors and thereby maintain and grow the organization.

Discussing his organization's position on advertising, Paul expressed the need to be "respectful, truthful, and effective." Being respectful and truthful were stated as very important objectives; he insisted, "we are not using the poor as pawns to support our fundraising." However, he did stress that "we have to be effective." If there were any doubt about what he meant, he clarified that it was necessary to get an "appropriate response" from donors (read: donation). Jacqueline made a similar point, saying "people are going to use the strategies that gain the most response."

This understanding of what it means to be effective helps explain a great deal about the promotional material of sponsorship programs. In this context, efficacy is perceived solely in terms of how much money the material secures. In other words, the value of communications between organizations and donors is predominantly perceived in terms of their fundraising ability, which largely sidelines (or simply disregards) other aspects of these communications, such as the "educational" component. It is not the truthfulness or respectfulness of sponsorship advertising that is brought into question here (although this issue is by no means straightforward); instead, it is the assumption that the indisputable role of these communications should be raising as much money as possible. From this perspective, even the very heart of child sponsorship, the emphasis on children, can be seen more as tool for fundraising than a target of intervention. After all, children are "the easiest way to hook a donor" (Pascal), "children sell; communities do not sell" (Brian), and "children appeal to donors; who does not want to help a child?" (Margaret).

Producing promotional material that attracts donors is a top priority for many NGOs that have set themselves the task of funding development projects overseas. However, when increasing revenue becomes ethically equivalent to the lofty yet vague goal of international development, this priority becomes so dominant that the financial draw of the material overshadows most other considerations. Despite Paul's initial comment on not using "the poor as pawns to support our fundraising," sponsorship seems to do exactly that. Arguments to this effect are presented in next chapter; for now, it should be noted that this understanding is not uncommon in the critical literature on development. In particular, there has been increasing reference to what has been referred to as "the pornography of poverty," which is generally understood to describe the use of extreme or sensational imagery to invoke compassionate (or voyeuristic) urges although it also implies the exploitation of vulnerable individuals (see Plewes and Stewart, 2007).

Powerless to "change the conversation"

The predominant concern for raising money produces a situation in which sponsorship promotional material is overwhelmingly aimed at attracting and maintaining donors rather than challenging their assumptions to any significant degree. Even though many staff expressed the need to be transparent and honest in their communications, it was also recognized that their material must be sanitized in such a way that donors are encouraged or cajoled but not confronted or offended. In reviewing his organization's messaging strategy, Brian remarked,

> we try very hard not to create a sense that you cannot enjoy your lifestyle in Canada. You have to somehow not be comfortable because all these

kids are dying. I want to come along and say to you, "You know what, enjoy your Tim Horton's coffee. In fact, you do not have to give it up. You do not have to give a coffee a day to help." ... We want to say, "You know what, enjoy life. Enjoy whatever you have earned, but in that, just share a little bit with the poor. Do not give it all away. You do not even have to give until it hurts, but just share a little bit." If everybody just shared a little bit, man, what an impact that would have on the world.

Similarly, Margaret mentioned being "very conscious of what our donors want to hear," although she also noted that this should not "override our basic mission and our need to tell the truth and be transparent." Jacqueline admitted that her organization "cannot use half the pictures because they are not appropriate"; they are "too sad" even though "it is the reality." She went on to explain one of the most important elements involved in the creation of material such as annual reports and success stories from the field:

> I always make a point to express thankfulness and gratitude, and I always make a point of speaking to them directly. So, I would not just talk about the child sponsorship program is providing [something]. I would say, "through your generous support, we are [doing x, y, or z]." Again, including them in so that they feel that connection. So, it is not just what we're doing as an organization. It is what they are doing with [or] through us so that they are supporting this and they are a part of this.

This need to constantly reaffirm the generosity of sponsors highlights the character of much sponsorship material. While this may include the "classic" image of a child with "flies-in-the-eyes," it will almost certainly include a statement about the role of the (potential) sponsor as wonderfully kind-hearted and as making an enormous difference in the world. It also illustrates, once again, the way programs feel compelled to interact with their donors given the discursive and organizational separation found within development and sponsorship. These two features, the need to focus on the impact of the sponsor's largess and the "Othering" of poverty found in the discourse of development, often go hand in hand. Irving explained, for instance, that negative imagery of destitute children is intentionally phased out over the "life" of a sponsorship. He noted how there is a "message track" in which the number of positive images are increased over time as the sponsorship "progresses"; "they [the positive images] grow as they [the sponsors] grow with their child."

Focusing on the role of sponsors within promotional material does not necessarily make this material positive and upbeat. There is still a great deal of suffering presented in sponsorship advertising. This does not mean that sponsorship programs and their staff are callous or unconcerned regarding the portrayal of

Southern children. What it does indicate, however, is that staff feel largely power-less to "change the conversation," as one participant repeatedly phrased it. Pascal expressed this feeling a number of times and always came back to the argument that he was compelled to use this imagery because it was effective in recruiting sponsors. He said,

> the whole flies-in-the-eyes-and-swollen-bellies type thing … From a fundraising perspective, I would say if the general public has such a problem with those advertisements, they should stop responding to them … If I could come up with something different that did not exploit that child, I would, and I am trying. And what kills me is we can go out with a positive message — and I have, in acquisition and direct mail, I have on a number of occasions because I am committed to testing, where we will tell the story of a community that faced X number of challenges, and because of Canadians, this community has completely changed … Hey, why don't you join a winner? No, [they] do not want to hear it, and it drives me bonkers.

In the face of the perceived need to acquire and retain sponsors and to increase revenues, almost no type of messaging is off-limits because it is not the content that is important to organizations, it is the "appropriate response" (in Paul's words). In other words, only one type of promotional material is deemed "effective" and there-fore useful — the kind that brings in donations. This viewpoint may be reproduced within NGOs that offer sponsorship, but the impetus for this perspective cannot be confined to them. Instead, it is linked to a broader imagining of how global poverty and inequality is manifested and what can and should be done about it. Rather than looking for explanation and resolution solely within the organizational contexts of sponsorship programs, then, it is necessary to examine how the problem of development is constructed, how Northern subjects respond to this construction, and how ethical action is situated within this response.

4

Consuming the Child Imaginary

Sally Struthers is famous. Even in Canada, where her role as Gloria on the 1970s American sitcom *All in the Family* may be less well known, she is still widely recognized as the celebrity face of child sponsorship. First appearing in American Christian Children's Fund (CCF) advertisements in 1976, she is often credited with revolutionizing the promotion of sponsorship. According to the *Chicago Tribune's* special report on child sponsorship, internal CCF studies have shown her to be "responsible for attracting more than 90 percent of its new sponsors" largely due to her ability to connect with women, who are thought to be behind a household's decision to sponsor a child (Zielinski and Jackson, 1998: 2-7). Struthers is not the only celebrity to be involved in marketing sponsorship; others such as Alex Trebek and Jan Arden have been seen on televised ads for Plan Canada and World Vision Canada, respectively. However, Struthers "is the undisputed queen of the genre, and her two-decade career as a spokeswoman mirrors the evolution of a fundraising strategy that markets altruism and guilt with the slickness of ad campaigns for car shampoo or exercise videos" (2-7).

Sponsorship advertisements have not always been universally associated with images of suffering children. Many early ads simply contained pictures of children to be sponsored or pleas from celebrities. After Struthers' introduction to the scene, though, the melodrama of sponsorship appeals increased exponentially. Whether related to the news fervour around the Ethiopian famine or the decrease in cable broadcasting rates, "hard sell" televised sponsorship commercials became popular in the 1980s and became associated with Struthers' image almost as much as those of malnourished children. In one of her now-iconic ads, she appears in front of a television showing images of children in horrible conditions. She is holding a remote and addresses the camera, saying "at times I have wanted to turn it off too." She goes on to declare that, through sponsorship, "I promise you can make these haunting pictures go away" (Zielinski and Jackson, 1998: 2-7). So it was that the style of appeal unofficially known as the "flies-in-the-eyes-and-bloated-bellies" came to prominence. While the prevalence of this representational form has declined in popularity over the years, often replaced by a more positive but still problematic idea of hope, it is still easy to find examples of it today. Apparently, the "effectiveness" of this type of advertising is not in dispute, only its appropriateness and truthfulness. The *Tribune* report relied on a California State University professor to explain this point with an oft-used though under-studied idea: "'you loosen wallets with guilt'" (2-7).

Apart from highlighting the emotion-laden and guilt-inducing character of Struthers' work for CCF, the *Tribune* report did not dedicate much space to discussing the content of sponsorship promotional material. In the only article devoted exclusively to the subject, the reporters detailed the cost of Struthers' participation, which is deemed to be high despite her technically working for free. Apparently, there were excessive costs associated with the insurance, the fees of the public relations firm that represented Struthers, and the first-class airfare required for her and some of her retinue (Zielinski and Jackson, 1998: 2-7). The report also discussed the self-serving motivations behind other celebrity involvement with child sponsorship (Zielinski and Jackson, 1998: 2-7). Apart from these critiques, the article used examples of Struthers' appeals, first for CCF and later for Save the Children US, to address some of the issues brought up in other parts of the report. These issues included the expense of sponsorship advertising, especially the television spots; the exploitative or undignified nature of how Southern peoples are portrayed; the use of images of children who are not receiving, and will never receive, any benefits from the sponsorship program; and the inaccuracy of representations of the lives of sponsored children and the benefits of sponsorship for these children.

According to *Tribune* staff reporters Zielinski and Jackson (1998: 2-7), "though disease and deprivation are realities in developing nations, child sponsorship commercials are frequently laced with wildly inflated claims about conditions facing children in these countries." They also note that "Often, the wrenching images of starving children … are plucked from file footage taken years earlier" (Zielinski and Jackson, 1998: 2-7). The use of such extreme or borrowed imagery in sponsorship promotional material is deemed justifiable by many organizations, though some have even acknowledged "that many of the children in ads do not directly benefit from their programs" (Zielinski and Jackson, 1998: 2-7). These organizations argue that the advertising content is "representative" of (some) situations in the South even though it may not reflect the specific situation of one's sponsored child; moreover, they commonly perceive it as "a means to a worthy end" (Zielinski and

Jackson, 1998: 2-7). Expanding on this latter idea, Zielinski and Jackson (2-7) cited Brian Anderson, Save the Children's marketing director, who apparently said,

> he had no qualms about showing dead children — even youngsters who may never have been sponsored by his group — if it proved effective in raising funds. "The public really decides what will be run and what won't be run through their response to the advertisements," Anderson explained.

Anderson's argument — the ends justify the means — definitely sounds extreme, and it played right into the journalists' depiction of sponsorship organizations as unscrupulous and dishonest.

The *Tribune's* depiction of the problems of sponsorship advertising, and the seemingly sluggish or intractable responses of sponsorship programs, once again emphasized organizational misconduct by placing issues of accuracy, transparency, and discretion at the centre of the discussion. Similar to other problems with child sponsorship, the *Tribune* critique suggested that the difficulties surrounding sponsorship advertising can be ameliorated through a concerted effort on the part of sponsorship programs to improve their methods and their ethics. Within this discussion, there was little concern with the processes that make these appeals so successful, although perhaps it is more accurate to say that what concern there is regarding the effectiveness of sponsorship advertising is too easily laid at the feet of several assumptions regarding the immediate emotional reactions of donors, such as the influence of compassion or guilt. Beyond a cursory explanation of stereotyping poor Southerners as passive and helpless, the *Tribune's* critique showed equally little discussion of why these portrayals of needy children might be problematic. While not to be dismissed, there is a need to move beyond the well-documented but time-worn criticisms brought up in the *Tribune* report. These criticisms leave us with little means of understanding the problems that are still present after the apparent transition to a more nuanced and more positive messaging strategy within much recent sponsorship promotional material. More importantly, they tell us little about the role of broader discursive forces in the representation of child sponsorship to donors.

Of all the aspects of child sponsorship, the area of advertising and its imagery has received the most critical attention from journalists and academics. Although not all of this attention deals directly with sponsorship advertising, there is substantial literature on the representation of people who are different from the intended audience (people who are Other), especially poor non-white people in the South (for example, see Bula, 2002; Doty, 1996; Dyer, 1993; Fabian, 1990; Giaccardi, 1995; Hackett, 1992; Hall, 1981, 1992, 1997; hooks, 1992; JanMohammed, 1985;

Jefferess, 2002a; Lutz and Collins, 1993; McHoul, 1991; Moeller, 1999; Nederveen Pieterse, 1992; Plewes and Stuart, 2007; Sontag, 2003; Wright, 2004). This literature covers an enormous variety of issues, and offers some valuable insights into representational practices and their influence on identity formation. Consequently, the present chapter will draw on some of this literature to help present an analysis of sponsorship promotional material with the aim of providing a critical reflection that sidelines the supposed insensitivity or dishonesty of sponsorship programs. Instead of an emphasis on inappropriateness or inaccuracy, this chapter will provide a critique of sponsorship promotional material that not only describes some of the discursive features of this material but also sheds light on how the practice of child sponsorship is ethically positioned in the contemporary world.

To facilitate this analysis, this chapter draws on a sample of sponsorship promotional material.[5] This sample represents items used both to recruit and retain child sponsors and includes televised ads, magazine inserts, brochures, newsletters, direct mail appeals, web pages and examples of sponsor updates. This sample was selected purposively and contains items from the following organizations: World Vision Canada (ten items), Plan Canada (five items), Christian Children's Fund of Canada (four items), Compassion Canada (four items), Food for the Hungry Canada (three items), and Canadian Feed the Children (three items). A list of the items in the sample can be found at the end of the book.

It should be noted that this sample is not used in an attempt to summarize the entirety of sponsorship advertising across all organizations. There are many different kinds of sponsorship promotion, and no one organization is exactly like another (although there are many similarities). Neither is this sample used to present an argument regarding the imagined effects of this advertising and its imagery on the minds of Northerners. While some general inferences can be made about the implications of sponsorship on Northern worldviews, it is problematic to assume any specific influence of individual sponsorship advertisements. Unless the viewer of an ad is asked directly, it is impossible to adequately describe what any individual advertisement means to a viewer, or what the effect of this meaning on the viewer will be (Hall 1981, 1997). The discussion presented in this chapter does not, consequently, follow traditional lines of content analysis, in which images and text from advertisements are commonly broken down into their constituent semiotic elements or assessed for their latent meanings. This means that even though advertising is the focus of this chapter, the purpose is not to present and analyze specific ads, and the fact that individual ads and their associated images are not reproduced in this chapter is intentional. This decision is based on a desire to highlight the discursive *contexts* involved in interpreting sponsorship promotional material in general rather than examine the *effects* of any particular advertisement.

Typical ads and typical critiques

A World Vision Canada televised advertisement for child sponsorship provides a good starting place for this analysis. The one-hour infomercial, entitled "Africa's Children," opens with a title sequence comprising a series of images. We first see a woman walking on a dirt road with what looks like a load of firewood on her head. This context-setting image, which shouts "Africa" as loud as the drum-laden background music, is accompanied by a few seemingly random flashes of people working with their hands before leading into a sequence of shots focusing on the sad faces of black children. These moving portraits — the last of which features a young girl at the door of her daub-and-wattle hut overlaid with the title of the "episode" — are followed by no less than nine separate shots of white World Vision spokespersons in the process of comforting children, lifting babies, talking with local health care professionals, or simply posing with some now-smiling African youngsters. After this brief introduction, which seems to last forever but takes no more than a minute, Susan Hay greets us directly:

> Hi everybody, I am Susan Hay in Southern Africa, and I came here with World Vision. I wanted to find out how the children here lived, and I wanted to find out how I could help. I can tell you ... it has been a life-changing experience for me.

Later in the same program, after Susan has taken us "into the life" of Rosalia, a five-year-old girl whose family is suffering from a drought, she informs us that

> What we can do to help is open up our eyes and our hearts as wide as we can and just sponsor a child. A dollar a day ... and you can send them to school; health care is there; you put food in their tummy, and they have clean water, and you know, just a dollar a day can go a very, very long way here. I have seen it for myself. We just need you to sponsor, and maybe you do not think you can make a difference — you cannot change the world — but if we all get together, one person can make a difference in the lives of little ones like this.

This World Vision infomercial continues with three additional heart-wrenching narratives of misery interspersed with four vignettes featuring Canadian sponsors and the apparent impact they have made on the lives of their sponsored children (as well as the considerable effect it has had on their own lives). Reports by celebrity spokespersons and appeals to sponsor a child are spliced in between these segments. The entire program ends with another few words by Susan, who is sitting beside a young girl she has just met that day. Susan talks about the "special connection" she has formed with this eight-year-old, and how she now wants to sponsor her. After we witness the presumably joyous reaction of the girl being told this on film (through the help of a translator), Susan closes with the following words:

> So, go to your phone now and do something extra special for yourself. And for just a few pennies a day, you are giving these kids hope for the future, sending them to school, better health care, just ... being a better person, and we all need that in our lives. So, thank you so much for watching us; this has been an amazing experience, and we are going to say a big goodbye from Africa. Ciao, say ciao [to the girl]. Thank you for watching.

This infomercial is typical of those produced by World Vision and very similar to those of Plan Canada, the only other Canadian sponsorship program to use long-format commercials on television.

Despite its undeniable allure, many problematic elements of this ad stand out, and some of these definitely resonate with the criticisms brought up in the *Tribune* report. During the course of the ad, for example, we are introduced to four children who are (apparently) in desperate need of sponsorship. The stories that we are told about these children are indeed heart-wrenching, filled with descriptions of illness, hunger, and neglect. Major segments of these stories seem very reminiscent of the "flies-in-the-eyes" style of appeal, where we are confronted with a very harsh depiction of need and a grim prognosis if this need is not addressed. Other parts, however, focus on the purported benefits of sponsorship and the joy that these benefits will supposedly bring. There are almost as many images of smiling children and vibrant communities as there are images of despair. This reflects a significant change in recent years across most sponsorship programs; there is a much greater emphasis on messages of hope in sponsorship promotional material. These positive messages, however, are tied almost exclusively to the intervention of sponsors and not the actions of Southerners. The children and families in this ad, and many others like it, are still portrayed superficially both as helpless objects of unfortunate circumstance and as passive recipients of Northern generosity. No more complexity than these simple tropes is offered (or, it seems, required). So, despite the increasing prevalence of "positive" messages in sponsorship promotional material, the issue of stereotypically negative representations of Southern peoples and places in such advertising is still a pressing concern.

This problem of negative stereotypes is a common theme in the literature on representations of other "races" and places (for example, see CCIC, 2004; Crewe and Fernando, 2006; Hall, 1997; Hoijer, 2004; Oliver, 2006; Rothmeyer, 2011; VSO, 2001). In particular, the need to simply avoid the use of stereotypical images and stories, as if this were a relatively straightforward decision, figures prominently in both lay commentaries and academic critiques. For example, the Canadian Council for International Cooperation (ccic) published a report from a 2004 workshop for fundraisers regarding "images of Africa." This workshop dealt with how to put ccic's Code of Ethics around "respectful communications to the public" into practice (5). The Code stipulates that member organizations should avoid "messages which generalise and mask the diversity of situations; messages which fuel prejudice; messages which foster a sense of Northern superiority; messages which show people as hopeless objects for our pity, rather than as equal partners in action and development" (5). Arguably, all of these elements were contravened by the infomercial under discussion despite World Vision Canada being a participant at this workshop. The key word here is "arguably." While it seems obvious that these points from the ccic Code should be avoided, it is not obvious what exactly qualifies as one of these points. The story of Rosalia definitely dwells on the misery of poverty and links the foremost possibility of hope to Northern support. However, does it foster a sense of Northern superiority or fuel prejudice? How could this determination be made?

While some examples of stereotypes are readily apparent, many are not so clear cut. The heart of the problem is that stereotypes are an intrinsic part of cultural and cognitive processes and, to some degree, are unavoidable. According to Brubaker, Loveman, and Stamatov (2004: 38–39), for example, much recent work on stereotyping indicates that they

> are no longer defined in terms of cognitive deficiencies — in terms of false or exaggerated or unwarranted belief — but more neutrally as cognitive structures that contain knowledge, beliefs, and expectations about social groups. Nor are stereotypes seen as the distinctive and pathological propensity of particular kinds of personalities … but rather as rooted in normal and ubiquitous cognitive processes.

Furthermore, while stereotypes can undeniably be harmful, knowing the direct and long-term effects of stereotypical representations is difficult, if not impossible. As Crewe and Fernando (2006) point out, stereotypes do not simply act externally on individuals with directly foreseeable results; instead, they are complexly modified and integrated into people's identities and their perceptions of the world. Consequently, stereotypes can apply in some cases, but are more often simply "cultural reference points that act as a backdrop for people to pass around, dispute, modify and even abandon as cultural identities change" (Crewe and Fernando, 2006: 43).

Stuart Hall (1981, 1997) makes some similar points. He notes that we should not assume any particular understandings or effects of apparently stereotypical representations. Assumptions about the interpretation and subsequent effect of stereotypical portrayals of Others can go both ways, leaving the way open to claim, for example, that particular representations are not racist despite having no empirical research on the issue (Hall, 1981). Hall encourages us to recognize that stereotypes can only make sense via reference to already established discourses. In this way, stereotypes can best be seen as part of the construction of symbolic boundaries that help structure desire and regulate collectivities. Consequently, rather than see stereotypes as the chief instrument of racism, it is more useful to see underlying processes of racialization as the mechanism that facilitates the production, legitimization, and interpretation of stereotypes.

This problem of stereotypical representations and their long-term consequences on Southerners will be discussed later in the chapter; for now, there are also some more immediate concerns with the World Vision infomercial and other ads. For one thing, there is no way of knowing if these particular children are actually "available" for sponsorship (it is not likely they are). While these images are not obviously borrowed from some general pool of past footage (as might have been the case in previous years), there is still no connection between the children whose representations are used to sell the idea of sponsorship in this ad and their actual sponsorship. Knowing how sponsorship generally functions overseas, a pertinent question in this case might be why these particular children are not already receiving services from the sponsorship program's local partners. Since it is rarely, if ever, the case nowadays that a sponsored child is excluded from the local work of the NGO funded by a Northern sponsorship program (whether or not they are awaiting sponsorship), where is it that these "real" children are located within the mechanics of sponsorship-funded development work? How can these children technically, not to mention ethically, be left without access to services when the organization is supposedly working in their midst (this is not dissimilar to the critique of photographers, such as Kevin Carter, when they take pictures of starving children rather than immediately intervene)? This begs another rather straightforward but difficult question: what is the compensation for their presence on camera? Can they be left to starve even as the production crew that is filming them eats through an obviously substantial budget (one that could "sponsor" these children many times over)? If not (and hopefully not), then how accurate can the stories presented be?

The issue of accuracy, of course, is a common point of contention regarding sponsorship advertising, and it was raised repeatedly in the *Tribune* report. This issue entails two distinct, albeit related, questions: first, to what extent are the stories of specific children in this ad, or others like it, "true" stories? Second, to what extent are the presented stories representative of both the general conditions in the South and the development interventions funded through sponsorship? The first question is important because one cannot, after all, be accused of misrepresenting sponsored children if the representations presented are "true," even if they are not representative of conditions in the South. However, even if one could determine the legitimacy of the stories presented in the advertisement's vignettes, which is nigh impossible given the information involved, there would be little benefit. If the story of Rosalia, for example, were found to be completely fabricated, what would be the consequence of this deception, and what would be gained by its alteration? Plan US has admitted to using generic photos coupled with made-up names and stories of children's lives that are "composites drawn 'from the histories of many children'" (Dorning, 1998a: 2-13). This was not seen as scandalous and did not result in retraction of the ad because, said the Plan US marketing director, "'the reading public does understand what the real message is'" (2-13). Even if it were a scandal that could not be brushed off with arguments about the need to raise money in the cheapest way possible (and producing "representative" stories is definitely cheaper and probably more effective than using "real" ones), then the fabricated story could just be replaced with a "true" story — inasmuch as any packaged story can be true. But what would be gained? Would the content and style of the ad be significantly different? Probably not. Telling any story, fact or fiction, is necessarily telling part of a story, one interpretation of events.

Even more than the first question, the second question gets to the heart of the problem of accuracy in sponsorship promotional material. This problem is not as much related to the complete misrepresentation of the organization's work or the people with whom it works, which is probably very rare, as it is to the level of representativeness of what is portrayed in sponsorship ads. If the tragic story of Rosalia is not common within the program areas funded by World Vision even if it is "true," or if the successes of sponsorship depicted in the commercial are not usual, then the organization is still vulnerable to critiques of inaccuracy and misrepresentation. The testing of representativeness in advertising seems straightforward: go overseas and examine some project sites, as did the *Tribune* staff. There are some conceptual pitfalls, however, that make the determination of accuracy difficult. For one, how many children's lives or how many project sites have to reflect the advertised stories before they are deemed representative? Even if an organization could show that a simple majority of cases are similar to those advertised (which they probably cannot), they would still have to deal with almost half of their donors sponsoring children whose conditions are not reflected in the ads. Two, how does one go about comparing hunger in one place with illness in another or, for that matter, vaccination with microcredit? Though it is often regarded as central to the problems of sponsorship promotion and though it cannot be completely dismissed, the question of accuracy begins a cycle of critique that is complicated by theoretical and practical difficulties and, in the end, has little possibility for any real change within the advertising practices of sponsorship programs. Even after well-publicized critiques like those in the *Tribune*, we are largely left with similar ads that have slightly more smiles, somewhat fewer flies, and much more carefully scripted appeals.

"Little more than props"

Clearly, problems of stereotypical and inaccurate representations of Southerners within this World Vision ad, and others like it, should not be dismissed. However, it is equally clear that such conventional critiques have neither resulted in substantial changes in advertising practices, nor have they adequately dealt with some of the thorny epistemological difficulties in such representations. Consequently, let us turn to a slightly different avenue of critique, one that will hopefully provide an alternate basis for the critical evaluation of sponsorship promotional material. This line of thought is introduced in the *Tribune* report but is not fleshed out. While the *Tribune* is generally quite uniform in its discussion of the problems of sponsorship, a single statement hints at something deeper than the incorrect or inappropriate representations of people from the South. Dellios (1998) comments that "the children whose somber faces grace those appeals amount to little more than props in a massive industry that privately rationalizes the myth of sponsorship as a necessary, if well-intentioned, fiction" (2-8). Unfortunately, there is little explanation of this statement in the article; it seems to simply be one more shot at the organizations that use children's faces to support what is seen as a bloated and ineffective infrastructure. This sentence too quickly glosses over the seed of a broader critique of the mechanisms that attract donors to child sponsorship and their relationship to an overarching discourse of development that structures thought and action in this area.

An understanding of sponsored children as props on an elaborately constructed stage, rather than as fully participating actors in the process of sponsorship, is a powerful metaphor to help explain some of the success of sponsorship as a fundraising tool as well as some of the problematic nature of its use. While somewhat simplistic, this metaphor does an excellent job of highlighting the generic quality of the representations featured in sponsorship promotional material — the way in which the children are relatively interchangeable set pieces in a narrative that is as much, if not more, about the experiences of the sponsors than about the lives of the children. Numerous instances in the infomercial "Africa's Children" highlight this point. Not only is the story of Rosalia's hunger, explained simply as an issue of drought, identical to those in a hundred other appeals, but what help is apparently offered (via the sponsors' charity) is so general that it is both indispensable and indisputable: "you can send them to school; health care is there; you put food in their tummy, and they have clean water." This generic story of hunger and response is quickly subsumed by another story, that of the "life-changing experience" offered to sponsors. After each vignette emphasizing the need, we are introduced to staff and sponsors who describe how wonderful it feels "to make a difference in the lives of little ones like this." What could be a better experience than doing "something extra special for yourself," than accomplishing so much good for "just a few pennies a day"? Few other experiences offer the opportunity to become a better person with so little effort. As Maren (1997: 140) writes in his critique of Save the Children US, "the sponsor is seduced by the possibility of getting something valuable on the cheap. What sponsors are really buying is, as stated in Save's brochures, a sense of well-being and 'deep satisfaction.'"

So, despite being a universal ingredient of sponsorship advertising, children do not seem to be the principal subject of these ads. Their sad (or smiling) faces may fill up advertisements to the point of overflowing, but they are not the protagonists. They play a principal role in a story other than that of their own need — a narrative centred on the personal development of the sponsor through the experience of sponsorship. Echoing the financial mechanics of sponsorship, wherein the sponsor and organization in the North have a well-defined relationship facilitated by a child that is only an (imagined) object of benevolence, sponsorship promotional material positions the sponsor within a tale of their own (ethical) transformation surrounded by the cast of characters that make this story possible. As props, then, representations of sponsored children simply supply a context in which the story of the sponsor and their experience can be made both comprehensible and compelling.

The key here is that this context is not a unique product related to the narrative of sponsorship. Rather, its significance comes from historical relationships and cultural conventions that imbue the practice of sponsorship with particular meanings. By far, the most important relationships that inform the reading of sponsorship advertisements are those related to the history of racialized divisions of the colonial era. The "civilizing" mission of colonial interventions provides a powerful but uncomfortable backdrop to present understandings of sponsorship. That said, this very history, which plays a significant role in making sponsorship intelligible, is not one most sponsorship programs or sponsors want to be associated with. A far more comfortable context for the rationalization of sponsorship is provided by another category of difference between sponsor and child — that of age.

The understanding of sponsorship promotion as largely focused on the sponsor rather than the child is not novel (for example, see Jefferess, 2002a; Maren 1997; Plewes and Stuart, 2007). This understanding should not imply, however, that the child is immaterial to the advertising. More accurately, it should not imply that the concept of childhood is immaterial. Because representations of sponsored children are largely generic, it is not the actual child itself but the concept of the child generally — of the period called childhood and of normal child development — that is pivotal in the story of sponsorship. Despite long-standing studies, such as Aries' (1962) *Centuries of Childhood,* that highlight the socially constructed nature of childhood, the discursive location of the child in modern liberal societies has become so naturalized that it is commonly taken for granted. It is the particular construction of appropriate child development and its contexts that, to a large degree, shapes both sponsorship programs' production of their ads and donors' responses to these ads. It is only because of the discursive space children occupy in many Northern societies that their representations can be used to tell (or sell) the story of sponsorship in the way it is often told (sold).

This relationship between sponsorship and the idea of the child is more than simply an understanding that "children sell," as a senior manager at a sponsorship program worded it. The themes of child development, international development, and the personal (ethical) development of the sponsor articulate with each other within the promotional material of sponsorship programs such that it is the liberal understanding of the child that facilitates the ethical transformation of the sponsor. In other words, (sponsored) children are props in a story of the sponsorship experience not because their representations are devoid of specific meaning (if they are deemed to be inaccurate for example) but because their representations convey a very particular set of general meanings to Northerners. This set of assumptions, which includes such elements as the (economic and political) innocence of childhood, allows for the easy integration of the stories of sponsored children into the stories of sponsors. Through this lens, we can understand sponsorship not so much as the commodification of children — as might be assumed from an initial critical appraisal of sponsorship advertising — but as another aspect of the link between consumption, identity, and ethics in modern liberal societies. While the following chapter takes up this argument regarding the relationship between the sponsorship experience and the personal development of the sponsor, the remainder of this chapter will discuss the role of children (and the concept of the child) in sponsorship promotional material *as it relates* to the aforementioned focus on sponsors and their transformation.

Generic representations for formulaic advertising

The promotional material of child sponsorship programs is formulaic; in fact, its formula is one of its most distinguishing features. After watching or reading a number of ads, it becomes difficult to tell the various agencies and appeals apart. The same components and the same themes seem to blend into each other, creating a drab procession of children's faces, earnest spokespersons, and repetitive thank-yous. These advertisements often contain one or more of the following main elements:

representations of the need for the sponsors' charity (i.e. displays of poverty or other difficulties among communities and children in the South); the benefits that sponsors can expect to receive, be they emotional, informational, or otherwise; a description of what the sponsors' donations will supposedly provide to a child and/or community; and expressions of gratitude for the sponsors' (future) support.

A single short commercial by Christian Children's Fund of Canada illustrates each of these main elements. The text of the commercial, read by a slow and sonorous male voice, is as follows:

> Innocent children of war, famine, and disease. Will you help them? For only $33 a month, you can sponsor one of these little ones, saving him or her from malnutrition and death. Call the number on the screen right now to sponsor a child in desperate need through Christian Children's Fund of Canada. By providing food, medicine, and a chance to go to school for one child, you will help that child's family and community.

At this point, the accompanying images switch from a slideshow of black-and-white pictures of sad black children to a full-colour video of a white sponsor family sitting around a table looking at some papers. The voice continues:

> Within ten days of your call, you will receive a photo and a story of a child in need and information on how to become a sponsor. Call now and sponsor by pre-authorized cheque or credit card and receive your choice of a free gift — our way of saying thank you. The children of war, famine, and disease are depending on you. Please call now.

There are many aspects of this ad that touch on points relevant to this chapter, including a basic concern with stereotyping the South as conflict- and disease-ridden. The most salient point related to the formula of sponsorship promotion, however, is the exceedingly general level of information that is conveyed about both the children in need of help (not to mention their families and their communities) and the role of sponsors' contributions in providing that aid. As with many sponsorship ads, there is no information about the children whose images are used in the ad or what is happening on the ground with donated money. While this level of generality is likely used to encompass the wide variety of work done overseas or to account for the variability in the audience, the lack of any specific information leaves many such ads without any significant context except that provided by the accompanying images and stories of children and their sponsors. In most cases, these images and stories are, by necessity or expediency, as generic as the other components of the ads.

Take, for example, a brochure produced by Canadian Feed the Children. This document, entitled "Childhood: The Chance of a Lifetime," includes five pictures with a total of nine (black) children. None of these children are named, and we are not told where they come from or the circumstances that make them require sponsorship. Instead, the words "supported," "protected," "respected," and "nourished" are inscribed on each picture. While the use of such words may distinguish this brochure from others, the images certainly do not. The same brochure could easily have been made using the images of other children; the text within the brochure reads as follows:

> Every child has potential. But poverty can stop it dead, keeping children from wellness, strength and success. With careful attention to everyday needs, Canadian Feed the Children helps remove the barriers imposed by poverty, so a child has the chance of a full, healthy life.

Such a universal description could apply to almost any situation or any child.

This same level of generality is present in many other types of sponsorship promotional material. In a letter sent to Compassion sponsors about their newly sponsored child, there is a short section introducing Edilson Borda from Bolivia. While the inclusion of a name and location is encouraging (and expected) in this kind of document, the background provided is sparse on details:

> Edilson makes his home with his father and his mother. Running errands is his household duty. His father is sometimes employed and his mother is sometimes employed. There are three children in the family. Playing with cars is Edilson's favourite activity. In primary school his performance is average and he regularly attends church activities. Your love and support help Edilson to receive the assistance he needs to develop his potential.

This is the kind of information that could be (and probably was) produced through a fill-in-the-blank style of storytelling that is written by a remote and removed individual and applicable to a host of other children and their families. The same is true of a sample Food for the Hungry Canada letter describing an upcoming celebration in the sponsored child's community:

> Very soon, Rhea's community will be having a celebration for just one reason — Rhea, and all the children in her community. Just take a peek at what an exciting time it will be: It is a wonderful celebration, where sponsored children and their families gather — with unsponsored children, too — and we celebrate the value of children and their families. Games, food, fellowship, and fun. You should see it! … Many children in Rhea's community do not know their actual birthday, but we do not want

to leave them out of the celebration! I believe that every child should be celebrated ... Your donation offsets the cost of the party and helps meet additional needs in the community. Your gift will provide practical things that your child and the unsponsored children need to stay healthy, keep learning and grow strong.

This generic solicitation letter is surely sent to all Food for the Hungry sponsors irrespective of the situation in their sponsored child's community. While this is understandable from an administrative point of view, it does not change the fact that such letters tell recipients next to nothing about who or what is actually involved in sponsorship.

The generic nature of the representations of children in sponsorship advertising may go unnoticed, however, because of the extremely personal way in which promotional images are captured and arranged. As viewers, we usually see the children (whether smiling or not) in the most vulnerable of circumstances; we are privy to a distressingly private look at their bodies — most often singled out from all but their base material contexts. In the sample of promotional material, there are no less than twenty images of children that have altered or deleted backgrounds to bring them into greater focus (literally and figuratively). This does not include the dozens of images of children photographed or videotaped on their own, more often than not staring directly at the camera/audience. Despite the powerful illusion of intimacy and connection, we rarely know more about their lives than their crushing poverty. When we are introduced to them, it is in a way that tells us everything and nothing — everything about their apparent needs and nothing about the specifics of their history, their community, or their lives. Even children such as Rosalia from the extended vignettes in "Africa's Children" could be replaced at any moment by another (or, at least, a black Other) because what seems to be important for selling child sponsorship is not who the child is but what they represent for the audience. It is this imminent exchangeability of the children in almost all promotional material — and in the practice of sponsorship itself where one sponsored child can be easily substituted for another from one day to the next without interruption in donations or services — that confirms their generic status.

As noted, the generic representations of children involved in sponsorship serve an important administrative function; they allow sponsorship programs to create promotional materials that are seemingly applicable to most situations in the South where the organizations or their partners work. This facilitates the sponsorship of thousands of different children without having to explain the specific situation for each child. Arguably, this practice of providing only the most superficial information is defensible because it saves money for the more important work being done on the ground and because it is commonly perceived that sponsorship audiences get turned off by too much information. It is possible, however, that this practice works precisely because no specific information is present.

This generic status of children in sponsorship advertising may seem contradictory to received wisdom in the area. Within psychology, the understanding that information and images of specific people raise more money and awareness than statistical descriptions of harm at a general level is well documented in the literature on the so-called identifiable victim effect (see Jenni and Loewenstein, 1997; Lee and Feeley, 2016). However, there is still some disagreement about the relevance of the effect and the mechanisms at play behind it (Lee and Feeley, 2016). For example, does it have to do with the amount of information given (Small and Loewenstein, 2003), the emotional response of the donor (Kogut and Ritov, 2005), or simply "less-analytic" personality traits (Friedrich and McGuire, 2010)? Whatever the case, it is apparent that how much the audience is told about the "victim," and who that "victim" is, has some moderating influence on the effect. Identifiable children, for instance, seem to generate more response than identifiable adults (Lee and Feeley, 2016), and this effect is present even without any significant information about the individual in question (Kogut and Ritov, 2005). What this implies is that specific knowledge about the "victim" is not itself what drives this effect; rather, contextual elements seem to play the largest role. Moreover, what seems to be missing from most psychological accounts of this phenomenon is a consideration of how the sociocultural contexts of the viewer (and the discursive contexts of the viewing itself) informs what they think and do. Simply locating the identifiable victim effect in a personal characteristic or reaction, such as emotional response, does not help us understand the thought processes of the viewer as they make sense of the appeal. After all, identifying an individual is not a wholly straightforward process. Adding a story to a face still requires some processing on the part of the viewer, such as a determination of why that person needs assistance, why they cannot provide it themselves, and why the viewer should help. For this part, it is just as likely the viewer who provides this information as it is the identification of the "victim" itself.

The lack of specific information on its own, then, may not be the most important feature of the generic nature of advertising; instead, it is the way this lack of specific information requires sponsors to generate interpretations using the cultural repertoires that are available. If there is little context from which to understand the representations of poor black children, it is left to the sponsor to fill in the blanks. For sponsorship to be successful, this process must both universalize and essentialize the relationships between individuals in the North and the South. While being paradoxically personal and superficial, the generic child image highlights an important similarity between sponsors and sponsored children and, simultaneously, an almost insurmountable difference of material (and perhaps cultural) circumstances. It must combine these elements to build a perceived connection between child and sponsor while maintaining the essential disparity that sees one in need of help and the other able to provide that assistance (see Dogra, 2012).

The similarity that fosters the perceived connection between sponsor and child, however, might come from more than ideas of a common humanity, which would seemingly engender an obligation to right injustice or to charitably assist fellow humans in distress. At least in part, it seems to come from the Northern viewer's (supposedly universal) understanding of the child and their appropriate roles and responsibilities in life. In this way, the difficulties and remedies of Southern poverty are made both personal and intelligible through ready-made assumptions about relationships between children and the individuals and institutions that surround them. The assumed universality of what children mean, then, allows sponsors to identify — not necessarily with the child itself, but with the practice of sponsorship. After all, feeding, educating, and maintaining the health of children is deemed a natural responsibility of the liberal family and state. In this way, the connection between sponsor and child seems to be maintained more through a universalized category of difference (that of age) than a common bond of humanity.

For this argument's purposes, age is taken to be the most salient category of difference in sponsorship. As noted above, however, age is by no means the only category of difference that plays a role in the connection between sponsor and child. Apart from the obvious category of wealth or class, the perceived category of race (or perhaps ethnicity) directly informs the sponsorship experience. Just as it would be short-sighted to ignore the connections between (past and present) imperialism and international development, it would be foolish to ignore the influence of representational practices of racialized groups on child sponsorship promotional material. While it is true that children occupy a particular place in the imagination of many Northerners, the same can equally be said of Southern Others. Racialized groups in the South have overwhelmingly been associated with cultural, moral, and economic "backwardness," consigning them to a history of "necessary" interventions (Escobar, 1995; Sachs, 1999). In fact, it is likely the intersection of age and race within child sponsorship that allows for the almost effortless categorization of sponsored children as being in need of developmental aid (and of sponsors being able to provide it).

From social construction of children
to the ethical constitution of the sponsor

It is no longer terribly controversial to assert that the concept of the child and the special period called childhood are social constructions. There is substantial scholarly recognition, at least within sociology, of the significant cultural and temporal variations in what it means to be a child (Aries, 1962). This does not negate the biological and psychological maturation of the human body and mind, but it does illustrate the highly variable way that this period of maturation is understood and delineated. As Bell (1993: 391) notes, a "sociology of childhood has long propounded the argument that childhood is not a natural category but one constructed via social ideas and institutions that create boundaries irreducible to physical or maturational difference." This understanding of the child as a constructed category is not always widely shared outside academia, however. For example, David Jefferess (2002b) discusses the idea of the child in relation to the universal child rights discourse. He writes that "despite the assumed universality, ahistoricality and naturalness of 'childhood,' the 'child' is an ambiguous and paradoxical concept, whose status as not (yet) adult is much more complex and fraught than child rights discourse suggests" (76). If the concept of the child is problematic in the discourse on child rights, it is possible to see how simplistic assumptions around childhood could unduly influence sponsors and their perception of sponsorship.

The representation of a Southern child, then, is not simply about that particular child. Such representations divide (potential) sponsors and (sponsored) children into essentialized categories laden with cultural connotations. That which defines the child provides the context for the definition of the viewer. Just as sponsors are the "surrogate" parents to these suffering children, they are also the wealth to their poverty and the charity to their need. More controversially, they are also the white to their black and the saviour to their salvation. By inhabiting these well-worn binaries, images of children in sponsorship ads and the people who view them are brought together — as much as they are separated — via their differences. More than any inaccurate depictions of chronic helplessness or hopelessness, the recurrent use of essentialized categories is what makes these sponsorship ads problematic and "Orientalist."

One of Edward Said's great contributions was his emphasis on the role of essentialist representations in practices of power. In *Orientalism*, Said (1979) examines representations of "the Orient" within Western, particularly British and French, culture and politics. Although most of the book is spent uncovering the thinly veiled chauvinism within Western literature that, for Said, forms the basis of these representations, he also wants to demonstrate how the "network of interests" that are always present in discussions about the Orient work to constrain every instance of "writing, thinking, or acting on the Orient" (3). Through illustrating this link between representations of the Orient and the political, economic, and military history of interaction with the Orient, Said sets out to explain how "European culture gained in strength and identity by setting itself off against the Orient as a sort of surrogate and even underground self" (3). Consequently, beyond the academic discipline of Orientalism and beyond a particular "style of thought" that falsely distinguishes between the two monolithic categories of Orient and Occident, Said understands Orientalism as "a Western style for dominating, restructuring, and having authority over the Orient" (2, 3). Said points out, however, that there is no such thing as a "real or true Orient," and although his political standpoint remains one of humanistic tolerance for diversity, he is primarily critiquing a way of seeing the world through reductive binaries (322).

As with "Orientalist" literature, sponsorship ads are commonly constructed around similarly reductive binaries. Within these ads, sponsored children become synonymous with Southern poverty; each of their images comes to represent — at a panoptical glance — the entire story of the South and its relationship to the North. Each child is, therefore, the embodiment of the development narrative of progress. Thus, while occupying the role of an imaginary yet threatened child(hood) to the Northern sponsor, these representations also take up the burden of distilling all economic relations between North and South to those of Northern generosity in response to Southern privation.

The universalized and essentialized representations of sponsored children seem to provide a certain level of continuity through change, a stable element amidst an overwhelming sea of global forces and sad faces. These representations, then, serve as a useful foil to help create the sponsor identity. The idea that the Other is a definitive component in the construction of the Self — or in other words, that locating difference is a crucial aspect of positioning oneself — is a long-standing notion in psychology and sociology (Cooley, 1998; Lacan, 2006 [1977]; Levinas, 1969). This concept has also been taken up by several postcolonial scholars in order to understand the consequences of colonialism on both the colonized and the colonizers (for example, see Bhabha, 1994; Said, 1979). In fact, one of the central contributions of postcolonial scholars has been foregrounding the role of representation within issues of identity and power. This in-depth treatment of representation not only highlights the way Others are constructed in the North but also the way this construction shapes how Northerners see themselves. Antonio Callari (2004: 113), for example, notes that "one of the key contributions of post-colonial thought has been the registering of *the other* as a moment of theoretical definition *of* the West" (emphasis in original).

This same process can be seen to occur in microcosm via the representations of children in sponsorship promotional material. The images of the sponsored child, and their geographical and economic context, appear to serve as the Other against which the (potential) sponsor can locate him or herself in the discourse that surrounds the practice of sponsorship. Even though the children themselves can be shuffled in and out of programs and advertisements, their meaning for the sponsor does not need to change. In fact, it is because of what such a racialized child means to them, given the common absence of much significant personal information, that sponsors are able not only to understand the ethical imperative to help but also to position themselves in the role of generous donor. Just as the representations of children are reproduced for the process of sponsorship fundraising, so too are sponsors reconstructed through the reading and viewing of sponsorship-related material. To facilitate the necessary uniformity of this reconstruction, one in which diverse sponsors can be equivalently transformed into better — more ethical — people, it is essential that sponsored children are able to fill the appropriate role as innocent and grateful objects of charity.

In her account of the Somalia Affair, Sherene Razack (2004) provides a useful illustration of this process of meaning-making involving representations of Southern Others and the construction of ethical Northern subjects. Drawing on a different trope related to Southern countries and their people(s), she highlights the perceived chaotic nature of the South and the effect this is seen to have on the health of Canadian soldiers. In this instance, vague representations of the South as inhospitable psychological terrain for Northern sensibilities allows the concrete racist and imperial practices of Canadian soldiers to be rationalized as "natural" reactions to difficult circumstances. In a parallel vein, fuzzy representations of vulnerable Southern children (who are directly situated within this chaotic environment) help provoke a different "natural" response among Northerners (i.e. charity). The effects on the construction of Northern identities, however, are surprisingly similar, allowing sponsors to ethically position themselves as doing good despite (or perhaps because of) the lack of any specific evidence.

The concept of the "gaze," with all its associated academic commentary, provides a useful way of linking the content of sponsorship promotional material to the experience of viewing it (see Foucault, 1989 [1966], 1973 [1963]). In social theory, a gaze is more than an intent look; it describes how the way something is represented affects its meaning and how the act of looking at something can give meaning to the observer as well as what is observed. In their book, *Reading National Geographic*, Catherine Lutz and Jane Collins (1993) discuss pictures from the *Geographic* as intersections of gazes, such as the photographer's gaze, the reader's gaze, the non-Western subjects' gaze, and the gaze of "Westerners" in the images. Looking at these pictures through the concept of the gaze, Lutz and Collins highlight how images of distant Others can tell us more about the institutional and national culture that created the images than about the Others represented by them.

This concept of the gaze seems an apt way to analyze sponsorship imagery. One of the most arresting qualities of the images of children used in these ads is the way they seem to stare at the viewer from inside the picture. Not only does this feature make these images particularly engrossing in a mass-mediated environment principally defined by its passive voyeurism, but it also facilitates the feeling of the (illusory) personal connection between viewer and viewed that draws attention away from the specific (spatial and historical) location of the sponsor as the viewer. This is especially relevant when the representation being viewed involves a person in distress. Susan Sontag (2003: 7) has written eloquently on this subject in her book, *Regarding the Pain of Others*, in which she states that "no 'we' should be taken for granted when the subject is looking at other people's pain." With this statement, she is referring to the way images both create Others who are seen but do not themselves see and place these Others squarely within the consciousness of the viewer. In other words, these images generate compelling connections between individuals while simultaneously separating observers from observed. In this way, images (can) distort both personal and politico-economic relationships to suffering, making it both proximate and distant, both apparently embedded in social practices and strangely singular and fragmented. As Sontag (2003: 102) writes,

> the imaginary proximity to the suffering inflicted on others that is granted by images suggests a link between the far-away sufferers — seen close-up on the television screen — and the privileged viewer that is simply untrue, that is yet one more mystification of our real relations of power.

Sontag's emphasis on power in this statement is important because it highlights how the different gazes involved in sponsorship promotional material are not all equivalent to each other. Some gazes, such as that of the sponsor, stand out.

Images of children in sponsorship advertising are accompanied by a cast of sample sponsors and narrators or spokespersons, each with their own gaze but all subsumed under the watchful eye of the sponsor as viewer. The primacy of the sponsors' gaze should be obvious despite the power of a poor child's pleading eyes, especially if we endeavour to keep in mind the purpose behind all sponsorship advertising. Although it is often eclipsed by the nature of the content, what sponsorship advertising is selling is the sponsorship experience itself. The collection of seemingly ethical experiences, such as building houses for Habitat for Humanity or attending the Live 8 concerts, has been made increasingly desirable within contemporary economic and cultural systems. While these practices obviously involve an object at which they are directed, like a house in Latin America or a poor African child, it is the experience itself which appears to hold the most value. Who asks a volunteer about the kind of house that was built or a sponsor about the community where the child comes from? "Why did you decide to do that?" or "What was it like?" seem to be more appropriate questions. Consequently, while sponsorship can be said to result in the commodification of black children, it seems to deal at least as much with the commodification of experience aimed at the sponsor. Perhaps it is more accurate to say, however, that the former can never really be separated from the latter. In other words, the very ability of the sponsorship experience to be successfully sold to Northerners relies on the racialized position of Southern children, even when they simply serve as an object of the sponsors' story of themselves.

It may be the case that sponsorship advertising revolves around the sponsor more than the child, but this is neither an original nor terribly profound insight. What must be considered in addition to this emphasis is how the focus on the sponsor as a sales technique interacts with the discursive context of the ads, including the practices that make up the politico-economic backdrop in which they are produced. This interaction plays off of — and itself facilitates — a distinctive view of the world and the place of individuals within it. In particular, the present nature of sponsorship as a fundraising technique that highlights the personal charity of Northern donors simultaneously with the economic responsibility of Southern recipients (a hand up not a handout; not giving a fish but teaching to fish) emerges out of — and coincides with — a global order that privileges individual liberty and private property above all else. Ignoring this interaction between text and context, or between meanings and practices, leads to an analysis of sponsorship advertising that disregards Foucault's insights about discourse and that neglects the relationship between the problems of so-called underdevelopment and the rise of neoliberalism.

5

"Change a life"

It is a powerful and seductive idea that it is possible to radically alter a child's life with very little effort. Believing you are able to help feed, clothe, heal, and educate a child must provide a person with a particular feeling of fulfillment. An old World Vision slogan, "Change a life. Change your own," neatly sums up this supposedly reciprocal relationship. The difficulty with this scenario, as the reporters from the *Chicago Tribune* would have it, comes when the recipient (sponsored child) does not get the help they were imagined to receive and the benefactor (sponsor) loses faith in the mediating organization or even in the process (of sponsorship) itself. For example, take the case of Kelley Schuster, who was looking "to take a journey of hope and restoration" after the death of her husband (Tackett and Jackson, 1998b: 2-13). She approached Christian Children's Fund (CCF) "seeking a new relationship, one with a child" (2-12). According to the *Tribune*, however, problems with the projects run by CCF hindered Schuster's efforts "to forge a lasting relationship with her sponsored child" (2-13). Apparently, these problems were a result of local mismanagement such that when Schuster tried to visit her sponsored child, Anthony, not only did the local staff of CCF not even show up to talk to Schuster, but she also found out that he "had received essentially nothing from Schuster's $21-a-month sponsorship payments" (2-13).

Understandably, this situation upset Schuster, and she quickly cancelled her sponsorship and sent a letter of complaint to CCF's president. In her mind, CCF's negligence in this case ruined any possibility of her building a relationship with her sponsored child. Despite the fact that CCF was clearly at fault, "Schuster blamed herself. 'I was so gullible,' she said. 'I did not check it out. I guess I had really high hopes of getting to know this boy and developing a relationship with him'" (Tackett and Jackson, 1998b: 2-13). This story seems to offer a clear example of how child sponsorship can go wrong for both the sponsored child and the sponsor. It highlights the pivotal role of the sponsorship program in validating the relationship between sponsor and child. It also somewhat obscures the fact that this social relationship is wholly predicated upon the financial relationship between the sponsorship program and the sponsored child and, more importantly, between the sponsorship program and the sponsor. Although Schuster's "heart is right," although she is "not trying to hurt anybody" and "really trying to help," and although she "even placed Anthony's photo on a table alongside pictures of her children," she could not maintain her relationship with Anthony due to the breakdown in her relationship with CCF (2-13).

In this example, the *Tribune* wrote of a sponsor frustrated in her desire to help a child in need. As with many of the *Tribune's* critiques, the blame is laid at the feet of the sponsorship agencies. By failing to provide the imagined benefits to sponsored children in exchange for the sponsorship fee, these organizations have breached the trust of their donors. The role of these donors needs little explanation; they are good people prompted by "charitable instincts" and are simply "trying to help." The disappointment felt by Schuster is thus envisioned as something related more to the inappropriate actions of sponsorship programs than to the (inappropriate?) expectations of sponsors. However, it seems to be these expectations as much as the actual results of sponsoring a child that fuel the practice of sponsorship. After all, the promotional material of sponsorship programs routinely encourages sponsors to expect profound, almost miraculous changes in the life of their sponsored child. These imagined changes are not only supposed to affirm the generosity of the sponsor, but they are also, somewhat paradoxically, supposed to be financially effortless.

In some apparently unrelated articles, the *Chicago Tribune* took up this issue of sponsorship results. The *Tribune* journalists did not attempt to completely deny that sponsorship can be helpful for some individuals. Instead, they highlighted the fact that child sponsorship is only a minor player in the global development industry. According to one inside source, a professor of development and former Childreach board member, "'child sponsorship agencies are very small players even in very small countries. It is really very arrogant to say we have had a major impact'" (Dorning, 1998b: 2-14). Despite the fact that sponsorship agencies are successful in securing millions in donations from private sources, their "contributions to the people they help are dwarfed by foreign aid and the countries' own resources" (2-14). More important than the scope of sponsorship dollars in the grand scheme of development assistance is the simple issue that, in many if not most cases, the impact of sponsorship on children and communities is largely unknown. In an extensive article on the legacy of sponsorship, Dorning and Goering (1998: 2-10) point out that "Although all sponsorship agencies highlight individual successes, the major groups say they do not know of any available data showing how formerly sponsored children have fared." Drawing on the stories of several former sponsored children, they conclude that "personal initiative, the support of family, the vagaries of circumstance and the actions of local authorities have as much impact as sponsorship" (2-10).

At first blush, this paucity of wide-spread, evaluative data on sponsorship seems as though it might hinder sponsor recruitment. How is it possible to convince sponsors to donate their money to "change a life" if there is little knowledge of whether or not this actually occurs? One answer lies, of course, with the notion that sponsorship organizations simply mislead sponsors regarding the effectiveness of sponsorship. As noted above, another answer may be found in the second half of World Vision's formula, the part where the sponsor changes their own life through the generous and miraculous process of sponsorship. Arguably, this promised transformation for the sponsor forms an equal — if not greater — part of a sponsor's expectation of sponsorship. The effectiveness of sponsorship on the ground in the South, then, seems to fade slightly into the background as it is substituted by the effectiveness of sponsorship as a way for the sponsor to become a different — a better — person. This consideration of the relationship between the transformation of a child's life through sponsorship and the transformation of the sponsor's own life in the process provides an alternate explanation to Schuster's disappointment, which may, in some way, be related to her unmet expectations of personal transformation. It also offers a fruitful entry point into the question of the role of sponsorship in sponsor's lives. Consequently, the next two chapters explore the relationship between the discourse of development and the way child sponsors perceive themselves and their actions in relation to sponsorship. These discourses allow sponsorship organizations and sponsors to promote and understand their international development contributions in terms of personal fulfillment and growth. In other words, these chapters will look at sponsors' understanding of child sponsorship, their reception of sponsorship promotional material, and ultimately, their motivation to sponsor a child through the lens of personal development.

To examine these issues, this chapter and the next draw on in-depth interviews with thirty-one people who sponsor, or have previously sponsored, children through Canadian NGOs. Of these participants, the majority are women (twenty-five), the majority are current sponsors (twenty-six), and the majority sponsor(ed) children through World Vision Canada or Plan Canada (twenty-five). The participants were recruited using posters placed in churches, libraries, community centres, and on the local university campus, as well as advertisements in the local paper and online (three of the interview participants were also recruited through referrals from other participants). Interviews with participants lasted between one and two hours and, with few exceptions, took place in the home of the sponsor.

The interviews were structured around a set of open-ended questions dealing with participants' thoughts and feelings about their sponsored child, about the process of sponsorship, and about their conceptions of global poverty and international development. Pseudonyms are used to help protect the confidentiality of participants.

Meetings whose needs?

Building on the arguments from the last few chapters, which explored the international development components of child sponsorship in light of perceptions of organizational and child development, the remaining chapters continue to look at sponsorship as something that is more than a way to simply address the needs of Southern children. As with promotional material that makes use of generic understandings of Southern children to provide context to the role of the Northern sponsor, child sponsorship nowadays seems to be as much about the satisfaction of sponsors' needs as it is about providing development assistance overseas. Despite the cynical nature of this statement, it makes perfect sense in terms of an understanding of the sponsorship experience as a product that is marketed to Northerners to raise money "for a good cause." This cause, the "development" of poor children, seemingly justifies almost any promotional strategy as long as it is successful at attracting sponsors. This is arguably more than a simple ends-justify-the-means scenario. What makes it successful in attracting Northern sponsors may be as important as what supposedly makes it successful in helping Southern children.

As noted in the last chapter, the understanding of sponsorship as focused more on the sponsor than the child has an ample history in the critical literature on foreign aid (for example, see Jefferess, 2002a; Maren 1997; Plewes and Stuart, 2007). This history almost exclusively draws on emotional concepts to describe sponsors' thoughts and actions. For example, Maren (1997: 140) argues that when someone decides to sponsor a child, they are really buying "a sense of well-being and 'deep satisfaction.'" Summarizing several studies on the psychological implications of the marketing of overseas aid, Campbell, Carr, and Maclachlan (2001) make a similar argument. They posit that the most common fundraising strategy "is the use of shocking pictures to arouse emotion and guilt" (426). Drawing on a study by Bozinoff and Ghingold (1983), they also argue that while "high-guilt" ads can result in more guilty feelings, these kinds of appeals are also likely to result in "counterarguing," rationalizations for not donating despite these feelings of guilt (426). They conclude that "guilt-arousing foreign-aid campaigns may indeed cause so much counterarguing that attitude and behavioural intention change are unlikely to occur" (426). Consequently, even if guilt is present upon the reception of sponsorship promotional material, it cannot simply be assumed to account for the decision to begin or maintain sponsorship.

While emotional factors obviously play some role in the thoughts and actions of sponsors, it is equally important to look beyond these transient states to the discursive contexts that contextualize them. These discourses — of global poverty, charity, and personal growth — inform sponsors' understandings of what child sponsorship is and what it accomplishes; they also help determine what it means to be a good person in modern liberal societies. Through this lens, one can begin to question what it might mean to be transformed by the sponsorship experience. How exactly is a sponsor's life changed? Is it simply a feeling of lessened guilt or increased satisfaction? Although we may be moved to action by an emotion, we first must interpret the world in such a way to account for that feeling. To feel guilty at seeing the face of a starving African child, for example, one must first understand the situation both as distressing and unfair. Furthermore, such emotional states are not permanent and are likely not experienced in the same way at every future encounter. Instead, it is probable that our emotional responses shift over time or simply give way to rationalizations about any action previously taken.

This does not mean that affective reactions to the imagery presented in sponsorship advertising are unimportant. These reactions, or personal interpretations of these reactions, definitely play a role in audience responses to such advertisements. There is a substantial literature on the nature of emotion and its relationship to bodily states of arousal (for example, see Gorton, 2007; Tompkins, 1995). Part of the debate is centred on the very definition of emotion, with some scholars arguing that it should be conceived of as separate from the bodily (affective) states that are interpreted as emotions. This implies that what are called emotions are a product of personal interpretation, and therefore subject to the influence of discourse, but it also implies that there are some more basic affective states that occur prior to the level of interpretation (perhaps at the level of instinct). Whatever the case, these debates fall somewhat outside the scope of this project. Suffice it to say that immediate emotional reactions are likely not the only factor involved in decisions to sponsor a child, and non-emotional elements seem to be neglected in much of the literature discussing why sponsorship is so successful.

Understanding the decision to begin or maintain sponsorship as more than a straightforward result of an emotional response is, arguably, an important first step in appreciating the complex role of the sponsor. Instead of looking primarily to sponsors' desire to *feel* good about themselves, it is enlightening to look at how sponsors *imagine* themselves as better people because of their participation in child sponsorship. The process of transformation that is supposed to occur through sponsorship can then be equally conceptualized as a process of formation, one that constructs sponsors (or facilitates their self-construction) as ethical subjects in relation to Southern poverty. This transformative process derives from both the messaging practices of child sponsorship programs and the (liberal) discourses of charity and responsibility that sustain them. This point may seem a little vague or trivial; however, it not only fits within much current literature on ethics and identity formation (see Appiah, 2005; Cruikshank, 1996, 1999; Hattori, 2003; Hoijer, 2004; King, 2003, 2006; Somers, 1994), but it also has several significant implications.

In his book, *The Ethics of Identity*, Appiah (2005) discusses the complex relationship people have with their identity, especially when it comes to the moral value they assign to the elements of social life. In particular, he notes how identity is both something that helps determine what people do and something that people adopt as a result of their actions. This reciprocal relationship means that identity not only plays a part in informing one's ethical decisions (as with the concept of a moral compass), but it also encompasses the way in which people perceive themselves as ethical individuals. In this manner,

> There are thus various ways that identity might be a source of value, rather than being something that realizes other values. First if an identity is yours, it may determine acts of solidarity as valuable, or be an internal part of the specification of your satisfactions and enjoyments, or motivate and give meaning to acts of supererogatory kindness. (Appiah 2005: 25)

The subtle distinction that Appiah is making reflects the movement away from traditional conceptions of identity as relatively stable and passive to a more postmodern notion of identity as fluid and active. This perspective highlights the fact that the decision to sponsor a child should be understood as more than simply a product of an individual's generous nature (an aspect of who they are). Instead, the motivation to sponsor must in some way also be built upon the desire to take on a certain (moral) identity.

Samantha King (2003: 295) employs a similar logic in her discussion of "new technologies of ethical citizenship" and the Race for the Cure (for breast cancer). In her article, "Doing Good by Running Well," she draws attention to the way contemporary capitalist society associates moral worth with "volunteerism and self-responsibility" such that taking part in a "physical activity–based fundraising event" can be seen as a significant and unproblematic reflection of one's generosity and civic participation (307). In this way, such fundraising events not only allow individuals an opportunity to "do good," but they also provide a powerful framework for understanding what it means to "be good" in contemporary society — a framework that permits and encourages "national identification and inclusion at the same time that [it denies] the unequal material conditions and violence of everyday life under capitalism" (305). Consequently, such "thons" help redefine ethical action in contemporary society such that "publicly celebrated, personal acts of generosity mediated through — and within — consumer culture [have] attained hegemonic status" and "dissent or criticism of dominant socio-economic relations is marginalised" (312). King concludes, then, that far from simply being a way to raise money for and awareness about breast cancer, "the Race for the Cure is an ideal technology for the production of proper American citizens" (311).

King's (2003) analysis of the ethical landscape of the Race for the Cure provides a useful comparison to the case of child sponsorship. Just as "thons" occupy a discursive space that allows them to construct participants in a certain light, simultaneously as moral people and good citizens, sponsorship provides individuals with an opportunity to see themselves, and be seen by others, as generous Canadians, Americans, etc. who make a difference in the world. Once again, these perceptions are more than the product of guilty consciences or "charitable instincts," and they culminate in more than straightforward feelings of well-being or accomplishment. They are the artifact of a powerful and purposive "technology of ethical citizenship," a technology that does more than raise money for poor people in the South. It is also part of the system that helps define what it means to be a good person in contemporary Northern society. Akin to running for the cure, child sponsorship seamlessly merges notions of societal/global development with those of self-development. Sponsorship represents a way to become a better person (as opposed to simply an expression of one's good nature) as much as it represents a way to help a poor child. In fact, because there is little knowledge about the actual effects of sponsorship on the child, the former component becomes all the more important — so much so that this lack of knowledge ceases to be a major issue and sponsorship becomes more about what the sponsors think of their own actions than about what their donations accomplish.

Perhaps the most important implication of the way the practice of sponsorship constructs (or facilitates the self-construction of) sponsors as ethical individuals is that this aligns it with, and not against, the processes that structure the modern world in all its violence and inequality. In other words, far from being a definitive solution to the problems of world poverty, sponsorship is yet another way that contemporary relations of power are expressed. These are the same relations that organize the relative locations of sponsors and sponsored children, informing their economic and geo-political separation. Sponsors understand, and are constantly reminded, that their comparatively minor donations have miraculous consequences in the lives of Others. Precisely because sponsored children occupy the place they do in the world, sponsorship not only plays a prominent role in the ethical identity of the sponsor but also serves as a mechanism that helps reproduce the categories (such as race, nation, gender, class) that structure our lives. Contrary to many other practices that connect self-improvement with charitable action, sponsorship offers "average" people the chance to do something (be someone) extraordinary with minimal effort. Relying on neoliberal discourses of charity and responsibility as much as those of development, this opportunity makes it possible to fulfill personal goals of morality at the same time as meeting collective expectations for engaged citizenship.

Perceptions of child sponsorship

The remainder of the chapter will expand on and clarify these arguments regarding the ethical character of child sponsorship, with the principal objective of exploring how sponsors articulate their understanding of sponsorship. Rather than focus on sponsors either as benevolent individuals duped by desperate sponsorship programs or as self-serving donors looking to ease their guilt, the analysis that follows tries to shed light on some of the discursive connections between the practice of sponsorship and the perception of doing "good" in the world. In the next chapter, themes such as poverty, charity, religion, and race are brought in to help explain these connections. To appreciate the way sponsors negotiated these themes, it is useful to consider what the participants talked about in relation to their sponsorships more generally. Not only will this provide a glimpse into how sponsorship is seen to work from a sponsor's perspective, but it will also underscore the surprising complexity of the participants' responses.

An important point to bear in mind is the varied and often contradictory way sponsors explain sponsorship and their thoughts and actions in relation to it. In many cases, participant responses were unexpectedly insightful in their evaluation of the practice of sponsorship and their participation in it. Some sponsors mentioned that sponsorship was largely an emotional ploy aimed at getting their money, but it worked on them. Sometimes, this insightfulness took the form of frank admissions of ignorance. Several sponsors noted, for example, that they really did not know much about their sponsored child, where they lived, or how they benefited from sponsorship. These responses were mixed in with a wide array of comments ranging from first-hand knowledge of what sponsorship agencies do abroad to exhortations against helping Muslim children. Despite this diversity of sponsor observations and perceptions, or perhaps because of it, it is possible to pull out some enlightening points of similarity.[6]

The sponsors discussed the nature of child sponsorship in a variety of ways. Most often, however, they mentioned that it was a way to help someone out, a way to do something concrete for a child and their family or community. This could be accomplished, moreover, with minimal effort on the part of the sponsor, so it was presented as somewhat of an obvious choice. For example, Abby explained that "we give World Vision $35 a month and they move [their sponsored child's] family into a community where they teach them to be self-sufficient and provide them with ways of getting education and help them to learn." Despite not necessarily portraying what actually happens as a result of sponsorship, Abby described what she imagines the results to be as both tangible and direct. Consequently, she went on to say,

> I always thought it was a really great idea. I mean why not help somebody out for, you know, when you can put that little amount in, and it seems to make so much of a large difference in somebody's life, why not?

This connection between the ease of sponsorship and the potentially extraordinary benefits is a theme that will be returned to in a moment. First, it should be noted that many sponsors also described sponsorship as a way to help that was relatively minor but something they could manage. For instance, Jolene mentioned that sponsorship is

> just helping to make someone's life better. If you look at what Oprah has done in Africa with the kids who came from poverty … To me, this is just a small way to do the same thing. It is being able to take someone who had no hope of a future and give them that hope of a future.

Consequently, even though sponsorship is sometimes recognized as only being "a small way" to help poor children, its apparent simplicity is one of its biggest draws.

The perception of valuable and straightforward benefits to the child and their family existed even though many sponsors were not exactly sure what happened with their sponsorship fees. Lana explained,

> The child is not an orphan, but his village is very poor. His family is very poor, and I feel that World Vision not only helps my sponsored child with clothing, school supplies, school fees if there are any, but also it sounds like what he gets filters down into his family. Plus, they are always asking me for extra money now. Whether it goes to his village or elsewhere, I am not sure.

Making the same point more frankly, Leah said,

> my donation goes toward helping the child and his immediate community — to improve life for that community and for the child. That is what I believe is supposed to happen and according to the commercials or the TV broadcasts, it is the whole child. It is education, it is medicine, it is food, it is water. That is what they say. Now, whether it is the truth, I have not taken the time to truly investigate it.

This lack of specific knowledge about what happens on the ground, coupled with a perception of direct benefits, is likely a factor in the way the sponsors sometimes linked sponsorship with adoption (unintentionally in some cases). Donald, for example, made the remark that "it is the same with [a] kid for adoption. Oh, I keep saying adoption, I mean sponsorship." The reference to adoption as a cognate for sponsorship, just like the use of the term foster parent, reveals an aspect of sponsorship that not only defines the sponsored child as a metaphorical orphan but that also defines the sponsor as the metaphorical parent. This erroneous association is significant not simply because it speaks to the paternalism of the sponsorship relationship, but primarily because it highlights the common pairing of conventional and imaginative elements of sponsorship. For instance, Pamela directly compared adoption and sponsorship in the following description:

> When a child is in need in another country, and somehow, through some connection, somebody meets that child and decides that this child's progress in life [would be improved] if they had a sponsor, like the way you would adopt a child, but since you cannot adopt, you would take on that child for life and ... be the donor to them, so they can carry on in life and have money ... usually until they are able to take care of themselves.

Because of gaps in information, sponsors are left to use their imagination to fill in the missing pieces of the story that is routinely left out of sponsorship promotional material. It seems natural, then, for sponsors to draw on experiences that appear similar to them, such as adoption, to help understand the practice of sponsorship. This is obviously problematic, however, because the families of these children are negated by this comparison. Their struggles to improve their child's life are hidden or downplayed, which — apart from being disrespectful — gives an incomplete picture of challenges involved in poverty alleviation. The lack of information that leads to this situation allows sponsors to draw mistaken, or simply imprecise, conclusions about the effects of sponsorship.

Understanding sponsorship as a way of solving the specific problems of poverty for Southern children was a recurring topic among sponsors' description of sponsorship. Commonly perceived deficits including food, health care, and, most prominently, education were seen to be the reason behind the need for child sponsorship, which was thus seen to be a solution. For example, Robert described sponsorship as

> supporting a kid who if you do not sponsor it [sic] may well not get education or may not get some food to live on. Secondly, it shows to the child and his family that there are people out there who are concerned about them.

Harriet reiterated the importance of solving the problem of education, saying,

> it is really all about going to school ... I link up there because I am a
> teacher and these children would be at home working, whatever that is.
> Subsistence farming is usually what the families are about. They have got
> a couple goats, couple chickens, maybe a tiny plot of land.

Discussing what he perceived to be the reason why sponsorship is a useful tool
to address poverty, Trevor stated,

> it is a way of seeing what your money does as opposed to something like
> United Way or so on where there is a huge pot of money that you throw
> yours in with, and you have no feedback. I think that the feedback is
> very gratifying.

In his mind, the perceived concrete relationship between sponsor and child
separates it from other forms of charity because of its individualized character.
"It is not just giving charity," he said, "but it is giving it in a way that allows them
to leverage it themselves and do something with it." At the same time, Trevor
admits that "it is hard to find common ground" and, therefore, does not write to
his sponsored child.

Trevor was not alone in finding it difficult to discover "common ground" with
his sponsored child. Harriet also noted that

> there is a great distance between us and these children ... So, you want
> to look for connections, but let us face it, there really are not very many
> connections except on the human level. And so, they do not speak English,
> and you cannot really talk about your life, so it is not like having a pen
> pal like some people might think ... I am not looking for that though.

This "distance" did not stop many sponsors from discussing sponsorship in
terms of the connection between sponsor and child, however. From her perspective, Alexis thought sponsorship "seemed to be a fairly trouble-free way of making
a connection with a child." Other sponsors mirrored this view, such as Gail who
said, "I think it is the personal connection. It is receiving these little pieces of paper
that gives me a sense that this person is benefiting from what I am doing." Donald,
a man in his forties, stated that "it is very important [that] I feel like a have a connection with the child. My little guy is 17 now." The connection with his "little
guy" did not seem quite as strong later on, though, when he said,

> I approach it [sponsorship] in a very loose way ... so I will just write a
> cheque and send it off. I probably should look at it more carefully and

say, what does sponsorship mean, but to me, it is just like helping this kid in this village.

Despite understanding that sponsorship is a "construct" to raise money, in his words, Tom expressed the desire for connection in a very similar manner, saying that "there is the hope that there will be at least some kind of relationship developing between the two [sponsor and child]." However, when discussing his own relationship to his sponsored child, he noted that "it is pretty limited ... because of the age differential between the child and myself and a huge cultural gap as well, so there is less of a relationship." Patty commented on her connection to her sponsored child in what could be considered a more emotional, if still possibly one-sided, way. Describing her state of mind when she learned that her sponsored child was being changed after years of sponsorship, she said, "Oh wait a minute, she has been part of my life for seven years. I do not want to just lose this friend, this person." It became easier, she admitted, even though "it was hard at the beginning to lose kids and have them replaced with new ones ... It is kind of sad, but that is the nature of the program."

Whether the sponsors described sponsorship as a way to connect with a child or simply a way to do their part in improving a child's life, they unanimously agreed that sponsorship was easily something they could do. In fact, this sentiment was so common that it was not surprising to hear Patty's initial response to the question of why she sponsors a child: "a dollar a day is nothing." She went on to say,

> at one point, I was so strapped for cash, and I thought, "how am I going to keep a roof over my head? How am I going to eat?" And so, I was looking at the budget, and I thought maybe I am going to have to cut the kids ... but then I just thought "no, that [$44] will buy me a few more groceries, but it gets so much more for them." And so, it is just that bit of money for them. [It] just means so much more, so I just kept doing it.

Donald echoed Patty's statements, saying that "It is not a huge amount of money. I mean my finances are always stretched ... but I look around where I live, and I am so goddamn lucky. Of course I can afford that." Perhaps Harriet summed it up best when she observed that sponsorship

> does not cost very much ... Practically anyone in North America can do this kind of support. It is very cheap, and they do not even want you to give a lot of money, and it is very easy to do ... so it was something that we could do and feel like we were making a difference.

The combination of financial and logistical ease with the feeling of "making a difference" was something many sponsors alluded to again and again. For example, Gail asserted that sponsorship

> is not a hardship, financially. I kind of look at it like direct giving at that point in time, similar to the panhandler in the street. I kind of like [it] because there is a sense of making a difference ... What I am doing really takes zero effort on my part, you know. It is so minimal as to be ridiculous, but for whatever reason, I think it is making a big difference in her life.

While Phyllis agreed that "it is a small amount of money ... to help a child and their family improve their life to have an opportunity for education, to improve their health, to improve their community," Alexis described a different aspect of how easy sponsorship is. She admitted that "they make it fairly painless, and it comes right off my Visa card. So, I even get Air Miles [laughs], and the price has not gone up in two years." Sponsorship was considered so affordable and effortless, in fact, Leah even confided,

> in some ways, I see it as a cop out because it is so easy. Just to give thirty-three bucks a month or whatever to support this child ... it is easier than me actually going over and getting my hands dirty and trying to make a difference ... it is just an easy way to help without getting too involved.

Leah's comments about sponsorship being a "cop out," not to mention Alexis's offhand remarks about Air Miles, uncomfortably highlight the psychological consequences of something being so easy. When the enormity of the task of addressing Southern poverty (or the disparity between the North and the South) can be accomplished for so small a "price," as Alexis says, one must wonder about the product being sold. Is it really significant change, or is it better understood as a way to engage with donors' perceptions of wanting to "make a difference"?

As noted above, the ease of sponsorship for the sponsor was often juxtaposed with the perceived benefits to the sponsored child, their family, and their community. When asked to describe what their money was used for, however, a sizable majority of the participants had an extremely difficult time articulating what exactly these benefits were. Beyond mentioning some broad areas such as education, health care, and food, these sponsors commonly — and rather calmly — admitted to not knowing where their money went. For example, when asked this question, Tom exclaimed, "gosh, I am sure they have told me. From what I can remember off the top of my head, I have the impression it is paying for at least education [and] some other necessities like food and clothing." Similarly, Donald responded, "I do not ask details [and] say, 'okay I want a breakdown,' but I have heard education being pointed out, help them go to school otherwise he might have to go to work." He immediately followed this statement, somewhat incongruously, with the assertion that "people have to be careful to understand what is happening with their money." Another participant offered a comment that could be a reiteration of this point or an explanation of it. She revealed,

> we do not see anything really more than what just shows up in the mail ... so we do not really know how the organization handles things, but there has not been anything that has left me wondering what is going on.

Toby, on the other hand, put it as simply as possible. When asked what he thought his sponsorship money was used for, he replied, "I really do not know how to answer that."

Instead of specifics, then, sponsors often relied on variations of the general idea of "helping" to describe what went on in the South with their donations. Interestingly, the word "hope" also came up repeatedly in the same context. For example, Phyllis noted that as a sponsor you have to "hope that you have given some improvement in their life. You have not answered all their questions. You have not taken care of everything, but you have kind of helped them get up a notch." Using similar language, Leah said,

> I am believing it [her donations] goes to the child and the community is what I hope because that is what the commercials lead us to believe ... I am hoping that a portion goes directly to the child for education, health, etcetera ... [but] I just honestly do not know how effective it is.

Alexis also made the same point:

> Well, I am hoping it is used for things like digging wells and providing sanitation and healthy cooking stoves because that is another problem in the developing world ... I really do not know; I have not investigated. I write the cheque [and] look at the stuff peripherally.

Valerie added,

> I think just the knowledge that somewhere, you may never meet them, that hopefully you helped to make a difference. I do not know whether that is educationally. I am hoping it is. They told me it is true. Apparently, his father works to support the family, but they are very, very poor. I do not know what work is in that area, probably what his dad's doing, farming, but it would be nice to think he had have more education perhaps than his parents, but I do not know what education. They do not tell me that.

From these statements, it may seem as though these sponsors were not terribly curious about, or engaged with, their sponsorship. Given the rest of their responses, however, this did not appear to be the case. Rather, the hope of doing something good, something they understood to be of help to poor Southern children, was enough of an incentive to overlook (or disregard) the unknown. Alexis expressed both desire and uncertainty with the following rhetorical question and answer: "Where do you begin? I do not have a clue where to begin. Well, in my own little way, I do not know where to begin, but at least I can write a cheque and a letter or two." Coming from a slightly different angle, Leah seemed to see the purpose as overshadowing the details. "I see them [children] as innocent," she said, "I see them as born into a world, into circumstances that were not very kind to them." Therefore, she helps "because I am in a position to ... I definitely recognize how fortunate I am not to be in those other circumstances, [and] being part of the solution even in such a small way is definitely a motivator." Leah's statement accents the issues brought up in the previous chapter regarding the generic role of the child in sponsors' narratives of themselves. It also highlights the asymmetrical importance of sponsor perceptions and desires relative to the actual information they possess about child sponsorship in general and the lives of sponsored children in particular.

Wanting to "make a difference"

Language about "helping," "making a difference," or "being part of the solution" came up repeatedly when participants discussed why they chose to begin and maintain their sponsorships. In addition, many sponsors noted that the personalized aspect of sponsorship was a major draw, as was the desire to follow through on a commitment they had made. Some sponsors, although fewer than one might expect, also talked about the apparent emotional draw of sponsorship. Leah, for example, frequently mentioned guilt throughout her interview although she expressly noted that sponsoring a child was the result of a "combination" of guilt and compassion. Campbell spelled it out clearly when he said, "I feel almost guilty living in the lap of luxury in this beautiful part of the world that it eases my conscience somewhat that I am contributing, even though it is in a minute way, to a child of the Third World." Like Leah, Campbell's guilt seems to stem from a perception of how fortunate he is to have what he has (or perhaps, to live where he does).

Guilt or compassion were not the only emotions mentioned, however. In reference to why she began sponsoring a child, Gail spoke about the "admiration" she felt for someone she knew who sponsored a number of children. Talking more generally about the emotional aspect of sponsorship, Margery, a former sponsor, admitted that she was "sucked into the whole gambit." She had decided to sponsor a child with two friends after seeing a promotional concert held by a sponsorship program. She remembered "the whole emotional side of it after the concert saying this is a way we can get involved and help these kids." She also drew attention to how the emotional aspect of deciding to sponsor a child blended into her feelings around the connection to the child. She said,

> I was totally sucked into that whole thing where you are writing a person so you do have that person's face and that connection … So I felt like, yes, stopping the financial support would be a bit of a betrayal to that somewhat relationship we had.

Once again, the idea of the connection — of the "somewhat relationship" to a sponsored child — played a motivating role for many sponsors.

Harriet laid it out succinctly, saying "I think that there is a great appeal to having this kind of aid personalized that really speaks to people that do this." Despite speaking of "the complications and the expense of the individual name [that sponsorship involves the idea of giving to an individual]," Alexis, who is relatively new to sponsorship, acknowledged that "the individual name is a real draw for people who want that sort of emotional connection." It was not clear if she included herself in this category of people or not. Instead, she stated that was "what drew me to [the organization], because I would have a foster grandchild somewhere." Alexis was not the only sponsor to personalize their sponsored child with reference to their own family. Valerie made the revealing comment that she sponsored a child

> because I have a daughter in England, and through marriage breakdown, I have no contact with my grandchildren any more. So, I thought I was very sad, and I do not have control, and I am hoping one day it will happen again, but that is okay. It [sponsorship] was a way for me to channel my desire to help. The little boy [sponsored child] is the same age as my grandson, and I could not have contact with him, but I could have with someone else. That was probably what the catalyst was.

This (psychological?) substitution of an actual or desired child with a sponsored child is fascinating despite its banality. It dovetails with the way sponsors sometimes conflated sponsorship with adoption, and it highlights the desired, although largely imagined, connection sponsors sought.

Sponsors were often drawn to the idea of either developing a relationship with a child or simply being able to directly connect their actions to the well-being of the sponsored child. Patty included both these elements:

> at the beginning, it was because I thought I can help one kid break out of that cycle of poverty by helping them to stay in school and not have to

quit and help out at home or go out and work or whatever. I can help at least one child, and if I could put a face to that child and get some letters from that child, so much the better.

Focusing on the perception of a direct financial connection, Jenny said of sponsorship that

> there is no doubt the money is going where it is supposed to go and the children are advancing and learning and happy. If you send a big amount of money to the Red Cross or some other big organization … somebody could be lining their pockets with that money.

Alternatively, Vanessa and Tom brought up the notion of a personal relationship with the child. Vanessa said, "I always had that [sponsorship] in the back of my mind. I like volunteer stuff, and making a contribution … Then of course the letters and the photos were something that inspired me, and I liked the personal connection." Tom began with a similar sentiment, saying "I guess I see the key difference between child sponsorship and giving money to some other organization is that relationship with the child." He ended, however, by noting that "I do not think that I have had that particularly deep or meaningful relationship with this child." In spite of the disappointment this apparently caused him, Tom did not stop sponsoring the child. Rather, he noted, "I felt like I made a commitment, and I wanted to honour that."

Tom was not the only sponsor to discuss their continuation of sponsorship in terms of personal commitment. Margery, Tom's partner and a former sponsor, also commented that "I had made that commitment, and I was not going to drop it." Recall that she considered it somewhat of a "betrayal" to stop her sponsorship. Interestingly, she said this despite first-hand knowledge that her sponsored child would not really lose any benefits if she stopped. This contradiction points to an interpretation that her commitment somehow combined thoughts of the child and desire to be a particular kind of person. A comment Valerie made supports this interpretation. She said that maintaining her sponsorship "was a commitment I made to myself." Adrienne, another former sponsor, also discussed commitment in a way that was not directly related to her perceived relationship to the sponsored child; she discussed her decision to sponsor as associated with the stability it provided in her own life at the time. She said,

> That was a way I could do it [give money to charity] monthly, and there was a commitment involved. So instead of just saying, "oh, I will give money without a commitment," it is just easier to have it [like that]. That way it's organized.

While the sponsors routinely talked about things like connection and commitment as to why they sponsor, the most common response was that they wanted to "make a difference" in the world. Valerie drew on this language, saying "we were not rich at all by North American standards, but I felt we could make a difference." Phyllis made a similar comment that highlights the personal desire to do some good almost irrespective of what it is. She declared,

> I think it is really important that we are playing this kind of part sponsoring something that can help someone move on in their life. It is really dear to my heart, and I think it is very strong in me, and that is why I wanted to do it.

On the other hand, a comment Tom made emphasizes the extremely general — or perhaps vague is a better term — character of "making a difference." He said, "I just had a sense of wanting to do something to help out, something in a developing context, you know, overseas kind of idea, and thought that this was one way to do that."

Imagining sponsorship as a practical (and often sufficient) way to help was not only a common theme in participants' decisions to sponsor, but it was also one that was frequently linked to a sort of pessimism about the state of the world. Donald, for example, assumed that "you cannot change the world. You can only do little things to try and make it work. You do what you can do." Sponsorship was seen as particularly valuable way to do something, then, because other efforts to help did not seem as useful — at least for Donald, who was heavily engaged in the anti-war movement. "That is exactly why I am supporting a kid," he noted. "it is exactly why I want to do one thing at least that I know is having an effect because the other things you do, sometimes it does not make any difference." Martha echoed and expanded on this sentiment:

> I think sometimes we get overwhelmed like when they say there is a million children starving in Africa and that [you] cannot do anything. But if you take one person with one child, you can do something, and so if ten people do ten children you can do something. So, to me, that was an important thing — that you can do something instead of being overwhelmed by everything that is going on in the world.

Donald and Martha's comments not only highlight the noteworthy overlap between the ambiguity of the perceived benefits of sponsorship and the vague explanations of their motivation to begin sponsoring, but they also juxtapose the imagined hopelessness of global poverty with the hope of sponsorship. This union of hopelessness and hope does not seem entirely coincidental. Recall the World

Vision advertisement where Susan Hay pleads,

> We just need you to sponsor, and maybe you do not think you can make
> a difference — you cannot change the world — but if we all get together,
> one person can make a difference in the lives of little ones like this.

Toby's perception of the situation encapsulates these views about "making a difference":

> I am pretty well-off, but there is a lot of the world [that] is not, and there
> is nothing that is ever going to be done. So, I like knowing that, okay, now
> there is a village that has a well, and they will do okay after all. I like that.

While not necessarily profound, Toby's comment neatly combines the perception of a world in disrepair and the ability of one person to make a concrete difference.

In taking on a sponsored child, sponsors such as Toby do not see themselves as saving the world (at least not on an individual basis) but simply improving the lives of their sponsored children and the communities in which they live. The key here, of course, is that when faced with global poverty that seems like an insurmountable challenge, sponsors turn to child sponsorship not only to provide that element of concrete improvement but also to locate themselves ethically in relation to this challenge. While this chapter has largely examined how sponsors think about the specific solution (they imagine) sponsorship provides, the next chapter explores the second half of this equation: what does it mean for them as sponsors?

6

"Change your own"

In the article "A girl's sweet gesture turns sour," the *Chicago Tribune* described how eleven-year-old Whitney decided to become a sponsor after watching a moving Children International (CI) advertisement (Tackett, 1998: 2-10). She made a deal with her parents to help with the low-cost $12 per month fee and began sponsoring eleven-year-old Angelina from the Dominican Republic. As is common practice among some sponsorship programs, Whitney was soon inundated with additional requests for donations to supply such things as holiday gifts and special medical treatments. Whitney's parents were angered by the continuous emotional appeals, which they felt manipulated their daughter and which almost doubled the amount of monthly donations. Moreover, her parents were surprised to hear that, via one of these additional donations, Angelina received a towel as a birthday gift. "'If I want to send $25,' Ferguson [Whitney's mother] said, 'which buys far more there than it buys here, I want Angelina to get a personal present — a dress, new shoes, a doll, something besides a towel'" (2-10). According to the *Tribune*, then, Whitney's "charitable instincts had been encouraged by CI's descriptions of Angelina's urgent needs," but the "continuous pleas" and allocation of funds ultimately left a "bad taste" (2-10). The fact that Whitney's "sweet gesture" was soured by CI's actions is simply seen as a consequence of a well-intentioned sponsor coming into contact with a greedy, desperate, or simply inept sponsorship program.

This story, which encourages the reader to empathize not with marginalized individuals in the South but with apparently disappointed or defrauded sponsors in the North, seemed to be the most common type of article in the *Tribune* series. It continues the trend of blaming particular practices of sponsorship programs as if getting the sponsorship program "right," or finding the "right" program for that matter, would solve the problems of child sponsorship. Is this really the case, however? Do sponsorship programs just need to get their collective acts together to provide higher quality service to sponsors and sponsored children alike, or is there something problematic about the practice itself? How might the perceptions and expectations of sponsors, and the discourse of development that informs them, be related to this problematic nature of sponsorship?

Building on the observations from the last chapter, this chapter further explores this issue of sponsor perceptions and expectations. Drawing on the same set of interviews with current and former sponsors, it continues an analysis of child sponsorship that probes the discursive link between the perceived development of the sponsored child (or their community) and the personal development of sponsors. To highlight some components of this link, most of this chapter is spent looking at participants' responses in relation to the themes of poverty, race, religion, and to a lesser extent, gender. While these are certainly not the only important themes related to sponsorship, they are ones that shed light on significant aspects of the practice of sponsorship as well as ones that represent very common areas of inquiry within the study of international development. Consequently, looking at participant responses through these thematic lenses provides a useful way to tie some fundamental components of the discourse of international development into the analysis of sponsors' expectations. Before looking at these themes in more depth, however, let us first turn to a more general issue — the rewards of sponsorship perceived by sponsors themselves — that will serve as a useful preface to the arguments presented later in the chapter.

When asked what the most rewarding aspects of sponsorship were, most of the sponsors talked about the good feelings associated with helping others, particularly others who are as destitute (or exotic) as the sponsors imagined their sponsored children to be. Like a number of sponsors, Tom used the word "satisfaction" to refer to the rewards of sponsorship. Tom said, "The initial motivation for doing it was to help, and so I am not really looking for a reward out of it. I guess one could say that the satisfaction of having done something [though]." Other sponsors, such as Vanessa and Pamela, simply described the good feeling they got from what they were doing. Sponsorship provided "that warm fuzzy feeling that I was doing something," commented Vanessa. "Because you came along this child's life is forever changed … and that is a really good feeling," stated Pamela.

Again, the manner in which these feelings are expressed is not coincidental. Organizations such as Christian Children's Fund, Harriet explained, do "a great job of making you feel like you are making a difference." No matter the precise impact one is making, sponsorship programs (justifiably?) ensure sponsors feel like their donations are significant. In yet another instance of combining general notions of help and hope, Harriet described this quality of child sponsorship:

I crossed my fingers and prayed that at least somebody was getting something positive out of it. Maybe it was our family; maybe it was somebody else ... You do not learn much about the country, but you learn a little about your child. And what you learn is that you are making a difference, and that is why you are doing it ... It is nice to feel you are doing something, whatever that is.

In recounting this experience, Harriet not only highlights the role of the organization in facilitating these feelings of satisfaction, but she also calls attention to two important themes regarding the rewards of sponsorship. The first relates to the somewhat familiar notion that the good feelings associated with charity are valuable in and of themselves and, therefore, remove some of the selflessness from apparently altruistic acts. The second deals with the idea that sponsorship is a learning experience for sponsors. A comment by Abby epitomizes the first point. "It is almost just like we are helping these people and we do not know them that well, we are just kind of giving them a hand," she said. She continued,

I like it. Well, helping people is not entirely unselfish, you know, you get a good feeling. Well, I do anyways. I get a good feeling when I do it, and I am proud of myself. I mean that is why I do it.

In a very telling turn of phrase, Abby went on to express what might be considered the limits of this egocentric facet of sponsorship. Discussing the selection of her sponsored child, she commented on the peculiarity of the experience, saying "you almost feel like you are, I don't know, like you are a god deciding that, oh, this is the one that is going to all of the sudden have this better shot at life." Although not quite as extreme, Beatrice made a similar point when she admitted,

it certainly makes me feel good to know that a child is being educated, fed, supported. For me, that is the best thing: that I am still able to be part of — I don't know, humanity I suppose. I do not know what word to use — that I have still got a certain amount of usefulness ... I have to have that need of being wanted also by a child. It is a two-way street.

Harriet, Abby, Beatrice, and many other sponsors acknowledged this "not entirely unselfish" element to their sponsorship. Perhaps the most significant — and most unusual — example came from a woman named Jenny, who sponsors eighteen children through World Vision.

An elderly woman, widowed and retired, Jenny had recently moved from Toronto, where she had sponsored fourteen children and where, she said, there were "too many immigrants." Although not necessary from an organizational standpoint, she stopped her sponsorships before moving, and began again when she arrived in Victoria. "Now I have eighteen children whose pictures are on my wall," she read from a statement that she had pre-written for the research interview. "This makes me very happy," she went on, "I know I am changing their lives forever. Almost all of the children are from Africa because African children are the most in need." She repeated both these points several times throughout her statement and the conversation that followed. "It made me so happy to think I was helping kids. It gives a lot of pleasure to help people" she said. Jenny went on to note,

> They thank me very much for my letters and say, "God bless you for help-ing me," and the parents say the same thing. I do not know what else you could do to make you feel better than to sponsor a World Vision child.

Happiness was not the only emotion she referred to when discussing her extraordinary engagement with sponsorship. She declared, "I am awfully proud of what I am doing," before mentioning that her two grown sons were also "proud of me because of it." Jenny seamlessly blended (conflated?) the benefits of spon-sorship for the children with her self-perception. For example, she recounted the following story:

> one little girl would have died if I had not been her sponsor. She lived in Malan, Mawali, [Interviewer: "Malawi?"] Malawi. She was seven or eight, and she took pneumonia, and because I was her sponsor, they managed to get her to a hospital to save her life. So that was a good day *for me.* (emphasis added)

She concluded the interview with the revealing remark — which will be con-sidered in more detail later on — that while she would like her efforts to inspire other people, she would "not want them to be jealous of [her]." Although few sponsors were as forthright about the personal rewards of sponsorship as Jenny was, her responses could be said to reflect the ideal-typical sponsorship experience. The notion that Jenny's comments are ideal-typical is important both in locating her case within the participant responses overall and in highlighting what could colloquially be seen as the exception that proves the rule. The analytical value of Jenny's comments lies not in their representativeness — because they are obviously not representative of all sponsors — but in their overt reflection of the often-subtle subjective processes that are at play within the sponsorship experience.

Feelings of satisfaction, happiness, or pride were not the only elements men-tioned by sponsors that speak to the personal rewards of sponsorship. Several sponsors also simply talked about it as an "experience," as something that is "fun" to do or something that fills a space in one's life. "I always thought it was just fun and interesting," Jaime said. Upon hearing about the unplanned changing of her sponsored child, Vanessa noted that it took "some of the fun out of it for me." In her response to the question about the rewards of sponsorship, Alexis mentioned the fun of it along with many of the issues discussed above. She said,

> I do not know that there are a whole lot of rewards. It makes me feel that I am doing my little bit. It is also nice when you get telephone solicitation to say, "Thank you. I am already involved" and not be telling a lie. It is not a whole lot of money. It is $33. That is not even a coffee a day these days. Its supportable; it is doable; it is one little thing ... making a difference even to one little person's life is a nice thing to do and definitely [the] connection because I volunteer and travel ... I thought it would be kind of fun to have another reason for going [to the country where her sponsored child lives] ... I think it will be fun to see where she lives.

Alexis was not the only sponsor to talk about visiting her sponsored child as a gratifying part of the experience. Trevor "strongly recommend[ed] anybody who is doing this to visit their sponsored child. I think that is an incredible part of the experience." Alexis was also not the only sponsor to mention the fact that her sponsorship allows her to hear about poverty in the world and feel like she is already doing her part. Erica, a former sponsor, noted that "when I would see the commercials come on TV, I would feel a little like, 'I do that.'" She continued to comment on her former sponsorship, talking about the experience she got out of it and what happened when she was done. She said that she did not feel guilty about stopping because, "I don't know. Been there, done that, and that was cool, and that was it."

In addition to talking about the personal rewards of sponsorship, Erica also touched on an issue that seems to be a frequently cited (but largely unknown) aspect of sponsorship. This is the idea that sponsoring a child is a good way to learn about other places and the problems of development that plague them. In this regard, however, Erica and many other sponsors found sponsorship to fall short. "I was expecting more," she said, "I do not know what more I was expecting ... more information ... like what was happening in their community. It was kind of like, 'Thanks for your money; here is a picture of the kid.'" Harriet spelled it out more directly, observing that "you get very little information, honestly ... I do not think it really does work to teach you much." Gail — a white, middle-aged, middle-class, immigrant Canadian with two grown children, like Harriet — just said, "Do I learn a lot from it? Not necessarily." A response from Tom provides a possible explanation for this lack of educational benefit. He conceded that "the level of correspondence is very rudimentary." Adrienne explained, there are just check marks [on the yearly updates]. There is really not much written out [about the child], so I think it [the reason for sponsorship] was my telling myself that I was giving something back. I was doing part of my tithe and being connected.

Despite the general lack of confidence in the educational ability of sponsorship regarding the sponsored child, their country, and their circumstances, more than a third of all participants thought that sponsoring a child was a great way to teach their (grand)children about the value of charity. Even though Harriet did not believe that sponsorship worked "to teach you much," she was quite adamant that her children benefited from the experience. She said,

> I know that I thought at the time that this would be something that a) was nice to help others and [b)] I thought it would be something my children would be able to relate to. And so, that is part of the, maybe, Christian teaching, and that is part the teacher thing: understanding that personalizing things for children makes it much more real, much more of an experience they can relate to.

Like Harriet, Gail described sponsorship as

> an example of walking the talk, right? So, this is something we do as a family, and that just helps solidify part of who we are as a family and demonstrating our value ... I think if we do not have these sorts of demonstrations of doing that then it becomes something like it is not real, it is not part of who you are.

Gail's use of the term "value" in the singular is fascinating. Provided Gail meant to say "values" rather than "value", this statement may be a simple recognition of the desire to put one's values into practice as a lesson for one's children. Even if this is the case, however, it could also represent an amusing insight into the way ethical identity is constructed because of the discursive slippage between her family's values and their value as a family. Either way, this helps demonstrate the predominantly social, as opposed to psychological, character of ethical identity construction, highlighting the connection between moral self-perception and participation in particular social practices (as opposed to simply espousing certain opinions).

From these responses, it seems as though the educational experience of sponsorship is more about showing one's (grand)children how to be a good person in contemporary times than about learning something concerning the roots of global poverty or the lives of sponsored children. Donald, for example, expressed this outlook:

I wanted to go see him [the sponsored child] actually, but then I have got mixed feelings about that too. I think, God, maybe I should just give the money to the community, but I would love my son to see it, to go there with me, just so that he could continue on thinking about these kids … and then he will have a conscience as he grows up.

While Harriet's, Gail's, and Donald's remarks are similar to those of other sponsors, Beatrice provided some comments that seem to epitomize this notion of the desired moral education of child sponsorship. Not only did she mention that sponsoring a child is "a great way of teaching my grandchildren that we are not the only people in the universe" and that through this process "they benefit [her grandchildren], we benefit and the kids overseas benefit," but she also described the situation in more depth:

my husband and I will give X amount of dollars to the children to give to [the sponsorship program], and in return what I am trying to get [the program] to follow through is to acknowledge to our grandchildren what kind of difference it made … because this is the only way we can teach North American children "look what you have done" … And the only way, I think, for North American children to pick up on that, is to read it, to have their name on it.

This comment by Beatrice, as with almost all participant responses, contains several intriguing statements about sponsorship that call out for analysis. It is fascinating to look at the way she and the other participants imagine the Others they are "helping," how they conceptualize that help, and how they see themselves in relation to it. These connections become clearer, however, when examining participant's comments in relation to specific topics such as poverty, development, race, and religion. While the general comments of participants considered above and in the last chapter have laid the groundwork for an argument about sponsorship that focuses more on the construction of ethical identities than the solving of problems of poverty, the following discussion of themes provides some analytical connections that hopefully make this argument more persuasive.

Poverty in the South

Sponsors characterized the conditions of their sponsored children, along with the children's communities and countries, in a variety of ways. Although a surprising number of participants were well acquainted with complex explanations of global poverty as well as the potential problems of stereotyping Others, the majority of sponsors still drew on mainstream assumptions regarding the South. These assumptions, a staple element of the discourse of development, commonly take the form of monolithically envisioning the South (and particularly the continent of Africa) as a place teeming with hungry, sick, and conflict-ridden people(s), who are the product of barren environments and bad choices. For example, Lana described where her sponsored child is from as follows:

> they do not have very many resources. I am not sure about the government; they have had dictators who have absconded with what funds were available. The climate can be harsh ... I think economics is what their problem is. They do not have a very large economic base to their country. There is not a lot of jobs that pay well. There is not enough community for young people to get to university, so they might not, in many cases, have any chance to get an education at all.

Introducing another common stereotype, Penelope explained what she saw to be the root problem of development in the South:

> we cannot make any progress as long as people keep producing ten or twelve children ... It is an endless thing in Africa. You feed one generation, and unless we send out birth control, they have babies, four hundred babies in the next few years and everyone is starving.

Jolene not only provided a very similar picture as Lana and Penelope did, but she also included a comparison of Canada and the South. She said,

> we can grow everything we need, but I think in many countries they cannot. And I think in a lot of countries, they are small countries with lots of people. We are just so blessed we have room, we have crops, we have everything we need and a lot of countries do not. They do not have the room, they do not have the climate, whatever. [Dictators are] prevalent in a lot of countries, that they have corrupt governments, and those in power are living high off the hog, and everybody else is living in poverty.

These somewhat stereotypical accounts of what life is like in the South do not, of course, spring from the ether. They are propagated through a variety of (mass) media, including sponsorship promotional material. This complex relationship between stereotypes of the South and sponsorship is readily apparent in the invalidated expectations of sponsors.

Several sponsors were surprised by their sponsorship experience because the conventional representations that convinced them to sponsor were subsequently discredited through the very experience of sponsorship. For example, Harriet noted that "we were quite surprised our first child was in Haiti, and I was not kind of expecting that. I was expecting Africa or something like that." A more detailed version of this issue was recounted by Adrienne, who visited her sponsored child in Brazil. She said, "we go into the house [of her sponsored child] and they have this brand-new stereo system and a brand-new fridge and a brand-new stove." She explained that the child

> happened to be in an urban area, and World Vision showed mainly Africa. And so, this was Latin America. It was very different than what was on television, and so we always picture this African child with flies on their face. And I knew it was not that, but I guess I expected a higher level of poverty.

The expectations of sponsors do not simply highlight the stereotypes that circulate regarding conditions in the South, they also reveal what sponsors expect from sponsorship. In this regard, it is once again revealing to introduce Jenny's rather candid viewpoint.

While her sincerity was undeniable, Jenny's discussion of Africa was replete with what, from most social scientific perspectives, would be deemed overly generalized or racist comments. She explained that "African children are in the need the most. Many of their parents have died. Many still live in mud huts. Many have very little to eat, and many have health problems." Jenny went on to link these stereotypical portrayals to the practice and experience of sponsorship. She said,

> the first picture is one of a sad, often frail, child. One who needs help each year. You receive a new picture, and what a difference. You hardly recognize the child; she looks so happy. The child is always smiling. Her face is bright and interested. She even looks healthy, and you will know you are giving for this fortunate child a new life, for a chance for education and happiness. It will make you happy too. You will feel as if you have done something special. This is the most rewarding action you can do … you know you are helping a child live a good life. You're saving it. Those little girls have an awful time over there. They end up as sex slaves, lots of them. Nothing else they can do, and if they avoid that, they still have a terribly hard life, have about fifteen children, many die of AIDS. They just have a dreadful life, so why would not I want to help them?

Jenny's description of the problems confronting children in Africa, and the help that sponsorship provides, may seem a little too simplistic to be representative of many sponsors. However, there were several other participants who echoed her assessment in similar, if not identical, ways. Abby admitted that she is "kind of ignorant about what their life is like," saying do they live in a hut? ... Niger, I do not know anything about Niger really. Where is that in relation to some of these horrible things that you hear about happening over there, and is somebody going to come in and wipe out this village that World Vision has worked so hard to set up?

Based on what "you hear about things and read about them," she explained that "it is not lush and green and that sort of thing. There are challenges to even getting yourself started with something, and ... there is not — I guess probably not really — a public education per se." Because of these kinds of perceptions, Abby could then locate the "proper" solutions that she imagined sponsorship to provide. She said,

> I like that they teach them to be self-sufficient. It is not like you are just throwing money at a problem, and they are not solving it. They are working towards getting them up and moving on their own, and then they can move on and help somebody else because I think that is really important. You know, you cannot just hand people cash, here you go, and let them sort it out for themselves because a lot of times, I do not know why, but they just never seem to get themselves up out of anything.

These comments, and many others like them, are interesting not necessarily because they provide evidence of the use of stereotyping and the presence of paternalistic ideals in relation to the South. Although these comments may support such an interpretation, they also reveal the relationship between the way sponsors imagine Others and the way they see themselves.

Significantly, this relationship relies on the liberal values that are thought to counter discriminatory patterns. In particular, the overwhelming emphasis on education (on both the personal and communal levels), and the ideas of individual responsibility and prosperity that are linked to it, as a solution to the problems of "underdevelopment" serves not only to reinforce the separation of Southern poverty from Northern wealth but also to legitimize the practice of "individual" child sponsorship. Because of the interventions that sponsoring a child is seen to provide (education being the chief among them), sponsorship is able to play a special role in facilitating this relationship between the way Others are imagined and the way sponsors see themselves. The importance of these connections between stereotyping, liberal values, and sponsorship lies in the fact that no amount of cultural sensitivity — and no amount of "public education" or "awareness-raising" about the South — will be able to simply eradicate the use of stereotypes without some consideration of how they are enmeshed with identity processes in North.

The focus on education and its central role in sponsorship was repeatedly apparent in sponsors' responses. Like many sponsors, Valerie cited the main benefit of sponsorship as "more education." Regarding her sponsored child, Martha stated, "I want her to be educated … It is one of the main reasons we sponsored so that a girl could get educated, a Muslim girl." Jenny, straightforward as ever, said,

> I insist on them going to school. I remember last year some child could not continue on with their schooling for some reason, and they wrote to me asking me if I would pay anything. I said "no, there is no future for the child if she cannot go to school." I cannot pay for her.

Similar to Jenny, Lana drew a connection between the personal "effort" of sponsorship and the value of education, commenting that "the most rewarding part [of sponsorship] is just to see he is gradually getting an education … he will be literate and has had the opportunity. It is something that we are developing a literate, educated little guy." Once again, the thematic considerations are not necessarily the most important here. The focus on education merely serves to illustrate the processes involved in the way Northern identities are related to perceptions of poverty in the South.

In particular, these processes seem to hinge upon the characteristic relationships that individuals and collectivities (whether one's own or those of Others) are seen to have within modern liberal thought. These relationships — such as those that specify parental, governmental, or developmental responsibilities — help define the roles (including their limitations) that Northerners are expected to assume in light of Southern poverty. In this way, we can make sense of Martha's statement (quoted earlier) as an expression of how child sponsorship helps Northerners fulfill these roles:

> I think sometimes we get overwhelmed, like when they say there is a million children starving in Africa and that [you] cannot do anything. But if you take one person with one child, you can do something, and so if ten people do ten children you can do something. So, to me, that was an important thing that you can do something instead of being overwhelmed by everything that is going on in the world.

To understand this comment as both rational and reasonable, it is necessary to already have a set of pre-conceived ideas about the (in)abilities and responsibilities of individuals. For example, the fact that such things as starvation in Africa are seen to be separated from the personal lives of Northerners, except in terms of their emotional impact, means that the issue can be understood in terms of choice (rather than, say, obligation). This reliance on sponsor choice, and particularly the choice to sponsor, then becomes associated with a particular understanding of child sponsorship as a solution to the problems of Southern poverty simply because it is one of the principal choices that is available to sympathetic Northerners. Consequently, we end up with sponsors like Leah, who admitted that "I know what I am doing is better than nothing, but I know there has got to be something that is even more effective, more better [sic]," before she made the following revealing (and confounding) statement: "I am just hoping that there is enough sponsorship out there that one day we do not have to have hurting children." This comment could be taken as evidence of the inconsistency of among some sponsors' thought processes, but it could better be explained as the intentional product of a narrative of sponsorship that is pushed by the organizations offering it.

Race, nation, religion

The way sponsors described the conditions of the South and their role in improving them through sponsorship was not only indicative of particular understandings of choice and responsibility, but it was also animated by particular national and racial themes. It should be noted, however, that these themes were present in extremely subtle forms. Despite the concept's enormous socio-cultural significance, direct references to race by sponsors were few and far between. As has been recognized by many recent academic perspectives on race (for example, see Giroux, 1994; White, 2002; Wren, 2001), this is understandable given the way that cultural and political references have taken over much of the language of race (albeit with very similar consequences). On the other hand, the concept of the nation (including perceptions of the nation-state system and Canada's role in it) came up frequently in sponsor responses, but this concept is so naturalized in the understanding of human relations that it is difficult to separate from other themes such as poverty, religion, and childhood.

One topic that provides a useful inroad into the themes of race and nation is the sponsors' comparison of Canadian conditions with those overseas. These responses were mentioned in the context of discussing why sponsors help children in the South rather than Canadian children. The most common answer to this question was that, as Donald noted, "there is no comparison" to the levels of need. Leah put it more precisely, saying "I am under the impression that, internationally, the children are worse off than Canadian children." The notion that children overseas will be more grateful for this help was often added to this (reasonable) idea that the need is greater in the South than in Canada. For example, Shelley said, "it is really hard to know how to help the kids here … Southern kids are happy … smiling, playing with their sticks and stuff, not saying, 'I want. I want.'" Adrienne simply stated that "kids down there have a lot more appreciation for things than kids up here." Perspectives such as these are critical to the success of sponsorship because they help assign relative value to the objects of charity and because they link these values to the identities and desires of the sponsors. Such perspectives on relating to Canada and the world allow sponsors to still see themselves as good Canadians even though — or perhaps because — they are not necessarily helping Canadian children.

Valerie drew the connection between the perceived difficulties of life in the South and her awareness of herself as a North American. She said,

> I do not know the true extent of it [poverty in the South]. I suppose it is because you see these children and there is poverty and [then] there is [real] poverty, which must be horrible for the child to have to deal with it. And you do see these things about little black babies who've lost their mom and dad. And I do not know if it is true. Are these lies that people tell you about these children? … I am a resident of the world, you know what I am saying, so I have no problem doing something like this. I think it starts there. It is not like I just see myself as this North American and whatever, but I like having that experience of connecting with somebody somewhere else.

The desire to experience connection "with somebody somewhere else" and even the desire to be more than "just" a North American is likely linked to the desire for the Other that bell hooks (1992) talks about as an aspect of the commodification of race and ethnicity. This relationship between sponsorship and the desire for difference is evident in Jaime's description of her motivation to sponsor. She confessed,

> I have not been able to travel anywhere, so I guess I have — for lack of a better word — a fascination with other places outside of North America even though I have not been able to go anywhere. And so, I kind of like knowing somebody who has a different society than me, and so I like the connection that it is.

Erica, however, tried to explain the association in more depth, saying

> there definitely is an element of — I do not know what it is — exotic-liking or something. There is something going on like that that just makes people feel good to help out, makes you feel like life is so much harder for other people [in other countries], and it makes people feel better to help out little coloured babies than kids in their own neighborhood.

As hooks discusses, this desire is not simply an interest in something that is unusual or foreign, it is part of a practice of power that reinforces one's own position over Others. This practice is not only associated with the legacy of colonial thought but also with the concept of race-pleasure (Farley, 1997). "Race is the preeminent pleasure of our time," writes Farley. "Whiteness is not a color; it is a way of feeling pleasure in and about one's body. The black body is needed to fulfill this desire for race-pleasure" (458). In this light, the pleasure provided through the experience of child sponsorship, while it may not exactly mimic race-pleasure, can be understood in some way as related to the perceptions of wealthy (white) sponsors *because* of their relative position compared to poor (black) children.

The position of sponsors not only provides the pleasure of experience, and the relations of power that this implies, but also the presumption of knowledge. Alexis, for example, asserted that

> we are so fortunate here. I can turn on the tap and be confident about the water, and two-thirds of the world cannot do that. I just think we have spread our talents around, whatever they are, as far as we can.

While this statement seems innocuous enough, it is still laden with assumptions about where talent lies and, therefore, who knows best. Gail stated the same idea in more widespread terms, saying "we can take our technology and jump start it into those rural areas. They do not have to go through a linear process to build up to that technology." Why does Canada have this technology to offer? According to Gail, it is because Canada was "a huge, barren land full of incredible wealth," and it received the necessary infrastructure "from a civilized society." From Gail's perspective, then, development "has to do with education. As societies become more educated, particularly the women, they start improving culturally; they begin maturing." Trevor also expressed this perspective in a similar manner with his comment that "it may be popular to decry colonialism, but the British brought democracy and education to India, and I think that gave India a step up compared to a lot of the Asian countries." This presumption of expert knowledge is surely a product of the broader discourse of development — and its relationship to past and present colonialism. It is also likely reproduced in some manner through the structure of the sponsorship experience. For example, Pamela explained,

> what I like about [sponsorship] is that you can choose the country, and you can choose the sex of the child that you want. So, I figured a Palestinian Muslim girl was the lowest on the totem pole for getting any help, so that is why we wanted to sponsor a little girl.

The option(s) presented by child sponsorship, then, allowed Pamela to fulfill a very particular kind of desire. "Ever since I was eight years old," Pamela said,

> I wanted to go to Africa and help the poor people. I have always really been interested in kids in Africa, especially. It was my dream to go to Ethiopia,

and so it was like the only thing that I [pause] that was the closest thing I could do to help anyone.

This statement by Pamela ties together these seemingly disparate, but nevertheless interconnected, elements of perceived Northern superiority in terms of development knowledge and the seeking of personal pleasure through sponsorship.

Pamela's comment about wanting to sponsor a Muslim child touches on a final theme that is relevant to this study, that of religion. Participants were usually asked if faith played a role in their decision to sponsor a child, and how they would feel about evangelism being part of the sponsorship organization's work abroad. Predictably, sponsor responses consistently fell into two camps, those for whom faith was a major factor and those who were indifferent or wary of its role in sponsorship. For many sponsors, faith was described as something that played a significant role in their motivation to sponsor. Leah speaks for this group well, saying that "being a Christian is a motivator as well. Believing that God has blessed me and wants that I should give in return." Talking about her decision to sponsor, Adrienne noted, "for me, it was following in my father's tithing, giving back." Martha echoed this point, tying together the notions of Christian responsibility with those of identity: "most definitely because part of my Christianity is serving others because you do some service work. That is part of what being a Christian is." Christianity is not the only faith that might be relevant here, although it was the predominant one among the participants in this study. Gail may have been taking this into account when she said that "generally people that are more spiritual are more likely to look around them and see the need and think of ways to provide that help."

This emphasis on faith as a motivator is not terribly surprising and neither is the discomfort many sponsors expressed toward the idea of evangelism being part of sponsorship. Toby conveyed his concerns with the comment,

> sometimes I worry about if they are converting to Christianity. I do not really have anything wrong with Christians or anything, but I do not know how comfortable I feel about them being there. Maybe the people in these countries are a little more susceptible or vulnerable.

Toby's partner Jaime was uncomfortable with the "Christian aspect" as well, but thought that World Vision as a Christian organization may be more "fiscally responsible" because of their religious nature. Patty simply said that evangelism "would not sit well with me." Interestingly, these sponsors still decided to support World Vision, a choice that could be explained in part by the way the organization seems to present a relatively moderate image of itself where religion is concerned. Not all sponsors were completely against evangelism, however. Some, like Tom, felt that it is okay as long "as it is not done in an insensitive way." As Martha explained,

I do not mind them doing it, but I really hope they respect the people they are teaching. Like going to a Muslim and saying you are not going to heaven unless you make Jesus your personal saviour … I would not want them doing that.

These statements, especially the word "teaching" with all its moral presumption, highlight the complex challenge of disentangling evangelical from humanitarian elements of sponsorship.

Leaving aside the issue of what is an acceptable level of proselytizing, not all discussion of religion revolved around the sponsorship organization. The (perceived) faith of the sponsored child was also mentioned by a few sponsors as something that was relevant to their decision to sponsor. Alexis noted that she made the decision to go with Plan precisely because they are not faith-based. However, she felt that religion was still a factor because her sponsored child's family is devoutly Christian. "I find this kind of difficult actually," Alexis said,

because I am always getting these letters "heaping God's blessing upon you" and "the family loves and prays to God almighty they can meet you" … I am afraid she is got in the grip of one of those holy roller churches.

A similar sentiment, albeit with a different result, can be found in something Penelope mentioned. She said she would not sponsor a child from the Philippines because "the trouble with sponsoring in the Philippines is they are all Catholic … and I feel the Catholic Church is not doing what they should in the world, and I feel kind of strongly about it." Alexis' and Penelope's comments represent a small minority of participant responses that demonstrated concern with what is seen as too much religiosity in the South (at least in contrast with a North that is seen to be more discreetly religious if not wholly secular).

Rather than representing too much faith, it also seemed possible for sponsored children to represent the "wrong" faith in the eyes of sponsors. Once again, Jenny provided a rather blunt statement that is noteworthy despite, or perhaps because of, its unconventional nature. Jenny began by saying that "I would not turn away a child [even if they are not Christian]. I think they have better values if they are raised a Christian." She followed this *comparatively* reasonable statement, however, with the contradictory declaration:

honestly, I do not want Muslim children because half the Muslims seem to want to kill us. The others do not, but you know what they are doing a lot of them, they are terrorists. I do not want my money, I have not got that much money to spend to educate a Muslim child … I do not want them to spend all their days studying the Bible. I just want them to get good values, to have good moral values. This little girl said, "obey my father and mother and be honest in all ways." That is about all there is, is it not? Would not that be better than having a little Muslim kid with a dagger?

Jenny's statement is by no means representative of other participant responses — at least not on the surface. Her opinion is not unexpected, though, given the present level of Islamophobia in North America. Jenny's assumption that "good moral values" are inevitably associated with Christianity and that violence is synonymous with Islam could be taken as a straightforward expression of individual prejudice. Such an analysis, however, would neglect the systemic roots of racism, which are found in the historical legacy of a world that has been deeply segregated by the concept of racial difference and in contemporary ways of thinking, speaking, and acting that rely on the distinctions created by these perceived differences. Consequently, we should see Jenny's comments as an expression of these commonly circulating perceptions of human diversity that normally take on a less straightforward (and less sensational) form. What is remarkable about these comments, then, is the way they clearly highlight a common discursive process involving racist statements. Jenny is able to maintain a positive self-image ("I would not turn away a child") despite the obvious discriminatory content of her response ("I have not got that much money to spend to educate a Muslim child") through reference to some indistinct moral objective ("I just want them to get good values"). Through this process, the internal contradictions between positive ethical identity and overtly discriminatory opinions are overcome such that, as long as individuals are well intentioned, racism can be sanitized.

While all the above comments regarding the role of faith and evangelism in child sponsorship may not be terribly surprising, they do help demonstrate the perceived divisions of the world and their effect on sponsorship. As discussed in Chapter 2, there is a commonly understood categorization of the world into Christian and non-Christian areas (or, perhaps more accurately, Protestant and non-Protestant areas) that overlaps with the categories of "developed" and "undeveloped" (see Bornstein, 2002). This division further cements the status of Southern people(s) as Others and facilitates their simultaneous subjection to developmental and evangelical interventions. Moreover, it also facilitates the link between the imagined justification for developmental/evangelical interventions (the simultaneous economic and moral poverty of the South) and the motivation to provide these interventions (the economic and moral superiority of the North). The key point here seems to be that the perception of the South as economically "backward" often overlaps with the perception of Southerners as morally "backward" (be it non-religious, too religious, or wrongly religious). Consequently, even those sponsors who were skeptical of the role of evangelism in child sponsorship could place explanations of poverty, in part, at the feet of religion (morality). In this way, the very real connections between the economic prosperity of the North and the poverty of the South are once again elided, and Northerners are able to position themselves as good people not only by virtue of being economically "developed" but also by being either good Christians or, for that matter, good atheists.

The satisfaction of sponsor needs

Most of this chapter and the last has been spent reviewing some general thematic patterns in the way sponsors talk about their sponsorships. The descriptions and explanations provided by sponsors highlight the startlingly varied and complex nature of representation and rationalization that accompanies child sponsorship. They also highlight the field of power and knowledge (or, more accurately, power-knowledge) upon which the practice of sponsorship is located. While the many responses discussed above may seem either too disparate or too ambiguous to draw conclusions from them about the social and psychological processes that animate sponsorship, one thing seems to stand out above all others: the importance of sponsorship for the contemporary world is as much about what the sponsor thinks and feels (and acts) about sponsorship as it is about what happens to the money they donate. This focus on the sponsor is evident in sponsorship promotional material and is justified through the money it produces each year. This focus is also evident in the way sponsors referred to the feel-good experience of sponsorship.

In many instances, the pleasures of the sponsorship experience are not only taken for granted but taken as due. Describing why she sponsored a child and then why she stopped, Adrienne said, "I guess it was knowing that I was doing something to help. Maybe I stopped [because] I found other more rewarding things or ways that I felt more rewarded." Other former sponsors made similar comments. Erica mentioned that she "was expecting it [sponsoring a child] to be more fulfilling and it just was not … I was hoping to feel a connection with the kid, and I did not really. It was very strange and unfulfilling." Likewise, Pamela said, "I did not withdraw because I think that people should not sponsor children. I just withdrew because it was not meaning anything for me." Phyllis, on the other hand, helped explain the connection between sponsorship promotional material and the (unrealized?) expectations of sponsors. "I really like when I see Plan occasionally [on TV]," she shared,

> I really like the way … Plan will visit different children. Then they sometimes will make a tape of the child, and then they take it to the foster, the sponsor, and I think that is really nice … to see the close connection, and

to see the tears of the sponsors when they see this child smiling at them and speaking their gratitude.

These comments highlight the quest for personal meaning or fulfillment that is so often part of the motivation to sponsor a child. They also do a good job of illustrating the position of the sponsored child in these situations, a position that is largely apparent through its relative absence.

The focus on the sponsor within child sponsorship has a counterpart in the commodification — or, more broadly, the objectification — of Southern children. This objectification was a regular feature of participant responses. Perhaps the most telling example of the objectification of the sponsored child is the metonymy associated with an off-hand comment made by Harriet. She said, "then they just sent us the other day our new boy, and so I have not even gotten him out of his little envelope." The vocal (and arguably semantic) replacement of a whole, living child with that child's picture is indicative of the largely unidirectional character of the sponsorship experience. This replacement is often compounded by a language of possession (not to mention differentiation), as in when Harriet referred to "my Ghana girl." Interestingly, Harriet also explained that Christian Children's Fund had begun placing a fingerprint of the child on their annual progress report. This phenomenon, which ensures sponsors know that there is a real child involved, seems depressingly similar to some form of quality assurance for the goods one purchases. Harriet was not the only sponsor to speak in possessive terms. Phyllis recounted her thoughts when she was forced to change her sponsored child, saying "oh well, I will get another little girl, see if I can have another little girl from Malawi." This emphasis on selection, and the gendered emphasis involved in this selection, came up again when she said, "well, I just thought I would like a little girl" in response to the question of why she specified a child from four to eight years of age when signing up for sponsorship. Vanessa also made a similar decision, commenting that "they all look like boys; I wanted a real little girl."

The fact that several sponsors expressed a desire for a girl as their sponsored child could be a product of their own gender (most participants were women) or a product of the present emphasis on the "girl child" in development discourse (for example, Plan's "Because I Am a Girl" campaign). Arguably, however, this preference could equally be related to the oppressed position of femininity, which has a long history of being more readily possessed and bartered than masculine forms. Describing her experience with signing up for sponsorship, Abby commented on the bizarre nature of selecting a child (whether girl or boy) as if they were a commodity. "He [the organization representative who came to her house] gave me a few different kids to choose from," she recounted, "which is [a] very strange thing to have to do." The strangeness of this experience, however, is often lost in its banality, as is evidenced by Jenny's shockingly casual remark: "the best way to pay for these children is by using your Visa card."

Through these participant responses, it is possible to see how sponsorship transforms Southern children into objects for Northern consumption. This process may be unavoidable in order to raise funds, but it places an uncomfortable emphasis on meeting the needs of the sponsor to secure these funds. This may seem like a suitable trade-off to sponsorship agencies, who often judge themselves according to their revenue stream, but there is more at stake than simply trying to raise the maximum amount of money for development assistance. The practice of sponsorship draws on and feeds into a discourse of international development that has become increasingly associated with the personal development of the private donors who help support it. What this means, then, is that sponsorship constructs (forms) sponsors in such a way that they are transformed into seemingly more ethical people. Their ethical nature is thus not a simple quality of their personality but is confirmed through what is envisioned as ongoing action on their part (even better than a single donation, which cannot be thought about or talked about in the same way). This is significant (problematic?) because the action they are taking by sponsoring a child is, in reality, quite divorced from the underlying problems of poverty in the world. Instead, sponsorship represents a kind of feedback loop that is able to sustain its ethical integrity (and those of its sponsors) without the need for convincing evidence that it is ameliorating poverty. In other words, the choice involved in the simple act of sponsorship itself is able to be ethically substituted for the desired results of sponsorship — the so-called development of the child and community.

This connection between international development, sponsorship, and (ethical) identity is readily apparent in many of the participant responses noted above. The links between the way sponsors talk about the benefits of sponsorship in relation to the perceived problems of Southern poverty and the way they refer to the rewards of sponsorship, such as the feeling of "making a difference," is highly indicative of an imagined (or merely desired) world where their apparently discrete and concrete choices have a significant positive effect. This is important not because it is untrue (their choices do have significant effects) but because these choices are not the only ones, or even the central ones, that matter. It is the multitude of everyday, abstract choices — choices that help reproduce a particular vision of global life and its associated practices — that really define the ethics of individuals and represent the solution to global poverty. Instead, we are left with accounts of sponsorship that are littered with the readily available language of emotional satisfaction.

It is hard to believe that is all there is to it, however. For instance, Julia described sponsorship as "one of the best things I have ever done in my life ... I get so much pleasure out of feeling I can make a difference." Similarly, Pamela said, knowing that you have a child overseas almost makes the world kind of a smaller place, that you do not just have your own family, but you are also at the same time looking out for someone else you could not adopt.

Comments like these hint at deeper processes than simply good feelings. Gail offered an anecdote that hints at one such process. She said,

I was travelling to another part of the country on business and was meeting a particular lady and went into her office, and there she had her child with World Vision right? So, it kind of gives something to talk about as well … it was really an affirmation of what I was doing because this is a person I otherwise respect, right, and it is like "oh, you have got one too" [laughs].

The fact that Gail's positive perception of herself in this circumstance was linked to the social approval of the person she met is not groundbreaking, but the way sponsorship facilitates such encounters between individuals in the North does hint at something important. It indicates how processes of ethical identity formation are *socially* grounded in the circulation of certain ideas about what makes a person good and the practices that are seen to convey these perceptions.

A similar story can be read into another participant's response related to the fact that Tom could not "remember what it was that triggered" his desire to sponsor. His partner Margery, however, was able to supply the answer: "Tom's just a really generous person." In a similar vein, Erica noted that "people were impressed when they found out that I was sponsoring a kid when they saw the picture on the fridge." A former sponsor who started sponsoring on her own when she was fifteen, Erica went on to say, "I was really invested in my own niceness … It was part of my do-gooder thing to sponsor a child … I just wanted to do good things." As with many accounts of sponsorship, Erica's comments highlight the way that sponsors are commonly positioned, or position themselves, as good people by virtue of their sponsorship. Erica's unusually perceptive statements illustrate how child sponsorship operates as a mechanism of identity formation that allows sponsors to understand their desire to help a poor child in terms of their quest for personal growth and moral development.

Conclusion

"The hard sell of little faces"

This compelling title introduced the second part of the *Chicago Tribune's* 1998 exposé on child sponsorship. The paper went on to declare that

> child sponsorship organizations are often better at promising miracles than delivering them. Potential sponsors may find it irresistible to change a child's life with a few dollars a week. However, reality is not that simple and help is not that cheap. (1-1)

Despite some of the limitations of the *Tribune* critique that have served to introduce the arguments presented throughout this project, this phrase — especially the final line — does an excellent job of summarizing the central challenges to child sponsorship. The problems of global poverty and inequality and the solutions that sponsorship is supposed to provide can be neither easily articulated, nor easily addressed. They are systemic problems. Consequently, the difficulties with sponsorship stem from more than bad organizational practices (although these do occur) or misplaced standpoints on development issues (although these occur as well). At its heart, child sponsorship represents a problem of perspective; the discourses surrounding sponsorship help produce subjects that are inclined to understand and explain their role in "making a difference" in a very particular manner. As could be expected, these understandings and explanations draw on many mainstream conceptions of the problems of poverty (and development) as well as the nature of ethical action. As a philanthropic practice, child sponsorship encourages a vision of the world that is paradoxically disconnected and egoistic.

From this perspective, the success of child sponsorship is not related as much to the way it focuses on the needs of poor children as it is to the way it constructs a vision of ethical action in the work of international development that coincides with the personal development of Northern sponsors, the "natural" bio-psychological development of Southern children, and the organizational development of sponsorship programs. In other words, the desires to become better people(s), secure appropriate childhoods, and raise lots of money end up taking priority over the goal of living together well on a global scale.

The problem of child sponsorship revisited

If we remember how sponsorship programs are organized internationally (into fundraising offices and project offices) and nationally (as marketing powerhouses), we can situate the problematization of global poverty within its current neoliberal frame of reference. This frame of reference positions the dilemma of international development as requiring solutions that provide the correct blend of social and economic interventions in the South facilitated by funding from the North. This is a discourse about development that not only ignores the historical and contemporary relations of power between North and South but that even goes so far as to make unspeakable or unthinkable alternate understandings of human behaviour and the nature of progress. This discourse enables sponsorship organization staff to justify the disadvantages of child sponsorship and its promotional appeals (such as the administrative expense and the apparent exploitation of children) through the argument that the money is needed for a good cause (the ends justify the means). This discourse also enables sponsors to be deemed good and generous people precisely because they are not seen to be complicit in the problem of poverty and their support is therefore not compulsory within this framework. Child sponsorship, then, becomes understood as a solution to the problem of global poverty through its claims both to being a successful fundraising strategy and transforming lives.

Recall Susan Hay's comments from the World Vision advertisement discussed in Chapter 4, where she tells us that "we cannot change the world, but if we all get together, one person can make a difference in the lives of little ones" like Rosalia. This is a point brought home by such ads again and again; for little effort on the part of sponsors, they can make a profound impact in the world and on themselves. No matter their jobs, lifestyles, or political affiliations, sponsors do not just get to feel good about themselves temporarily, but they become better people. More than anything, this ridiculous ease with which we are invited to throw off history and injustice and to consume our individual portion of the liberal pie is what makes child sponsorship problematic. As part of a movement that sees people doing good by enjoying or improving themselves, child sponsorship and its advertising helps reposition what it means to live ethically in a terribly unequal and unjust world. Simply, it presents sponsors with an almost miraculous way of transforming themselves ethically, one that is far out of proportion to the actual change that is occurring.

This does not mean that child sponsorship programs set out to reform the ethical landscape or that they are not doing "good" in the world (at least in the short term). It simply means that we must see child sponsorship not only as a means to an end but also an end in itself — not only as a development fundraising technique but also as a process of subjectification set within dominant cultural, political, and socio-economic contexts. We should remember, borrowing from Foucault (2003 [1983]), that sponsorship may not be bad, but it is dangerous.

Through these perspectives on development and ethics, the organizations that offer sponsorship are seated squarely within the rubric of ends justifying means (although these ends are ill defined). Perhaps this accounts somewhat for the difficulty many sponsors and staff have in articulating the reasons behind global poverty and inequality and yet the ease with which they embrace the "obvious" good of what they are doing. Perhaps this accounts somewhat for the relative neglect of advocacy and development education on the part of sponsorship programs. Perhaps this accounts somewhat for the overwhelming lack of critical reviews of their own work with respect to anything but the bottom line. Perhaps this accounts somewhat for the fact that child sponsorship seems to be disproportionally concerned with satisfying the needs of sponsors over those of the sponsored child. After all, if sponsorship programs do good by raising money, then sponsorship of a child is automatically an ethical act since the sponsors are providing this money. This vision of child sponsorship as ethical action, however, has significant consequences: it elides the global connections between individuals and groups that form the basis of structural barriers to equality, it reproduces colonial relations of power and knowledge, and it allows for the deterioration of conditions in the South despite the appearance of enormous efforts in the North.

A future for child sponsorship?

The principal focus of this book on the ethical rather than the organizational or the overseas character of child sponsorship means that it is difficult to provide anything in the way of concrete recommendations. This was never the goal of the critique presented here, which is more about exploring the complex ethical relationships between the practice of sponsorship and the discursive contexts within which it operates. However, it is fruitful to reflect on the implications of this critique for the ongoing practice of sponsorship. While it may not be possible to readily turn this research into suggestions for improvement, there are a few points that could be taken into consideration with respect to child sponsorship and related practices.

Before anything else, it is important to recognize the distinction between short-term and long-term objectives for addressing issues of global poverty and inequality. It would be neither warranted, nor beneficial, to advocate that sponsorship programs immediately drop sponsorship as a fundraising technique or that sponsors immediately give up their sponsorships. It is undeniable that supporting organizations such as World Vision and Plan through child sponsorship is better than using that same money to purchase more consumer goods, for example. In the long run, however, it should not be too controversial to suggest that child sponsorship will never be the solution to Southern poverty its organizations often present it to be. In addition, the practice of sponsorship itself contributes to a pattern of thought and action regarding global poverty and inequality that is either insufficient or counterproductive. This is not necessarily, or perhaps not only, the fault of sponsorship programs as this book has pointed out repeatedly. What is problematic, then, is the continuing perception of sponsorship as an effective solution, or even a major part of the solution, to poverty. Whether it takes the form of believing sponsors can really "make a difference" in the world through sponsorship or believing that people "cannot change the world but can change the life of one child," this perception ignores the fact that "reality is not that simple and help is not that cheap" (see Kirk, 2012).

Despite not attempting to blame the organizations involved, the critique presented here is more damning in some ways because, if one accepts it, there is really no salvation for child sponsorship. These organizations cannot do much to address the problems that plague the practice of sponsorship; these problems are part of a broader set of issues that are cultural as much as they are economic or administrative. What can be done presently is to begin a search for alternate means to acquire the private sources of revenue that sponsorship taps into. In fact, many sponsorship organizations either make use of or have tested fundraising strategies similar to sponsorship but without some of its attendant difficulties.

UNICEF's "Global Parent" or Save the Children's "Child Guardian" programs represent such initiatives. There are no individual updates provided or letter exchanges facilitated though their programs. Instead, sponsors receive information about a "representative child" so as to save on the administrative costs of individual sponsorship. These programs draw on similar discourses as sponsorship does, however, and are therefore subject to a critique similar to the one outlined in this book. Organizations that have tried other variations on sponsorship, such as sponsor a village or sponsor a cause (education, HIV, vaccination, etc.), have not found them to be as financially successful as child sponsorship and have therefore discontinued them. Arguably, these variations are preferable to child sponsorship for reasons similar to the representative child programs. In addition, they may also be useful in removing some of the emphasis on individual ability and responsibility that often accompanies discussions of poverty or development.

Another significant trend in this field is the proliferation of "gift catalogues" wherein you can purportedly purchase goats, school supplies, and other services or items for a community overseas. While no figures are available to compare this technique to sponsorship, these catalogues seem to be successful in securing additional donations from current sponsors (at least according to the interview participants). Once again, these types of fundraising practices appear to do nothing to change mainstream (unidirectional and disconnected) representations of the problems and solutions to global poverty. In fact, they may even do a better job of promoting individual consumption as the dominant method of (imagined) social change and of separating the fundraising appeal from the development intervention. How is it that a person sitting in Canada should decide the number of goats needed relative to the amount of school supplies? The short answer is that they should not, nor could they really, since these catalogues work much the same way sponsorship does — as a fundraising tool. Logically, it does not make sense to have direct proportionality between what Northerners purchase in these catalogues and what is handed out overseas. In fact, since the Northern organization is often separate from its international partners, with these partners commonly (and rightly) setting development priorities, it is unrealistic to have any *direct* relationship between purchases in these catalogues and what happens on the ground.

The fact that many interviewed sponsors did not understand this tenuous connection between the organizations that raise funds and those than spend them, just as many did not understand the way their sponsorship fee was spent in the South, highlights an area of potential improvement for sponsorship organizations. While no sponsorship organization is explicitly fraudulent in their marketing about where sponsorship money goes — it is always in the fine print that this money does not go directly to the child — they are not terribly forthright about it either. The present system of distributing funds overseas does not match the marketing messages of individual child sponsorship very well, and sponsorship organizations seem to be keen to maintain these messages. However, there are benefits to spreading the word more widely about how sponsorship really works, and the costs associated with doing this may not be as high as organizations imagine. Bringing the promotion of sponsorship in line with current development practice, for example by focusing on community-level issues rather than on individual progress, should be seen as an aspect of public education (and therefore part of the organization's mission) rather than simply a dilution of marketing power. This perspective may help (potential) sponsors to displace the emphasis on individual achievement that is so often associated with liberal notions of development and to better appreciate the complexity of the issues involved. Judging from the interviews conducted for this research, sponsors who were not aware of how their donations were actually spent were generally positive about the community-level focus with some even expressing relief that their sponsored child was not being singled out for special attention.

As for the handful of sponsorship organizations, such as Chalice or Compassion, that send money directly to the families of children or provide benefits directed solely at children rather than the community, they must be considered within the framework of best practices in local community development. Due in part to the creation of disparity and the lack of focus on collective economic development, having an external benefactor provide individually directed resources is largely considered inappropriate. Consequently, revamping sponsorship to return to a more congruous but less desirable "cheque-to-child" model should obviously not be seen as an option to address the challenges presented here.

All in all, the alternatives to mainstream child sponsorship are often plagued by the same general issue: they neglect the importance of advocating for systemic (attitudinal or lifestyle) change in favour of increasing donations. Fundraising may have a place, but it cannot and should not replace a critical and sustained look at how everyday activities in the North, such as shopping for food or clothes, are tied to the continued exploitation of people in the South through such things as liberalized trade regimes, restrictive intellectual property laws, unethical labour practices, and artificially depressed wages. For example, while sponsorship organizations in Canada are subject to charity tax laws, which restrict political commentary and therefore some kinds of advocacy work, they are still capable of producing promotional or educational material that tries to get at the deeper issues involved in global inequality albeit at the possible expense of donor recruitment and retention. Once again, however, it comes down to not seeing raising money as the key element to combating global poverty and inequality. Rather, well-established organizations such as World Vision or Plan International need to come out of the closet (to borrow an apt phrase from the gay rights movement) and start being more openly vocal about some of the underlying issues, such as the historical and contemporary effects of imperialism, the amounts of defence spending compared to Official Development Assistance rates, the continued presence of so-called tied aid, the illegal or simply unfair practices of Northern corporations and multilateral organizations, etc. The phrase "From charity to justice," which became one of the slogans of the 2005 Live 8 concerts, is a good example of the shift that is necessary — although the concerts themselves are simply another example of Northerners doing good by enjoying themselves. This shift may alienate some donors and, taken far enough, threaten an organization's charitable status, but it is not impossible. In fact, the size of some sponsorship agencies, and the scope of their influence, is such that speaking out more forcefully to the public at large (and not simply having small advocacy teams aimed at governmental policy) is a way to lead the entire sector in a vital conversation.

This importance for sponsorship organizations to be more outspoken brings to the fore another potential area of improvement. It seems as though sponsorship organizations could really improve their work by producing, maintaining, and publicizing a consistent philosophy of development. As noted in Chapters 2 and 3, the staff of sponsorship organizations commonly expressed diverse and inconsistent perspectives on causes of global poverty and necessary responses. Having a consistent development philosophy and promoting that philosophy both internally and externally could go a long way toward ameliorating some of the negative side effects of sponsorship marketing. While any consistent philosophy would be better than none (in that it would at least allow for a frank discussion about priorities), it almost goes without saying that, ideally, this philosophy should not blame the poor or exonerate the wealthy, should express a reliance on securing political will as much as promoting education, and should argue the necessity for change in the North as much as in the South.

A final thought on the implications of this research relates to sponsors rather than sponsorship organizations. One of the most frequent questions sponsors asked before concluding the interview was whether or not they should continue to sponsor a child, whether it was "really helping." This is not an easy question to answer, and truthfully, this research provides no clear-cut answer. Often, however, being able to ask the right kinds of questions is as important as knowing the correct answers (provided these answers even exist). Consequently, current or potential sponsors can approach this particular question by asking themselves some different ones. For example, what rewards do I feel I get out of sponsorship, and how is this related to my perception of myself? Why should I feel generous about helping a poor child overseas when I feel obliged to help a poor child in Canada? Knowing I can accomplish the same things on the ground without the extra administrative burden of sponsorship, do I need the feedback I get from sponsoring a child to continue donating to the cause of mitigating global poverty and inequality? In addition to, or instead of, sponsoring a child, what can I do to effect change here in Canada rather than focusing on what needs to be done in the South? How much does sponsoring a child really have to do with my connection to someone in another part of the world; are there different ways to fulfill this desire that are less one-sided? If I want to maintain my sponsorship, how can I influence the sponsorship organization to focus more on advocacy or public education in the North?

Thinking ethically about child sponsorship does not necessarily involve stopping one's sponsorship immediately, but it should involve asking some difficult questions about what we know about the benefits of sponsorship and what we expect to get from it. In many ways, child sponsorship is akin to a customer care program. It is not dissimilar to the reward cards one uses to earn points in exchange for brand loyalty, where tangible but pre-selected goods or services are made available seemingly for free (the costs are incorporated into the original purchase price) to make sure people continue to support the company. Perhaps one question sponsors should ask themselves, then, is "do I really need this incentive?"

A future for our understanding of sponsorship?

Since the research for this study was conducted, there has been a marked increase in academic interest in the area of child sponsorship. Several empirical studies, and at least one edited volume, on child sponsorship have been published (for example, see Van Eekelen, 2013; Glewwe, Ross, and Wydick, 2014; Watson and Clarke, 2014; Wydick, Glewwe, and Rutledge, 2013). Brad Watson and Matthew Clarke (2014) pulled together a group of academics, development experts, and child sponsorship staff to produce a book titled *Child Sponsorship: Exploring Pathways to a Brighter Future*. The editors have collected a series of articles addressing many different aspects of sponsorship and a variety of sponsorship agencies. In a field where very little research has existed, this is an important volume improving our knowledge of a little-understood practice.

Similar to this study, the objective of Watson and Clarke's book appears to be something other than simply vilifying the activities and motivations of sponsorship organizations. In fact, the book largely presents a positive take on child sponsorship and its perceived role in the reduction of global poverty while presenting useful recommendations for child sponsorship agencies. In this way, it is significantly diverges from the work presented here, which has presented a critique of child sponsorship by attempting to locate it within the broader networks of power and knowledge referred to as the discourse of development. While both perspectives are useful in their own ways, it seems unlikely that the underlying tension surrounding the value of sponsorship will be solved by the simple increase of knowledge in the area. This tension comes from an ethical dilemma at the core of the idea of development: what defines a good life, who gets to decide this, and how can people best be allowed to achieve it? Seeing child sponsorship as playing a positive role in addressing this dilemma necessarily involves taking a particular stance within it, one that too often obscures the inherently political nature of the questions involved. Child sponsorship cannot avoid placing the problem of poverty at the feet of the sponsored and the power of change in the hands of the sponsors.

Just because more information will never let us fully determine the value of sponsorship does not mean that it cannot help guide us through the immediate future. In this way, perhaps the most significant recent study on child sponsorship is that by Wydick, Glewwe, and Rutledge (2013), which claims to offer quantitative evidence for the efficacy of child sponsorship. Despite only looking at the Compassion sponsorship program, this study has already been cited numerous times to justify the value of child sponsorship more generally. This may be telling because, as the authors mention, Compassion organizes their sponsorship programs somewhat differently from other major sponsorship programs. There appears to be a greater emphasis on the financial benefits of sponsorship being funneled primarily or exclusively to sponsored children (or those awaiting sponsorship). While this allows for a more accurate assessment of the impact of sponsorship, it is not significantly comparable to most programs funded by sponsorship that use their funds at the community level. In fact, this model of more direct funding of sponsored children was abandoned by most sponsorship programs because it was deemed counterproductive and prejudicial at the community level (due in part to the way it created local disparities among children and resentment among, and within, families).

The issue of direct funding to sponsored children aside, the main problem with Wydick, Glewwe, and Rutledge's (2013) study is that even if we take the effectiveness of the Compassion program at face value given the evidence they present, this does not tell us anything other than the fact that child sponsorship is better than doing nothing. Although probably outside the feasible scope of their study, the authors did not compare the outcomes of sponsored children (or the communities in which they live) to other potentially more beneficial approaches, such as the kind of community-level development projects funded by other major sponsorship programs. If other interventions are even more successful than the Compassion model by the same measures, then there is no incentive to promote it as something other than "better than nothing." Moreover, given the way Compassion is structured internationally (sending the money raised from child sponsorship to partners who oversee the actual "work" of development on the ground), all that can be concluded from the evidence is that when the partner organizations are funded, they can accomplish the presented results. No actual evidence about why this funding must, or even should, come from child sponsorship is provided; the same results may be possible from funding these partners through bilateral aid.

This issue of appropriately evaluating the effectiveness of child sponsorship highlights the first of three broad areas where we could improve our knowledge of sponsorship. Independent research into the effects of sponsorship on children, families, and communities in the South is needed. Given the fact that sponsorship is predominantly a fundraising technique, however, this needs to be more than an evaluation of the impact of sponsorship dollars on local development. Instead, the evaluative component could usefully focus on the personal effects of participating in the production of sponsorship promotional material including annual reports and letters to sponsors (perhaps in a manner similar to Glewwe, Ross, and Wydick [2014] or Watson and Ware [2014]). This kind of research might investigate the claim that sponsorship is psychologically beneficial to the children and families involved (above and beyond the psychological benefits that greater financial stability and security provide); it might also address the community-level effects of having organization representatives solicit children for sponsorship and then collect information about these sponsored children. There are also, of course, issues to investigate regarding the creation of disparities through sponsorship as sponsored children receive letters (and sometimes extra gifts) that other children, including siblings, do not necessarily receive. A challenge to this kind of evaluative data, however, lies within the individualizing tendencies of the contemporary development discourse. For example, assuming individual aspiration is a positive outcome of sponsorship, as Glewwe, Ross, and Wydick seem to do, might be taken to imply that clear goals and personal motivation is a root cause of global poverty in the first place.

A second area where there are still many questions about sponsorship relates to the paucity of independent information about the way sponsorship monies are distributed among partner organizations or dealt with once transferred to these organizations. Tracking sponsorship dollars from source to spending would help to investigate claims of organizational efficiency and to study the relationship between the stated goals of an organization and its structures and practices. There is also very little public knowledge around the way organization revenues and expenditures are tracked internally and reported externally. While organizations appear transparent by releasing their financial statements to the public and communicating their spending in easily digested pie charts, these resources tell us very little about where the organization acquires funds and how it spends them. Studies that highlight this (admittedly difficult to acquire) information would be beneficial not simply to reveal the inefficiencies and subterfuges of sponsorship organizations but also to shed light on how accepted and routine organizational practices relate to the way the problems and solutions of poverty are perceived.

Third, we could improve our understanding of sponsorship by further exploring the motivations and rationalizations of sponsors and sponsorship staff (and how these relate to development practice). It would be valuable to examine the relationship between the motivation to sponsor a child, or to donate money in another way, and the willingness to engage in either activism or lifestyle change. Highlighting the demographic or ideological characteristics of sponsors might help draw some conclusions regarding the relationship between sponsorship, worldview, and political values. Looking more in-depth at communications between sponsors, organization staff, and sponsored children (or their representatives) might help illustrate how aspects of personal and organizational identity are expressed and what this might mean in terms of investment in certain perspectives on development. Finally, more conversation with organization staff would be particularly helpful in examining both the "corporatization" of non-governmental organizations (especially their integration of for-profit business and marketing logic) and internal barriers to institutional change (especially the relationship between organizational structure and staff roles and expectations).

A future for developmentality?

Beyond the specific topic of child sponsorship, this book addresses several key issues in global sociology and the critical literature on development. The over-arching emphasis of this research — the production of ethical subjects as a facet of the discourse of development — continues a particular trend in the critique of international development thought and practice that focuses on the subjectivities of Northerners (for example, see Goudge, 2003; Heron 2007; Smith and Yanacopulos, 2004). Rather than focus on the economic, political, or cultural difficulties that appear to impede a country's increase in GNP or a higher placement on the Human Development Index, this research draws attention to the importance of studying the way everyday practices in the North, and their attendant rationalizations, contribute to an unequal and unjust global order. Furthermore, by expanding on the postdevelopment emphasis on meaning-making processes in international development (for example, see Rojas, 2001, 2004; Sachs, 2000), the discussion of developmentality in this study provides a specific way to look at how the discursive mechanisms of development operate to produce ethical subjects and how these mechanisms are tied to neoliberal modes of governance (Ove, 2013).

Developmentality was conceptualized as a tool to aid in the production of a novel critique of child sponsorship. It was never intended to develop a theoretical life of its own; it was merely used to represent a particular trend in our understanding and exercise of development, whatever its form. This objective appears to mirror Foucault's intent with governmentality, a shorthand for a complex concept that seemed to be waiting for a different expression that never materialized. The notion of governmentality has now developed a substantial life of its own, however, so the question is: can (or should) developmentality be used in a broader context to look at practices similar to child sponsorship?

It seems as though the answer to this question lies less in the value of devel-opmentality as an explanatory tool and more in its value as a descriptive one. As a way of articulating a set of connections between representations of develop-ment and their associated practices, developmentality offers a slightly unwieldy but convenient shorthand for describing a deeply entrenched aspect of modern neoliberal society: the linking of broader social and institutional goals to personal improvement. This aspect, which connects particular ideas of progress with particular practices of individualism, is so deeply rooted it does not appear that even the contemporary backlash against neoliberalism will counter it. As with governmentality, this emphasis on the individual over the social may have found a new expression in the era of neoliberalism, but it is an essential facet of liberalism itself. This means that the objective of using the concept of developmentality, similar to that of governmentality, lies in its ability to expose these connections in order to "think otherwise" about the issue (Foucault, 2003 [1980a]). Of course, it is first important to believe it necessary to "think otherwise," and for this reason, projects like this one on child sponsorship hopefully help to foster that discussion. At the end of this book, it now becomes clear that it is not developmentality that helps formulate an analysis of child sponsorship as much as it is child sponsorship that helps illustrate the nature of developmentality.

The evidence behind this inversion can be found in the plethora of international development–related practices that are now firmly entrenched in the North. Such things as the meteoric rise in popularity of microcredit, the "ethical" branding of goods and services, and the proliferation of so-called voluntourism activities can equally be understood through the lens of developmentality. Microcredit, for example, has been become so popular that its progenitor, Muhammad Yunus, won the Nobel Peace Prize. Supposedly a way for poor people to lift themselves out of poverty, microcredit provides small loans, encouraging entrepreneurial practices, to people who do not otherwise have access to capital. This practice has been called "credit-baiting," however, for the way it commonly draws people into a capitalist economic framework that simultaneously destroys many of the interpersonal connections that help sustain poor people (Spivak, 1999: 220; see also Rankin, 2001). At the same time, websites such as Kiva, which facilitates small loans (largely) between people in the South and the North, provide Northerners with yet another way to "solve" the problem of global poverty through a paradoxically disconnected, and disproportionately moral, gesture. While the microloans may help an individual in particular ways, the practice itself — like most development funding/fundraising strategies in the North — projects a particular narrative of Southern poverty and its causes. This narrative focuses on the way individuals, organizations, or businesses can help poor people with *their* poverty, as if it were simply a personal trouble with no broader social causes or consequences. As with child sponsorship, this lack of holistic understandings of poverty — facilitated by the contemporary discourse of development — allows the practice of microcredit to appear ethical.

Similarly, some aspects of the contemporary "ethical consumption" movement draw on an equivalent logic. While the discussion around, and demand for, fairly traded products has heated up over the past decade, so has the desire of corporate interests to cash in on a new niche market. The creation of a "transnational moral economy" around fair trade (Goodman, 2004) has not only changed consumption habits (and their subjective effects) but has also led to a situation where fair trade certification processes are increasingly subject to corporate influence (Renard, 2005; Macdonald, 2007) and where fair trade is fallaciously thought to provide a holistic solution to the problems of global poverty (Levi and Linton, 2003). Specific consumer campaigns such as Product (RED) are no different. (RED) is a celebrity-inspired fundraising strategy in which a wide variety of consumer products are "ethically" branded to raise money for the Global Fund to fight HIV/AIDS, malaria, and tuberculosis in Africa. It *seems* to make perfect sense. After all, Northerners want to spend money on cell phones and t-shirts, so why not raise money for "Africa" at the same time? It appears to be a win-win situation; Northerners get to feel good about themselves and Southerners get HIV/AIDS medication. However, while this strategy may be successful in selling products and therefore raising money, it not only reproduces particular (traditional) representations of Africa and its relationship to the North, but it also commodifies Southern poverty and illness (see Barnes, 2008; Hintzen, 2008; Jungar and Salo, 2008; Magubane, 2008; Wiragu, Farley, and Jensen, 2010).

This is problematic in that the simplicity of the messages conveyed through this campaign is detrimental to the broader understanding of social responsibility that is necessary to make significant changes in the world (see Young, 2006). Expanding on this point, Anderson (2008: 47) notes,

> Virtually every aspect of (RED)'s message is simplistic and the result of such simplicity is visible in comments about the organization. Africa, when discussed, is portrayed as a monolithic continent whose people are in peril, but whom we can save as long as we buy the right products. So lacking in centrality to (RED)'s advertising and messaging, Africa is the subject of only one half of one percent of all comments left at (RED)'s MySpace page. Only fifty-eight people mentioned the continent at all. Instead, the majority of comments were focused on the greatness of (RED), its fine products, or the general, unspecified cause. Finally, consumerism is touted as the means by which we can save Africa, without acknowledging the inherent inequalities existent in the global economy, some of which have helped to impoverish many Africans on the continent.

The simplicity of (RED)'s message should not obscure the fact that there are complex discursive processes at work. As with the developmentality inherent in child sponsorship, (RED) does not operate as an ethical brand *despite* the lack of specificity about Africa and its "cause" or *despite* the focus on (RED) products. Rather, (RED) is successfully presented as an ethical choice *because* of the generic way that "development aid" and its recipients are presented and *because* of the conflation of personal or organizational development with the purported goals of international development (e.g. "I am a better person when I buy these products because I am helping others"; "What is good for (RED) is good for Africa"). Van Niekerk (2008:65) subtly highlights this point by stating that (RED)'s intervention is both about Africa and not about Africa; whatever it accomplishes on the ground, it is also about "the desire for relief from the guilt of subjecthood and domination, manifested here in the form of relief from the guilt of consumerism." Through this relief, real challenges of global health and illness are simultaneously connected to and separated from personal consumption. They are connected through the belief that corporate social responsibility, and the consumption tied to it, is a sufficient mechanism to address these issues. They are separated by a failure to adequately explore the link between Northern lifestyles, especially Northern consumptive practices, and Southern hardship.

Although there are a multitude of related practices that highlight the nature of contemporary developmentality, such as the Aga Khan Foundation's "World Partnership Walk" or the proliferation of "socially responsible investing" houses such as Meritas and Ethical Funds, the last one that will be discussed here is the practice of "voluntourism." Voluntourism — volunteering for local (development) projects while travelling for pleasure (largely in the South) — once again reinforces the link between personal enrichment and the helping of others/Others. "VolunTourism is 'slow travel,'" promotes the website VolunTourism.org (Projects Abroad, 2012: n.p.), "The experience starts before it even begins — with Y-O-U! 'Know Thyself' is the first step in the process." Through what may be seen as quintessentially selfless tasks, such as digging latrines in Guatemala, voluntourism nevertheless reflects a view of the world in which individualism is naturalized and egotism is rationalized. According to Projects Abroad (2012: n.p.), one of the largest Canadian voluntourism agencies,

> By touring and volunteering simultaneously, your time and efforts will be greatly appreciated and your role will be important … Through your chosen voluntourism project, you will not only provide beneficial aid and services to your community, but you will also gain from your cross-cultural immersion.

The fact that such practices are unashamedly marketed as beneficial to the "voluntourist" as well as the local community is no by-product of the promotional process; it is part of the overlapping discourses of personal and international development that are central to constructing voluntourists as ethical subjects. When potential voluntourists are plied with the idea that their service overseas is extraordinarily (and disproportionately) meaningful to the people they are helping, they are being drawn into a narrative that makes sense precisely because it extends traditional (colonial) understandings of the relationship between Northerners and Southerners. This process locates individual acts of voluntourism within the broader project of development. As Barbara Heron (2007: 150) notes in her study of the "helping imperative" behind female, white, bourgeois development workers:

> The development enterprise, seen in this light, appears to be of constitutive importance for white Northern subjects, securing for us key aspects of colonial relations accomplished for our predecessors; thus the development narrative is not only produced through imperial relations, but it's necessary to their operation.

In this way, purportedly ethical activities such as volunteering abroad can be implicated in both historical and contemporary global relations of power. This means that voluntourists should, as Heron writes about her participants, "consider our investments in innocence in relation to the making of our selves, or, put more bluntly, in not seeing our participation in domination" (152).

Child sponsorship, then, is definitely not alone in helping reproduce the current global order. Rather, it is simply one aspect, albeit a significant one, of a broader pattern that continues to separate "us" from "them" through the dissociation of "I" from "we." In the end, the practice of child sponsorship helps construct a vision of ethics that should not be seen as truly transformative, or at least not for the children and communities involved. Rather, this vision is mundane and mainstream. It is a vision that reciprocally supports the contemporary discourse of development and animates governmental processes. It is a vision that is rooted in the same notions of charity and responsibility that have repeatedly failed to solve the problem of deprivation and global inequality and that are intimately associated with the current era of neoliberal capitalism.

List of sponsorship promotional material contained in sample

1. Canadian Feed the Children. No Date. "Childhood: The Chance of a Lifetime" [brochure]. No publication information. Available August 2007.
2. Canadian Feed the Children. No Date. "Sponsoring a child what a wonderful way to help!" [brochure]. No publication information. Available August 2007.
3. Canadian Feed the Children. No Date. "Birtukan Woldie" [pamphlet]. No publication information. Available August 2007.
4. Canadian Food for the Hungry International. No Date. "Celebrate!" [sample donation appeal]. No publication information. Available August 2007.
5. Christian Children's Fund of Canada. No Date. Untitled [YouTube video]. <http://www.youtube.com/watch?v=2IwQG0D6h8I>. Retrieved July 10, 2007.
6. Christian Children's Fund of Canada. No Date. "Easter Gift" [sample donation appeal]. No publication information. Available August 2007.
7. Compassion Canada. No Date. Untitled [YouTube video]. <http://www.youtube.com/watch?v=XF_gjd3ysbE>. July 12, 2007.
8. Compassion Canada. No Date. *Compassion Today,* 7, 2 [magazine]. No publication information.
9. Compassion Canada. No Date. "Edilson Borda" [sample introductory letter]. No publication information. Available August 2007.
10. Compassion Canada. No Date. "Question & Answer Booklet" [pamphlet]. No publication information. Available August 2007.
11. Plan Canada. No Date. "Susan is waiting for a sponsor" [pamphlet]. No publication information. Available August 2007.
12. Plan Canada. No date. "Destination Hope" [televised commercial]. CTV.

Aired January 13, 2007.

13. Plan Canada. No date. "Heart of a Child" [televised commercial]. CTV. Aired March 30, 2007.

14. World Vision. No date. "Africa's Children" [televised commercial]. Global. Aired January 3, 2007.

15. World Vision. No date. "Children of Hope" [televised commercial]. Global. Aired January 11, 2007.

16. World Vision. No date. "Sponsor a Child, Change a Life" [televised commercial]. Omni. Aired January 11, 2007.

17. World Vision. No date. "You and Your Sponsored Child: Helping Build a Bridge of Hope" [brochure]. No publication information. Available August 2007.

18. World Vision. No date. C"ome Celebrate: Ntiza, Malawi" [brochure]. No publication information. Available August 2007.

19. World Vision. No date. "Child Sponsorship Works ... I've Seen It!" [brochure]. No publication information. Available August 2007.

20. World Vision. *Child View* [magazine]. No publication information. Summer 2006.

21. World Vision. *Child View* [magazine]. No publication information. Winter 2006/07.

Notes

1   This book uses the terms North and South to describe the conceptual division of the world into wealthier countries and poorer countries. The South, or the Global South, refers to what has alternatively been called the Third World or the developing world (also developing countries or less developed countries) in contrast to the North, the Global North, the West, the First World, or the developed world (also developed countries). It is recognized that none of these terminological binaries are adequate to encompass the breadth of the geography or the heterogeneity of the people(s) involved. That said, most people — including the interviewed participants — still understand and talk about the world in terms of this conceptual shorthand; for the sake of producing something generally understandable, this book continues to use this division. The terms North and South are used to represent this categorization not only because they are increasingly common in the critical literature on global poverty and inequality, but also because they avoid some of the bias associated with more traditional terms (e.g. developed and developing).

2   The labels "black" and "white" are used in this book despite being problematic because they may be taken to reinforce socially constructed categories of race or because they may be seen to exclude some categories, such as Hispanic or Asian peoples. Obviously, the intent of using these labels is not to find accurate terms to describe human diversity. Instead, the point is to highlight how perceived racial categories have played, and continue to play, a formative role in the conceptual divisions that structure our world.

Despite the ostensibly colour-blind rhetoric of much development discourse nowadays, processes of racialization are central to the operation of practices such as child sponsorship. These processes continue to highlight particular socially salient traits, such as skin colour, and link them to historical (and paternalistic) narratives of race and social progress. Links to these historical narratives are often obscured, however, as representations of the South and its people are strategically repackaged to serve contemporary needs. The labels white and black are used here, consequently, not because they represent the actual skin colours of the people involved, but because they serve as a general reminder that processes of racialization are at play even as they are made invisible by the contemporary operations of the discourse of development (and are, therefore, largely absent from participant responses).

3   It is somewhat difficult to determine which child sponsorship programs are the largest in Canada (or elsewhere for that matter). Is a program "larger" because it has more sponsors, more sponsored children, more assets, higher revenue specifically from child sponsorships, higher overall organization revenue, higher actual expenditures on development projects (revenue minus marketing and administrative overhead), or simply a more recognized name in the sponsorship industry? It is not easy to answer this question, but what is clear is that World Vision Canada has the largest child sponsorship program in Canada by any of these measures, with about CAN$445 million in revenue in 2016 (all figures are based on returns to the Canada Revenue Agency). Plan Canada is a clear number two, with about CAN$213 million in revenue in 2016. After these two agencies, the situation is less clear, but the third, fourth, and fifth spots seem to go to Compassion Canada with CAN$64 million, Christian Children's Fund of Canada with CAN$37 million, and Chalice with CAN$25 million in 2016 revenues. There are many smaller sponsorship agencies including Canadian Feed the Children (CAN$11 million), Food for the Hungry Canada (CAN$8 million), and sos Children's Villages (CAN$5 million).

4   Even though the *Tribune* does not go into depth discussing executive compensation within non-profits, it was, and still is, a hot topic. Even though some organizations have policies regarding executive compensation that talk about discounted salaries for equivalent roles in business and industry (for example, see World Vision, 2017b), many sponsorship organizations pay their senior management more than CAN$150,000 a year. According to 2016 charity returns sent to Revenue Canada, both Plan Canada and World Vision Canada employed ten people who earned more than CAN$160,000 a year. In addition, many CEOs of major charities in Canada earn over CAN$300,000 per year, including the head of Plan Canada. While earning less than some of their American counterparts, Canadian NGOs have been under pressure to explain or alter their policies regarding executive compensation.

5   The term "promotional material" is often used instead of, or interchangeably with, "advertising." Both terms are meant to convey the entirety of the mass-mediated content that is witnessed by or sent to the (potential) sponsor/donor. This includes not only what are traditionally seen as ads aimed at garnering new sponsors, such as direct mail appeals, brochures, or TV commercials, but also the letters, reports, and reminders sent to current sponsors. While a little more awkward, the former term is useful because it appears to encompass some elements that the latter term neglects. In particular, it is easier to explain all communication to sponsors as a form of promotional material in that, even though they are not traditionally seen as advertising, the letters, brochures, reports, etc. still serve the purpose of promoting the program to the sponsor so that they continue their sponsorship.

6   Some of the diversity in participant understandings of sponsorship may be due to the fact that a seemingly disproportionate number of participants had extensive knowledge of sponsorship programs and/or issues of international development. At least two participants had worked for child sponsorship programs, sometimes in overseas offices. At least three participants (not always the same ones) had studied international

development issues at the graduate level. At least four sponsors had visited their sponsored children.

Because of this diversity, as well as the scope of the study, it is not possible to represent all participants' voices equally well. Consequently, the following account of sponsorship should not be taken as representative of the entire breadth of participant responses, just as it may not be representative of all sponsors' experiences or opinions. The goal, however, is not to generalize to all child sponsors, although many of the points are probably reflective of a majority of sponsors. Instead, the objective is to shed light on the social and psychological processes involved in decisions to begin or maintain sponsorship by exploring the ways this subset of sponsors understands what they are doing. These understandings can then be analyzed to highlight the way sponsors reproduce various discourses related to sponsorship.

Works Cited

Anderson, Benedict. 1991. *Imagined Communities: Reflections on the Origin and Spread of Nationalism*, 2nd ed. New York: Verso.

Anderson, Lisa. 1998a. "Charity's Probe Finds Sponsors Funded at Least 24 Dead Children." *Chicago Tribune*, March 15: 1-1, 1-9.

____. 1998b. "In search of Korotoumou." *Chicago Tribune*, March 15: B1.

____. 1998c. "Via Corporate Partners, You May Help Save the Children." *Chicago Tribune*, March 15: 2-7.

Anderson, Norma. 2008. "Shoppers of the World Unite: (RED)'s Messaging and Morality in the Fight Against African AIDS." *The Journal of Pan African Studies*, 2,6: 32–54.

Appiah, Anthony Kwame. 2005. *The Ethics of Identity*. Princeton, NJ: Princeton University Press.

Aries, Philippe. 1962. *Centuries of Childhood: A Social History of Family Life*. New York: Vintage.

Barker, Martin. 1981. *The New Racism*. London, UK: Junction.

Barnes, Teresa. 2008. "Product Red: The Marketing of African Misery." *The Journal of Pan African Studies*, 2, 6: 71–76.

Barry, Andrew, Thomas Osborne, and Nikolas Rose (eds.). 1996. *Foucault and Political Reason: Liberalism, Neo-Liberalism, and Rationalities of Government*. Chicago: University of Chicago Press.

Barthes, Roland. 1972 [1957]. *Mythologies*, Trans. Annette Lavers. New York: Hill and Wang.

Bell, Vikki. 1993. "Governing Childhood: Neo-Liberalism and the Law." *Economy and Society*, 22, 3: 390–405.

Bhabha, Homi. 1994. *The Location of Culture*. New York: Routledge Classics.

Biccum, April. 2005. "Development and the 'New' Imperialism: A Reinvention of Colonial Discourse in DFID Promotional Literature." *Third World Quarterly*, 26, 6: 1005–20.

Bornstein, Erica. 2002. "Developing Faith: Theologies of Economic Development in Zimbabwe." *Journal of Religion in Africa*, 32, 1: 4–31.

____. 2001. "Child Sponsorship, Evangelism, and Belonging in the Work of World Vision Zimbabwe." *American Ethnologist*, 28, 3: 595–622.

Bourdieu, Pierre. 1986. "The Forms of Capital." In John Richardson (ed.), *Handbook of Theory and Research for the Sociology of Education*. New York: Greenwood.

Bozinoff, Lorne. and Morry Ghingold. 1983. "Evaluating Guilt Arousing Marketing Communications." *Journal of Business Research,* 11: 243–55.

Braedley, Susan, and Meg Luxton (eds.). 2010. *Neoliberalism and Everyday Life*. Montreal & Kingston: McGill-Queen's University Press.

Bratich, Jack, Jeremy Packer, and Cameron McCarthy (eds.). 2003. *Foucault, Cultural Studies, and Governmentality*. New York: SUNY Press.

Brubaker, Rogers, Mara Loveman, and Peter Stamatov. 2004. "Ethnicity as Cognition." *Theory and Society* 33: 31–64.

Bula, Omega. 2002. "Images of Africa: Challenging Negative Stereotypes in Media and Society." *Making Waves* (Summer): 21–23.

Burchell, Graham, Colin Gordon, and Peter Miller (eds.). 1991. *The Foucault Effect: Studies in Governmentality*. Chicago: University of Chicago Press.

Callari, Antonio. 2004. "Economics and the Postcolonial Other." In Eiman O. Zein-Elabdin and S. Charusheela (eds.), *Postcolonialism Meets Economics*. London, UK: Routledge.

Campbell, Danielle, Stuart Carr, and Malcolm Maclachlan. 2001. "Attributing 'Third World Poverty' in Australia and Malawi: A Case of Donor Bias?" *Journal of Applied Social Psychology,* 21, 2: 409–430.

Canadian Feed the Children. No date. "Childhood: The Chance of a Lifetime" [brochure]. No publication information. Available August 2007.

CCIC (Canadian Council for International Cooperation). 2004. "Images of Africa Workshop for Fundraisers." Africa-Canada Forum Workshop March 29, 2004. Retrieved April 29, 2007. <http://www.ccic.ca/_files/en/what_we_do/002_images_in_africa_report.pdf>.

Chalice. 2017. "FAQ Sponsorship." Retrieved August 27, 2017. <http://www.chalice.ca/sponsor-a-child/faq-sponsorship>.

Chang, Ha-Joon, and Ilene Grabel. 2004. *Reclaiming Development: An Alternative Economic Policy Manual*. London, UK: Zed.

Chicago Tribune. 1998. "Searching for Miracles." March 15: 2-2.

ChildFund Alliance. 2017. "Who Are the Members of ChildFund Alliance?" Retrieved June 15, 2017. <https://childfundalliance.org/our-members>.

Children, Incorporated. 2017. "Our History." Retrieved September 1, 2017. <https://childrenincorporated.org/about/>.

Chouliaraki, Lilie. 2006. *The Spectatorship of Suffering*. London, UK: Sage.

Christian Children's Fund of Canada. 2017. "Finance and Accountability." Retrieved September 1, 2017. <https://www.ccfcanada.ca/about-us/financials>.

____. 2010. "New CEO to Spearhead Development of Leading Edge Solutions to End Extreme Poverty." Retrieved August 13, 2010. <http://www.ccfcanada.ca/AboutUs/PressCentre/press_releases/2008_June112009.aspx>.

____. No date. "Innocent Children of War" [online commercial]. Retrieved July 10, 2007. <http://www.youtube.com/watch?v=2IwQG0D6h8I>.

Christian Children's Fund US. 2008. "CCF History." Retrieved September 10, 2008. <http://www.christianchildrensfund.org/content.aspx?id=726>.

Comaroff, Jean, and John Comaroff (eds.). 2001. *Millenial Capitalism and the Culture of*

Neoliberalism. Durham: Duke University Press.

Compassion Canada. 2017a. "History." Retrieved September 1, 2017. <https://www.compassion.ca/our-history/>.

____. 2017b. "Frequently Asked Questions." Retrieved September 1, 2017. <https://www.compassion.ca/faq/>.

____. No date. "Releasing Children from Poverty in Jesus' Name" [brochure]. No publication information. Available August 2008.

Compassion International. 2017. "Donation FAQ." Retrieved September 1, 2017. <https://www.compassion.com/contribution/contributionfaq/#faq-tcm:5-453611>.

Cooley, Charles. 1998. *On Self and Social Organization*, Ed. Schubert Hans-Joachim. Chicago: University of Chicago Press.

Craig, David, and Doug Porter. 2006. *Development beyond Neoliberalism: Governance, Poverty Reduction, and Political Economy*. New York: Routledge.

Crewdson, John, and Laurie Goering. 1998. "Frail Girl Falls between the Cracks." *Chicago Tribune*, March 22: 2-14, 2-15.

Crewe, Emma, and Priyanthi Fernando. 2006. "The Elephant in the Room: Racism in Representations, Relationships and Rituals." *Progress in Development Studies*, 6, 1: 40–54.

Cruikshank, Barbara. 1999. *The Will to Empower: Democratic Citizens and Other Subjects*. Ithaca, NY: Cornell University Press.

____. 1996. "Revolutions Within: Self-Government and Self-Esteem." In Barry, Andrew, Thomas Osborne and Nikolas Rose (eds.), *Foucault and Political Reason: Liberalism, Neo-Liberalism, and Rationalities of Government*. Chicago: University of Chicago Press.

Crush, Jonathan (ed.). 1995. *Power of Development*. London, UK: Routledge.

Dean, Mitchell. 1999. *Governmentality: Power and Rule in Modern Society*. Los Angeles: Sage.

Dean, Mitchell, and Barry Hindess (eds.). 1998. *Governing Australia: Studies in Contemporary Rationalities of Government*. Cambridge, UK: Cambridge University Press.

Deb, Debal. 2009. *Beyond Developmentality: Constructing Inclusive Freedom and Sustainability*. London, UK: Earthscan.

Dellios, Hugh. 1998. "For Sponsors, Image and Reality Are Worlds Apart." *Chicago Tribune*, March 15: 2-8, 2-9.

Dellios, Hugh, and Lisa Anderson. 1998. "Greetings from Grave: 'We Are All Doing Well.'" *Chicago Tribune*, March 15: B6.

Derrida, Jacques. 1992. *Given Time: Counterfeit Money (Vol. 1)*. Trans. Peggy Kamuf. Chicago: Chicago University Press.

Dirar, Uoldelul. 2003. "Church-State Relations in Colonial Eritrea: Missionaries and the Development of Colonial Strategies (1869–1911)." *Journal of Modern Italian Studies*, 8, 3: 391–410.

Dogra, Nandita. 2012. *Representations of Global Poverty: Aid, Development and International NGOs*. London, UK: I.B. Tauris.

Donzelot, Jaques. 1979. *The Policing of Families*. New York: Random House.

Dorning, Mike. 1998a. "Tiny Fictions Bring Big Bucks." *Chicago Tribune*, March 15: 2-13.

____. 1998b. "Many Can Take a Bow in Developing Nations." *Chicago Tribune*, March 15: 2-14.

Dorning, Mike, and Laurie Goering. 1998. "Where Have All the Children Gone?" *Chicago Tribune*, March 15: 2-10, 2-11.

Doty, Roxanne Lynn. 1996. *Imperial Encounters: The Politics of Representation in North-South Relations*. Minneapolis: University of Minnesota Press.

Dutton, Michael. 2009. "911: The After-life of Colonial Governmentality." *Postcolonial Studies,* 12, 3: 303–314.

Dyer, Richard. 1993. *The Matter of Images: Essays on Representation*. New York: Routledge.

Easterly, William. 2006. *The White Man's Burden: Why the West's Efforts to Aid the Rest Have Done So Much Ill and So Little Good*. London, UK: Penguin Press.

Edelman, Marc, and Angelique Haugerud (eds.). 2005. *The Anthropology of Development and Globalization: From Classical Political Economy to Contemporary Neoliberalism*. London, UK: Blackwell.

Escobar, Arturo. 1995. *Encountering Development: The Making and Unmaking of the Third World*. Princeton Studies in Culture/Power/History. Princeton, NJ: Princeton University Press.

Esteva, Gustavo. 1992. "Development." In Wolfgang Sachs (ed.), *The Development Dictionary: A Guide to Knowledge as Power*. London, UK: Zed books.

Fabian, Johannes. 1990. "Presence and Representation: The Other and Anthropological Writing." *Critical Inquiry,* 16, 4: 753–772.

Fabre, Cecile. 2007. *Justice in a Changing World*. Cambridge, UK: Polity.

Fanon, Franz. 2008 [1952]. *Black Skin, White Masks*. Trans. Richard Philcox. New York: Grove.

Farley, Alex. 1997. "The Black Body as Fetish Object." *Oregon Law Review,* 76, 3: 457–535.

Fendler, Lynn. 2001. "Educating Flexible Souls: The Construction of Subjectivity through Developmentality and Interaction." In Kenneth Hultqvist and Gunilla Dahlberg (eds.), *Governing the Child in the New Millennium*. New York: Routledge.

Fieldston, Sara. 2014. "Little Cold Warriors: Child Sponsorship and International Affairs." *Diplomatic History,* 38, 2: 240–250.

Fishkin, James. 1986. "Theories of Justice and International Relations: The Limits of Liberal Theory." In Anthony Ellis (ed.), *Ethics and International Relations*. Manchester: Manchester University Press.

Foucault, Michel. 2007. *Security, Territory, Population: Lectures at the College de France 1977–78*. Ed. Michel Senellart. Trans. Graham Burchell. New York: Palgrave Macmillan.

____. 2003 [1984a]. "The Ethics of the Concern of the Self as a Practice of Freedom." In Paul Rabinow and Nikolas Rose (eds.), *The Essential Foucault: Selections from The Essential Works of Foucault 1954–1984*. New York: New Press.

____. 2003 [1984b]. "Polemics, Politics, and Problematizations." In Paul Rabinow and Nikolas Rose (eds.), *The Essential Foucault: Selections from The Essential Works of Foucault 1954–1984*. New York: New Press.

____. 2003 [1983]. "On the Genealogy of Ethics: An Overview of Work in Progress." In Paul Rabinow and Nikolas Rose (eds.), *The Essential Foucault: Selections from The Essential Works of Foucault 1954–1984*. New York: New Press.

____. 2003 [1982a]. "The Subject and Power." In Paul Rabinow and Nikolas Rose (eds.), *The Essential Foucault: Selections from The Essential Works of Foucault 1954–1984*. New York: New Press.

____. 2003 [1982b]. "Technologies of the Self." In Paul Rabinow and Nikolas Rose (eds.), *The Essential Foucault: Selections from The Essential Works of Foucault 1954–1984*. New

York: New Press.

____. 2003 [1980a]. "The Masked Philosopher." In Paul Rabinow and Nikolas Rose (eds.), *The Essential Foucault: Selections from The Essential Works of Foucault 1954–1984*. New York: New Press.

____. 2003 [1980b]. "Questions of Method." In Paul Rabinow and Nikolas Rose (eds.), *The Essential Foucault: Selections from The Essential Works of Foucault 1954–1984*. New York: New Press.

____. 2003 [1978]. "Governmentality." In Paul Rabinow and Nikolas Rose (eds.), *The Essential Foucault: Selections from The Essential Works of Foucault 1954–1984*. New York: New Press.

____. 2003 [1977]. "Truth and Power." In Paul Rabinow and Nikolas Rose (eds.), *The Essential Foucault: Selections from The Essential Works of Foucault 1954–1984*. New York: New Press.

____. 2002 [1969]. *The Archaeology of Knowledge*. Trans. A.M. Sheridan Smith. London, UK: Routledge.

____. 1990 [1984]. *The History of Sexuality, Vol. 2: The Use of Pleasure*. Trans. Robert Hurley. New York: Vintage Books.

____. 1990 [1978]. *The History of Sexuality: An Introduction*. Trans. Robert Hurley. New York: Vintage Books.

____. 1989 [1966]. *The Order of Things: An Archeology of the Human Sciences*. London: Routledge.

____. 1973 [1963]. *Birth of the Clinic: An Archaeology of Medical Perception*. Trans. A. M. Sheridan Smith. New York, NY: Pantheon Books.

Frank, Andre G. 1996. "The Underdevelopment of Development." In Sing C. Chew and Robert A Denemark (eds.), *The Underdevelopment of Development: Essays in Honor of Andre Gunder Frank*. Thousand Oaks: Sage.

Friedrich, James, and Acacia McGuire. 2010. "Individual Differences in Reasoning Style as a Moderator of the Indentifiable Victim Effect." *Social Influence*, 5, 3: 182–201.

Giaccardi, Chiara. 1995. "Television Advertising and the Representation of Social Reality: A Comparative Study." *Theory, Culture & Society*, 12: 109–131.

Giroux, Henry. 1994. "Living Dangerously: Identity Politcs and the New Cultural Racism." In Henry Giroux and Peter McLaren (eds.), *Between Borders: Pedagogy and the Politics of Cultural Studies*. London, UK: Routledge.

Glewwe, Paul, Phillip Ross, and Bruce Wydick. 2014. "Developing Hope: The Impact of International Child Sponsorship on Self-Esteem and Aspirations." *Economics*. Paper 9. Retrieved March 30, 2015 <http://repository.usfca.edu/econ/9>.

Goodman, Michael. 2004. "Reading Fair Trade: Political Ecological Imaginary and the Moral Economy of Fair Trade Foods." *Ethics in Political Ecology*, 23, 7: 891–915.

Gorton, Kristyn. 2007. "Theorizing Emotion and Affect: Feminist Engagements." *Feminist Theory*, 8: 333–348.

Goudge, Paulette. 2003. *The Whiteness of Power: Racism in Third World Development and Aid*. London, UK: Lawrence and Wishart.

Government of Canada. 2010. "Personal Income Tax Relief for All Taxpayers." *Canada's Economic Action Plan*. Retrieved May 29, 2010 <http://www.actionplan.gc.ca/initiatives/eng/index.asp?mode=5&initiativeID=51&clientid=5>.

Grillo, Ralph, D. 1997. "Discourses of Development: The View from Anthropology." In Ralph D. Grillo and Roderick L. Stirrat (eds.), *Discourses of Development: Anthropological Perspectives*. Oxford, UK: Berg.

Hackett, Robert. 1992. "Coups, Earthquakes, and Hostages? Foreign News on Canadian Television." In Marc Grenier (ed.), *Critical Studies of Canadian Mass Media*. Toronto: Butterworths.

Hall, Stuart. 1997. "The Spectacle of the 'Other.'" In Stuart Hall (ed.) *Representation: Cultural Representations and Signifying Practices*. London, UK: Sage.

____. 1992. "The Rest and the West: Discourse and Power." In Stuart Hall and Gieben (eds.), *Formations of Modernity*. Oxford, UK: Polity Press.

____. 1981. "The Whites of Their Eyes: Racist Ideologies and the Media." In George Bridges and Rosalind Brunt (eds.), *Silver Linings: Some Strategies for the Eighties*. London, UK: Lawrence and Wishart.

Hancock, Graham. 1989. *Lords of Poverty: The Power, Prestige, and Corruption of the International Aid Business*. New York: Atlantic Monthly Press.

Harvey, David. 2007. *A Brief History of Neoliberalism*. New York: Oxford University Press.

Hattori, Tomohisa. 2003. "The Moral Politics of Foreign Aid." *Review of International Studies,* 29: 229–247.

Heron, Barbara. 2007. *The Desire for Development: Whiteness, Gender, and the Helping Imperative*. Waterloo, ON: Wilfrid Laurier University Press.

Hindess, Barry. 2002. "Neo-Liberal Citizenship." *Citizenship Studies,* 6, 2: 127–143.

Hintzen, Percy. 2008. "Desire and the Enrapture of Capitalist Consumption: Product Red, Africa, and the Crisis of Sustainability." *The Journal of Pan African Studies,* 2, 6: 77–91.

Hoijer, Birgitta. 2004. "The Discourse of Global Compassion: The Audience and Media Reporting of Human Suffering." *Media, Culture, and Society,* 26, 4: 513–531.

hooks, bell. 1992. *Black Looks: Race and Representation*. Boston: South End.

Ilcan, Suzan, and Lynne Phillips. 2006. "Global Developmentalities." Keynote address, Technocracy@Development Conference, The University of Wageningen, The Netherlands. 26–28 June, 2006. Retrieved April 12, 2010 <http://www.ceres.wur.nl/old%20website/summerschool/papers/Global%20Developmentalities%20Keynote%20Address%202006.doc>.

Imagine Canada. 2014. "Fundraising and Administrative Expenses." *The Narrative*. Issue Sheets Series. Retrieved August 15, 2017 <http://sectorsource.ca/sites/default/files/resources/files/narrative-issue-sheet-expenses-en.pdf>.

Jackson, David. 1998. "Problems Roil Grass-Roots Work." *Chicago Tribune*, March 22: 2-11, 2-12.

Jackson, David, and Michael Tackett. 1998. "An Executive with a Golden Touch." *Chicago Tribune*, March 22: 2-4.

Jacobi, Juliane. 2009. "Between Charity and Education: Orphans and Orphanages in Early Modern Times." *Paedagogica Historica,* 45, 1: 51–66.

JanMohammned, Abdul. 1985. "The Economy of Manichean Allegory: The Function of Racial Difference in Colonialist Literature." *Critical Inquiry,* 12, 1: 59–87.

Jefferess, David. 2002a. "For Sale — Piece of Mind: (Neo-) Colonial Discourse and the Commodification of Third World Poverty in World Vision's 'Telethons.'" *Critical Arts,* 16, 1: 1–21.

_____. 2002b. "Neither Seen Nor Heard: The Idea of the 'Child' as Impediment to the Rights of Children." *Topia: A Canadian Journal of Cultural Studies,* 7: 75–97.

Jenni, Karen, and George Loewenstein. 1997. "Explaining the 'Identifiable Victim Effect.'" *Journal of Risk and Uncertainty,* 14, 3: 235–257.

Jungar, Katarina, and Elaine Salo. 2008. "Shop and Do Good?" *The Journal of Pan African Studies,* 2, 6: 92–102.

Kelly, Paul. 2005. *Liberalism.* Cambridge, UK: Polity Press.

King, Samantha. 2006. *Pink Ribbons, Inc: Breast Cancer and the Politics of Philanthropy.* Minneapolis: University of Minnesota Press.

_____. 2003. "Doing Good by Running Well: Breast Cancer, the Race for the Cure, and New Technologies of Ethical Citizenship." In Jack Bratich, Jeremy Packer, and Cameron McCarthy (eds.), *Foucault, Cultural Studies, and Governmentality.* New York: SUNY Press.

Kirk, Martin. 2012. "Beyond Charity: Helping NGOs Lead a Transformative New Public Discourse on Global Poverty and Social Justice." *Ethics and International Affairs,* 26, 2: 243–263.

Kogut, Tehila, and Ilana Ritov. 2005. "The 'Identifiable Victim' Effect: An Identified Group, or Just a Single Individual?" *Behavioural Decision Making,* 18, 3: 157–167.

Lacan, Jacques. 2006 [1977]. *Ecrits: The First Complete Edition in English.* Trans. Bruce Fink. New York: W.W. Norton & Company.

Larner, Wendy, and William Walters (eds.). 2004. *Global Governmentality: Governing International Spaces.* London, UK: Routledge.

Lee, Seyoung, and Thomas Feeley. 2016. "The Identifiable Victim Effect: A Meta-Analytic Review." *Social Influence,* 11, 3: 199–215.

Lemke, Thomas. 2007. "An Indigestible Meal: Foucault, Governmentality, and State Theory." *Distinktion: Scandinavian Journal of Social Theory,* 15: 43–66.

_____. 2002. "Foucault, Governmentality, and Critique." *Rethinking Marxism,* 114, 3: 49–64.

_____. 2001. "The Birth of Bio-Politics: Michael Foucault's Lectures at the College De France on Neo-Liberal Governmentality." *Economy and Society,* 30, 2: 190–207.

Levi, Margaret, and April Linton. 2003. "Fair Trade: A Cup at a Time?" *Politics and Society,* 31, 3: 407–432.

Levinas, Emmanuel. 1969. *Totality and Infinity: An Essay on Exteriority.* Trans. Alphonso Lingis. Pittsburgh: Duquesne University Press.

Lie, Jon. 2005. "Developmentality: CDF and PRSP as Governance Mechanisms." Conference presentation, *The Public Reconfigured: The Production of Poverty in an Age of Advancing Neoliberalism,* Rosendahl Barony, Norway. September 23–25, 2005. Retrieved September 5, 2008 <http://www2.warwick.ac.uk/fac/soc/csgr/events/workshops/2006ws/world_bank/papers/developmentality1._cdf_and_prsp_as_governance_mechanisms.pdf>.

Lomasky, Loren. 2007. "Liberalism Beyond Borders." In Ellen Paul, Fred Miller Jr., and Jeffery Paul (eds.), *Liberalism: Old and New.* Cambridge, UK: Cambridge University Press.

Lutz, Catherine A., and Jane L. Collins. 1993. *Reading National Geographic.* Chicago, IL: Chicago University Press.

Macdonald, Kate. 2007. "Globalising Justice within Coffee Supply Chains? Fair Trade,

Starbucks and the Transformation of Supply Chain Governance." *Third World Quarterly*, 28, 4: 793–812.

Magubane, Zine. 2008. "The (Product) Red Man's Burden: Charity, Celebrity, and the Contradictions of Coevalness." *The Journal of Pan African Studies*, 2, 6: 103–119.

Maren, Michael. 1997. *The Road to Hell: The Ravaging Effects of Foreign Aid and International Charity*. New York: Free Press.

Mauss, Marcel. 1954. *The Gift: Forms and Functions of Exchange in Archaic Societies*. Glencoe, IL: Free Press.

Mawuko-Yevugah, Lord. 2010. "Governing Through Developmentality: The Politics of International Aid Reform and the (Re)Production of Power, Neoliberalism and Neocolonial Interventions in Ghana." Ph.D. Thesis, University of Alberta

McHoul, Alec. 1991. "Taking the Children: Some Reflections at a Distance on the Camera and Dr. Barnardo." *The Australian Journal of Media Culture*, 5, 1: 32–50.

The Miracle Merchants: The Myths of Child Sponsorship. Series. 1998. *Chicago Tribune*, March 15, 22.

Moeller, Susan. 1999. *Compassion Fatigue: How the Media Sell Disease, Famine, War, and Death*. London, UK: Routledge.

Nederveen Pieterse, Jan. 1992. *White on Black: Images of Africa and Blacks in Western Popular Culture*. New Haven, CT: Yale University Press.

Oliver, Amy. 2006. "The 'Pornography of Poverty' and the 'Brothel Without Walls': Understanding the Impact of Art on Development." *Undercurrent*, 2: 18–25.

Ove, Peter. 2013. "Governmentality and the Analytics of Development." *Perspectives on Global Development and Technology*, 12, 1–2: 310–331.

Parpart, Jane. 2000. "Rethinking Participation, Empowerment, and Development from a Gender Perspective." In Jim Freedman (ed.), *Transforming Development: Foreign Aid for a Changing World*. Totronto: University of Toronto Press.

Pels, Peter. 1997. "The Anthropology of Colonialism: Culture, History, and the Emergence of Western Governmentality." *Annual Review of Anthropology*, 26: 163–183.

Plan Canada. 2017a. "Financial Overview." Retrieved September 1, 2017 <http://plancanada.ca/annualreview-fy16/financial-overview>.

____. 2017b. "Sponsorship FAQs." Retrieved August 22, 2017. <http://plancanada.ca/NetCommunity/Page.aspx?pid=1902>.

____. No date. "Susan Is Waiting for a Sponsor: Give Her a Future for Only $1 a Day…" [brochure]. No publication information. Available November 2006.

____. No date. "Heart of a Child" [televised commercial]. CTV. Aired March 30, 2007.

Plan International. 2017a. "How We Are Financed." Retrieved June 15, 2017 <https://plan-international.org/finance#raise>.

____. 2017b. "Our History." Retrieved June 15, 2017 <https://plan-international.org/organisation/history>.

____. 2008. "The Development Impact of Child Sponsorship." Retrieved August 3, 2010 <http://plan-international.org/about-plan/resources/publications/about-plans-work/the-development-impact-of-child-sponsorship>.

Plan UK. 2008. "History of Plan." Retrieved September 10, 2008 <http://www.plan-uk.org/about/planstory>.

Plewes, Betty, and Ricky Stewart. 2007. "The Pornography of Poverty: A Cautionary

Fundraising Tale." In Daniel Bell and Jean-Marc Coicaud (eds.), *Ethics in Action: The Ethical Challenges of International Human Rights Nongovernmental Organizations.* Cambridge, NY: Cambridge University Press.

Porter, Doug. 1995. "Scenes from Childhood: The Homesickness of Development Discourse." In Jonathan Crush (ed.), *Power of Development.* London, UK: Routledge.

Projects Abroad. 2012. "Voluntourism." Retrieved December 18, 2012 <http://www.projects-abroad.ca/voluntourism/>.

Rahnema, Majid. 1992. "Participation." In Wolfgang Sachs (ed.), *The Development Dictionary: A Guide to Knowledge as Power,* London, UK: Zed Books.

Rankin, Katharine. 2001. "Governing Development: Neoliberalism, Microcredit, and Rational Economic Woman." *Economy and Society,* 30, 1: 18–37.

Rawls, John, 1999. *The Law of Peoples.* Cambridge, MA: Harvard University Press.

_____. 1971. *A Theory of Justice.* Cambridge, MA: Belknap Press.

Razack, Sherene. 2004. *Dark Threats and White Knights: The Somalia Affair, Peacekeeping, and the New Imperialism.* Toronto: University of Toronto Press.

Renard, Marie-Christine. 2005. "Quality Certification, Regulation and Power in Fair Trade." *Journal of Rural Studies,* 21, 4: 419–431.

Rist, Gilbert. 2002. *The History of Development: From Western Origins to Global Faith,* 2nd ed. London, UK: Zed Books.

Rojas, Christina. 2004. "Governing through the Social: Representations of Poverty and Global Governmentality." In Wendy Larner and William Walters (eds.), *Global Governmentality: Governing International Spaces.* London, UK: Routledge.

_____. 2001. "'Development': What Is in a Word? Views from the Paradigms." *Canadian Journal of Development Studies,* 22, 3: 571–596.

Rose, Nikolas. 1999. *Powers of Freedom: Reframing Political Thought.* Cambridge, UK: Cambridge University Press.

_____. 1998. *Inventing Our Selves: Psychology, Power, and Personhood.* Cambridge, UK: Cambridge University Press.

Rose, Nikolas, and Peter Miller. 1992. "Political Power beyond the State: Problematics of Government." *The British Journal of Sociology,* 43, 2: 173–205.

Rostow, Walt. 1960. *The Stages of Economic Growth: A Non-Communist Manifesto.* Cambridge, UK: Cambridge University Press.

Rothmeyer, Karen. 2011. "They Wanted Journalists to Say 'Wow': How NGOs Affect U.S. Media Coverage of Africa." *John Shorenstein Center on the Press, Politics, and Public Policy Discussion Paper Series* #D-61. Retrieved March 12, 2011 (<http://www.hks.harvard.edu/presspol/publications/papers/discussion_papers/d61_rothmyer.pdf>.

Sachs, Wolfgang. 2000. "Development: The Rise and Decline of an Ideal." *Wuppertal Papers,* 108: 4–29.

_____. 1999. *Planet Dialectics: Explorations in Environment and Development.* London, UK: Zed Books.

_____ (ed.). 1992. *The Development Dictionary: A Guide to Knowledge as Power.* London, UK: Zed Books.

Said, Edward. 1994. *Culture and Imperialism.* New York: Vintage Books.

_____. 1979. *Orientalism.* New York: Vintage Books.

Save the Children US. 2008. "Our History." Retrieved September 5, 2008 <http://www.

savethechildren.org/about/mission/our-history>.

Schmetzer, Uli, and John Crewdson. 1998. "Nails, Plywood, Cement for an 8-Year-Olds Birthday." *Chicago Tribune*, March 22: 2-8, 2-9.

Scott, David. 1995. "Colonial Governmentality." *Social Text*, 42: 191–220.

Shanin, Theodor. 1997. "The Idea of Progress." In Majid Rahnema with Victoria Bawtree (eds.), *The Post-Development Reader*. London, UK: Zed Books.

Small, Deborah, and George Loewenstein. 2003. "Helping *a* Victim or Helping *the* Victim: Altruism and Identifiability." *Journal of Risk and Uncertainty*, 26, 1: 5–16.

Smillie, Ian. 1998. "Optical and Other Illusions: Trends and Issues in Public Thinking about Development Co-operation." In Ian Smillie and Henny Helmich (in collaboration with Tony German and Judith Randel) (eds.), *Public Attitudes and International Development Co-operation*. Paris, FR: OECD.

____. 1995. *The Alms Bazaar: Altruism under Fire — Non-Profit Organizations and International Development*. London, UK: IT Publications.

Smith, Matt, and Helen Yanacopulos. 2004. "The Public Faces of Development: An Introduction." *Journal of International Development*, 16: 657–664.

Somers, Margaret. 1994. "The Narrative Constitution of Identity: A Relational and Network Approach." *Theory and Society*, 23, 5: 605–649.

Sontag, Susan. 2003. *Regarding the Pain of Others*. New York: Farrar, Strauss, and Giroux.

SOS Children's Villages Canada 2017. "About SOS Children's Villages Canada" Retrieved September 1, 2017 <https://www.soschildrensvillages.ca/about-sos-childrens-villages-canada>.

Spivak, Gayatri. 1999. *A Critique of Postcolonial Reason: Toward a History of the Vanishing Present*. Cambridge, MA: Harvard University Press.

Stalker, Peter. 1982. "Please Do Not Sponsor This Child." *New Internationalist*, 111 (May). Retrieved September 29, 2008 <http://live.newint.org/issue111/keynote.htm>.

Stein, Janice. 2002. *The Cult of Efficiency*. Massey Lectures Series, Revised ed. Toronto: Anansi.

Tackett, Michael. 1998. "A Girl's Sweet Gesture Turns Sour." *Chicago Tribune*, March 22: 2-10.

Tackett, Michael, and Laurie Goering. 1998. "Step by Step, Family Pulling Itself Up." *Chicago Tribune*, March 22: 2-5.

Tackett, Michael, and David Jackson. 1998a. "The Low-Cost Leader." *Chicago Tribune*, March 22: 2-1, 2-3, 2-4.

____. 1998b. "Unable to Make the Connection." *Chicago Tribune*, March 22: 2-13.

Tompkins, Silvan. 1995. *Exploring Affect: The Selected Writings of Silvan S. Tompkins*. Ed. Virginia E. Demos. New York: University of Cambridge Press.

Turner, Mark, and David Hulme. 1997. *Governance, Administration, and Development: Making the State Work*. West Hartford, CT: Kumarian Press.

United Nations Development Programme. 2010. "Participatory Local Development." Retrieved August 10, 2010 <http://www.undp.org/poverty/focus_local_development.shtml>.

Van Eekelen, William. 2013. "Revisiting Child Sponsorship Programmes." *Development in Practice*, 23, 4: 468–480.

Van Neikerk, Marinus. 2008. "(Red) Mythology." *The Journal of Pan African Studies*, 2.6,

55-67.

VSO (Voluntary Service Overseas). 2001. *The Live Aid Legacy: The Developing World Through British Eyes — A Research Report.* Retrieved October 13, 2008 <www.eldis.org/vfile/upload/1/document/0708/DOC1830.pdf>.

Wallerstein, Immanuel. 2004. *World-Systems Analysis: An Introduction.* Durham: Duke University Press.

Watson, Brad. 2014. "Origins of Child Sponsorship: Save the Children Fund in the 1920s." In Brad Watson and Matthew Clarke (eds.), *Child Sponsorship: Exploring Pathways to a Brighter Future.* New York: Palgrave MacMillan.

Watson, Brad, and Matthew Clarke (eds.). 2014. *Child Sponsorship: Exploring Pathways to a Brighter Future.* New York: Palgrave MacMillan.

Watson, Brad, and Anthony Ware. 2014. "Through the Eyes of the Sponsored." In Brad Watson and Matthew Clarke (eds.), *Child Sponsorship: Exploring Pathways to a Brighter Future.* New York: Palgrave MacMillan.

White, Sarah. 2002. "Thinking Race, Thinking Development." *Third World Quarterly,* 23, 3: 407–419.

Wiragu, Jessica, Kathryn Farley, and Courtney Jensen. 2010. "Is Business Discourse Colonizing Philanthropy? A Critical Discourse Analysis of (PRODUCT) RED." *VOLUNTAS: International Journal of Voluntary and Nonprofit Organizations,* 21, 4: 611–630.

World Vision Canada. 2017a. "Frequently Asked Questions." Retrieved September 1, 2017 <http://www.worldvision.ca/about-us/frequently-asked-questions>. ___. 2017b. "Our Approach to Executive Compensation." Retrieved September 1, 2017 <http://www.worldvision.ca/about-us/financial-accountability>.

___. 2008. "History." Retrieved September 5, 2008 <http://www.worldvision.ca/About-Us/History/Pages/History.aspx>.

___. No date. "Heart for the Children with Dr. Tony Campolo" [televised commercial]. Omni. Aired December 7, 2007.

___. No date. "Africa's Children" [televised commercial]. Global. Aired January 3, 2007.

___. No date. "Sponsor a Child, Change a Life" [televised commercial]. Omni. Aired January 11, 2007.

___. No date. "You and Your Sponsored Child: Helping Build a Bridge of Hope" [brochure]. No publication information. Available August 2007.

World Vision International. 2017a. "Consolidated Financial Statements 2016, 2015." Retrieved June 15, 2017 <http://www.wvi.org/accountability/publication/consolidated-financial-statements-2016-2015-1)>.

___. 2017b. "Our History." Retrieved September 1, 2017 <http://www.wvi.org/our-history>.

Wren, Karen. 2001. "Cultural Racism: Something Rotten in the State of Denmark." *Social & Cultural Geography,* 2, 2: 141–162.

Wright, Caroline. 2004. "Consuming Lives, Consuming Landscapes: Interpreting Advertisements for Cafedirect Coffees." *Journal of International Development,* 16: 665–680.

Wydick, Bruce, Paul Glewwe, and Laine Rutledge. 2013. "Does International Child Sponsorship Work? A Six-Country Study of Impacts on Adult Life Outcomes." *Journal of Political Economy,* 121, 2: 393–436.

Young, Iris. 2006. "Responsibility and Global Justice: A Social Connection Model." *Social Philosophy and Policy*, 23, 1: 102–130.

Zielinski, Graeme, and David Jackson. 1998. "'At Times, I have Wanted to Turn It Off Too.'" *Chicago Tribune*, March 15: 2-7.

Index